ADI DA

The Promised God-Man Is Here

THE AUTHORIZED CONCISE BIOGRAPHY OF AVATAR ADI DA SAMRAJ

BY CAROLYN LEE, PH.D.
Written under the direction of
The Ruchira Sannyasin Order of Adidam Ruchiradam

THE DAWN HORSE PRESS

NOTE TO THE READER

All who study the Way of Adidam or take up its practice should remember that they are responding to a Call to become responsible for themselves. They should understand that they, not Avatar Adi Da Samraj or others, are responsible for any decision they make or action they take in the course of their lives of study or practice.

The devotional, Spiritual, functional, practical, relational, cultural, and formal community practices and disciplines referred to in this book are appropriate and natural practices that are voluntarily and progressively adopted by members of the practicing congregations of Adidam (as appropriate to the personal circumstance of each individual). Although anyone may find these practices useful and beneficial, they are not presented as advice or recommendations to the general reader or to anyone who is not a member of one of the practicing congregations of Adidam. And nothing in this book is intended as a diagnosis, prescription, or recommended treatment or cure for any specific "problem", whether medical, emotional, psychological, social, or Spiritual. One should apply a particular program of treatment, prevention, cure, or general health only in consultation with a licensed physician or other qualified professional.

This concise edition of *Adi Da* is formally authorized for publication by the Ruchira Sannyasin Order of Adidam Ruchiradam. (The Ruchira Sannyasin Order of Adidam Ruchiradam is the senior Spiritual and Cultural Authority within the formal gathering of formally acknowledged devotees of the Divine World-Teacher, Ruchira Avatar Adi Da Samraj.)

NOTE TO BIBLIOGRAPHERS: The correct form for citing Ruchira Avatar Adi Da Samraj's Name (in any form of alphabetized listing) is:

Adi Da Samraj, Ruchira Avatar

Produced by the Avataric Pan-Communion of Adidam
in cooperation with the Dawn Horse Press

New concise edition, August 2003

Printed in the United States of America

International Standard Book Number:

Library of Congress Catalog Card Number: 2003110212

Adi Da

Avatar Adi Da Samraj

CONTENTS

ABOUT THE COVER:

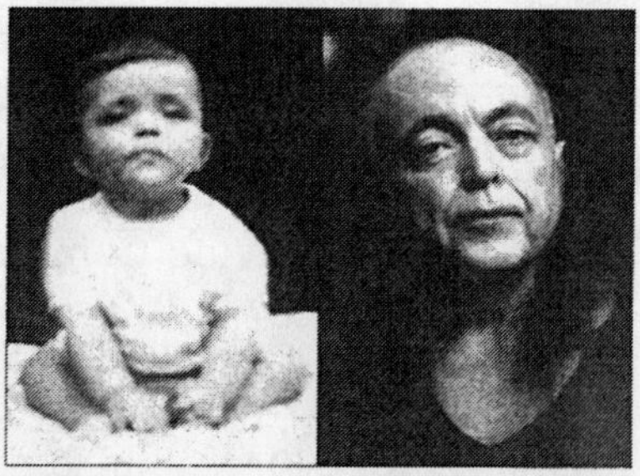

The two photographs of Avatar Adi Da Samraj on the cover both show Him in profound moments of Transmitting His Spiritual Blessing. The first photograph was taken in 1940 (when He was less than a year old), the second in 2000 (when He was sixty years of age). As the first photograph shows, even as a young infant, Avatar Adi Da was already Radiating the same Spiritual Depth and Force that He Radiates now. Thus, His Spiritual Blessing-Power is not the result of a lifetime of Spiritual practice, but was the case from birth. Such is the characteristic of the Divine Avatar—Who has "Crossed Down" from the Divine Domain (Appearing as a human being in the midst of this world), and Who is born only in order to Reveal the Nature of the Divine Reality and the Way of Perfect Liberation.

Avatar Adi Da Samraj
Adidam Samrajashram, 2003

INTRODUCTION

Adi Da, the Promised One, Is Here

The Divine Process of His Life and the Unique Way of Spiritual Awakening He Offers

The ancient traditions of humankind foretell a final Revelation, a God-Man promised for the "late-time", who will perfectly fulfill the deepest longings of the human heart. This book is based on the recognition that, by a Unique and Mysterious Process, this all-surpassing Event has occurred. Avatar Adi Da Samraj is the Divine Being of Grace and Truth Who authenticates the ancient intuitions, and is the answer to the heart-prayers of all beings.

While many great Spiritual beings have Realized our higher human potential through heroic effort, the Process by which Real God—or Truth Itself, or Reality Itself—manifests as a human form is entirely different. Avatar Adi Da Samraj speaks of this Mysterious Process:

There is another Process, Which Enters the conditionally manifested world from the Ultimate, Un-manifested, Perfectly Divine Domain. There is a Vast, Unlimited Domain of Existence, *not qualified in any sense, not qualified as this conditional world is, or as the infinite variety of conditional, cosmic worlds is. And there is a Movement Directly Out of That Divine Domain, That Realm of Very Consciousness and Very Light. The Living Being Who Appears within the human world, or within any other world, by Coming Directly Out of the Un-manifested, or Un-"created", Domain, the Heart-Light That Is the Truly Eternal Real-God-World, Is the Truly Heaven-Born One, Unique among the Great Siddhas.*[*1] *I Am That One.*

—Avatar Adi Da Samraj
The Divine Siddha-Method Of The Ruchira Avatar

This Unique Process is the Act of Divine Descent, which indicates the real meaning of "Avatar"—One "Crossed Down" to here from Above the mortal realms. While Appearing through this Act of Descent, Avatar Adi Da Samraj has also embraced human existence without reserve in order to enable everyone, one by one, to "wake up" from the "dream" of presumed-to-be-mortal existence. He is here to Awaken all to the Condition that is truly Real and Free—the Condition that exists now and forever, beyond death, beyond all religious myths, and beyond any gesture of mind.

Avatar Adi Da Samraj was born in New York in 1939. His Appearance at that moment in human history—the beginning of World War II—was not arbitrary. As this book will describe, Avatar Adi Da's human Appearance here required vast preparation that has come to fruition in this time of humanity's extreme need—a time when the globe is on fire with strife and suffering, and its very existence is threatened by ecological destruction and the modern weapons of war. In fact, the Divine Being and Reality is responding to aeons of human prayers, as to an immense magnet. Avatar Adi Da is here to transform humankind, and more than humankind. He is here to Illumine even all of manifest existence. This is what He has been doing since His birth—for His human birth was more than His association with a human body. His birth on earth was the initiation of an infinite and ongoing process. That process can be described as His "Emergence", as a tangible, identifiable Presence in the heart of all that exists.

*Notes to the text of *Adi Da* appear on pp. 334-39.

How was it possible for the Eternal Divine Being to enter into human manifestation as the Ruchira Avatar, Adi Da Samraj? By what Mysterious Process did His human birth occur, in 1939, on Long Island, New York?

From His early childhood, Avatar Adi Da described this Process in two words—the "Bright" and the "Thumbs".

From His early years, the "Bright"—His Prior Condition of Blissful Divine Light—literally "pressed" Itself into His infant body in waves of Force Descending from infinitely above His head. This intense Force would engorge His throat with a gagging sensation. It felt, as He said, "like a gigantic mass of Thumbs". Fevers and delirium would sometimes accompany the onset of the "Thumbs" as His young body struggled to adapt to the overwhelming Infusion of the "Bright". It was a Divine Yogic Event and utter Sacrifice—the "Bright" Combining with the mechanism of a mortal human being.

Throughout His Life, Avatar Adi Da has passed through extreme Yogic Events that have restructured His human mechanism and allowed His Spiritual Transmission to magnify. These Events are part of the uniqueness of the Divine Avatar's Revelation and they have profound significance for all human beings.

"An Unbounded Space of Joy"

This book is built on the testimony of many people who, over the last more-than-thirty years, have been Graced to have direct contact with Avatar Adi Da and to experience the overwhelming force of His Revelation. I, the author, will never forget the occasion of my first sighting of Avatar Adi Da:

The time was 1986, and the place was Maria Hoop, a village in southern Holland. I was in my late thirties. I had an academic career. From my childhood, I had traveled widely and I was familiar with the highest intellectual and artistic achievements of Western civilization. But I was quite unprepared for the power of what now occurred.

I was seated in the chapel of a former monastery with about one hundred other people, waiting for Avatar Adi Da to come into the room and take His seat in front of us. He was offering Darshan—a traditional word for the sighting of a Spiritually Awakened being. I had no experience of Darshan, or any real sense of what to expect. I was there because I had already read some books by Avatar Adi Da, and His Teaching had moved me to want to see Him in person.

Before Avatar Adi Da came in, we waited a long time—hours of devotional chanting and listening to recitations from His Teaching. This is how such great beings have been honored by their followers for centuries. But I had no real framework for that tradition of devotion to the Spiritual Master—except as it was reflected in Christianity, where the Master had been alive two thousand years ago. And so it felt somewhat strange to me.

When Avatar Adi Da entered the room, the whole room changed. He was of another Place, not of this place. At the same time, He seemed extremely human, and almost frail. He was dressed very simply in indigo, with His hair down to His shoulders.

I had never had a Spiritual experience in my life, never seen anything except the ordinary material reality. But the minute He sat down, His eyes held me and His face began to "melt". Another Reality was unveiled. Apparitions of Spiritual Masters of different times and places flowed over His features. I had no idea who these beings were, but I could see their distinct qualities—Chinese, Tibetan, Indian.

Eventually, the faces passed, and there was just His face. No more apparitions. But then I became aware that His whole body was a locus of Light. There was a Radiance around Him—but it wasn't just an aura. His body was dissolving in the Light. The Light seemed to be the source of His body, not an emanation of the body.

I blinked numerous times, but the process continued. It wasn't something happening inside me, a kind of mystical experience within, or a meditative vision. This event was happening right there in the room. The Light filled the room, and the shape of Avatar Adi Da's body disappeared and reappeared in the brilliant golden and white Light. The Light was not like ordinary light—electric light or daylight. It was infinitely more refined, and it seemed alive. It was Bliss, Radiant Feeling—heart-Feeling to infinity. The room was full and deep and bright, an unbounded space of Joy. And everything in the room had a fluid quality, not solid at all. I lost my sense of being located at a particular point in space, and I seemed to be viewing Him and everything else from different places in the room.

I was "gone" in amazement, and my heart was on fire. I was undone with a force of recognition. My heart said, "You are God"—the Divine Light in human form. And I loved Him—I felt that I had always loved Him, had always known Him, and yet not until now. I wept with an aching ecstasy in every cell of my being. And that was the real beginning of my relationship to Him as His devotee.

The next day, Avatar Adi Da sat again. This time, there was no noticeable magnification of Light but just the vision of His Form, as tender and exposed as that of a baby lying in its crib. I was shocked at His vulnerability. I could not comprehend the paradox. The previous day, I had seen His body as an appearance coalescing into Form out of pure Light. And now He was almost painfully present as a totally vulnerable human body, simply Radiating Love.

I felt unable, in that moment, to receive that intensity of Love—and immediately my life flashed before me, as happens (people say) at the moment of death. I saw everything unloving about my life from my earliest memories to that moment. I saw what I had done in all my relationships—with friends, family, lovers—that was all about my own satisfaction, my own agendas, the competitiveness, the anger, the heartlessness, the failure to be sensitive to anyone except myself. The intensity of this reflection grew and grew, until I felt I would explode. I wanted to run from the room.

Then I looked at Avatar Adi Da. His eyes were half-closed in Bliss, and it was obvious to me that He "knew" everything about me. And He did not care how it looked. He was there to Draw me beyond all of it. I knew that some profound, pre-verbal longing in my being had been boundlessly answered and satisfied—and that the rest of my life would be devoted to the Revelation that had just been given to me. It was the undoubted Revelation of God, yes—but not the "Creator-God" of my childhood religion. The "God" that had been shown to me on these occasions was not apart, not separate, not a great "Parent". That One was simply Light, the inseparable Source and Substance of everything. He was Bliss, Love, and Joy—humanly Present and yet Radiating from Infinity.

"Learning Man"

As this book describes, the purpose of Avatar Adi Da's early Life was for Him to "Learn Man"—to enter into the entire range of human seeking and experiencing. Around the age of two years, in a spontaneous gesture of Love toward those around Him, He relinquished His unbroken Samadhi[2] of the "Bright" and identified with the self-contracted state of human beings.

At first, in His childhood and during studies at Columbia College (New York), Avatar Adi Da imbibed the world of ordinary life, exoteric (or belief-based) religion, and scientific materialism—in other words, the gross, or merely physical, view of reality.

Later, with His Gurus, Swami Rudrananda (in New York) and then with Swami Muktananda (in India), He went beyond conventional life, and embraced the ancient Spiritual way of Guru-devotion. In the relationships with His Teachers, He became familiar with the esoteric point of view of the Yogis and their search for the Divine through the means of Kundalini Yoga. With Swami Muktananda (and under the guidance of Bhagavan Nityananda from the subtle plane), He Realized all the subtle experiences and Samadhis that are potential in the Siddha tradition.

While living at Swami Muktananda's Ashram in early 1970, Avatar Adi Da Samraj experienced the direct intervention of the Goddess-Power, or Shakti, revealing Herself as a Divine Personality present to guide the final stages of His Sadhana (or Spiritual practice). Appearing in the forms of the Hindu goddess Durga, and as the Virgin Mary of Christianity, the Shakti mysteriously led Avatar Adi Da on a pilgrimage of the major holy sites of the Middle East and Europe. There, He spontaneously experienced the depth of the Western psyche in mystical Christian visions of extraordinary intensity. Those visions, in their turn, faded, and His Sadhana entered into the causal domain, the deep root-place where attention arises. In that meditative seclusion, resting prior to all experience, He fulfilled the goals described in the highest forms of Buddhism and Advaita Vedanta.

But none of this was sufficient for Avatar Adi Da Samraj. He was not diverted or satisfied by any temporary experience or limited point of view. Only the "Bright" Itself, His Native Divine State of Perfect Love-Bliss, was Sufficient. And so He persisted in His unrelenting enquiry into Reality until the process fulfilled itself. Seated in the Vedanta Temple in Hollywood, California, on September 10, 1970, He suddenly Knew that His Realization was unqualified and irrevocable. He was fully re-established in the "Bright".

After Re-Awakening to the "Bright", Avatar Adi Da continued to relate to the gross dimension, continued to see visions associated with the subtle dimension, continued to be aware of the causal depth. But none of these experiences had (or have) any power to bind His attention. He Recognized that all these experiences (gross, subtle, and causal) were mere passing modifications of the "Bright" Reality Itself—unnecessary, temporary, and non-binding.

A Divine Transmission-Process

In His lifelong process of Revealing the "Bright", Avatar Adi Da Samraj has gone to the depths of the human condition. After going through His time of "Learning", He spent decades Submitted to the lives of His devotees, freely Instructing them face to face. By that means, confronted with every human quality and egoic tendency, He Gave form to His Divine Teaching in its universal scope.

One of the unique fundamentals of the Divine Avatar's Teaching is that human beings, themselves, are preventing the Realization of Reality—through something they are <u>doing</u>. Each one is <u>contracting</u> from Reality, presuming to be an ego, a separate self. This ego-act—the act of self-contraction—is the source of all suffering and unhappiness. The self-contraction makes human life into a constant drama of seeking—every kind of search to attain, or avoid, or identify with experience, high and low. And in fact, understanding oneself fundamentally as the self-contraction allows one to become available to Avatar Adi Da's Transmission of the "Bright".

While His own experience of the "Bright" and the "Thumbs" was unique, a similar process takes place in Avatar Adi Da's devotee. Just as He Combined with His own body-mind via the "Thumbs", Avatar Adi Da Samraj Spiritually Transmits to others His very Nature and Condition. The Spiritual Way that the Divine Avatar has Given to human beings—the Way of Adidam—is a Divine Transmission-Process, in which He is Moved to Radiate His "Bright" Condition to His devotees in Response to their demonstrated devotion.

AVATAR ADI DA SAMRAJ: The only Liberating discovery is that My Avataric Divine Spirit-Presence is Real, able to be tangibly experienced under any and all circumstances. It is not about imagining My Presence or manipulating yourself. None of that is satisfying, in any case. To searchlessly Behold Me and, in the midst of it, to notice My Avataric Divine Spirit-Presence tangibly Moving upon you in your real experience—this is the great and Liberating discovery, the only Satisfaction, ultimately, the only Satisfaction in life. Everything else is temporary, conditional, ego-based, and disheartening. Only the discovery of the tangible Reality of That Which Is Divine is heartening and Liberating and Satisfactory.

—March 24, 2003

The usual Spiritual endeavor is an effort "from the ground up", a search to refine the being so that it is capable of ascending to What is Above. The Way of Adidam—the Way of the Divine Avatar, Adi Da—demonstrates the opposite process. What is Above Comes Down to what is below. The Divine Person, Avatar Adi Da Samraj, literally Descends—in the form of His Spiritually Transmitted Presence—into the body-mind of His devotee.

The Spiritual Transmission of Avatar Adi Da Samraj is received as a tangible, Blissful Current of Spirit-Force, filling the body-mind from head to toe. To experience this undeniable Spirit-Force, coming upon you from Beyond, is incomprehensibly profound.

It is a "washing" of the entire being that purifies and opens the knotted-up body and mind.

In this process, the flesh body is literally "Brightened" by the Divine Avatar's Spiritual Radiance, and a fundamental shift occurs in the way one sees the world. The ordinary point of view about reality—that regards existence as merely gross, or material—is seen to be obviously untrue. Reality is seen and felt and known to be Spiritual in nature. This transformation of view is a Yogic event, not a mental process. It occurs directly through the Grace of Avatar Adi Da's Spiritual Infusion of the body. As this Spiritual process unfolds, one is no longer dominated by the conceptual mind, or bound to its chatter, because the being is drawn deeper—in meditation and daily life—to something more compelling and real. What is infinitely more attractive than the mind is the "Bright", the Radiant heart-Fullness of Reality Itself. Most ultimately, the "Bright" is Where one Stands perpetually—waking, dreaming, and sleeping.

The Primary Practice

Such Realization occurs only through the most profound devotional attention to Avatar Adi Da Samraj. The Way of Realizing the "Bright" is the Way of constant turning to Him with all the faculties of the being—the mind, emotion, body, and breath[3] because He Is the "Bright". This turning is true devotion, a relinquishment of ego. To persist in that turning means that you cannot avoid anything. All the contents of mind, emotion, the knots in the body, the obstructions in the breath stand out, more than ever, as the process of purification takes place. But the practice is to give attention to Avatar Adi Da Samraj, and not to struggle with anything that is arising in the body-mind. The practice is simply to feel toward Him, to allow His "Brightness" to Attract you. In that surrender, a door is opened to His Spiritual Blessing.

AVATAR ADI DA SAMRAJ: Your turning to Me and My Transmission of My own Avataric Divine Spirit-Presence—My "Bright" Spiritual

Transmission in Response to your surrender to Me, these two together—is Adidam.

Turning to Me is not consoling. It is a profound practice. It is not about being comfortable. It is about being profoundly uncomfortable, unable to be comfortable with the way things seem—unable to be distracted, unable to be just sort of pleasurized into a humming, whistling, mumming state.

The turning to Me I have Given to you will serve in the most difficult moment, as well as in the most ordinary moment. It will require the same thing of you in both occasions. It will be equally profound on both occasions, if you truly practice it.

When there is Realization of Me, that never ends. You cannot get away from it. The same with this devotion to Me. It is moment to moment. The obligation is constant. The practice is constant.

To move Me to Respond to you is the essence of that devotion. Come to Me in the Body. Move Me to Bless you.

—March 24, 2003

AVATAR ADI DA SAMRAJ: The Way of Adidam, in practice, is not about relinquishing the body. It is about surrender as the body. The means of Realization is the relationship to Me, whole bodily turning the faculties to Me, entering into Communion with Me on the basis of surrender as the body-mind. On that basis, I am able to Do My Blessing-Work of Transmitting the "Bright", Transmitting the Divine Self-Condition. And, in that surrendered disposition, the devotee becomes combined with My Transmitted Person. This becomes a more and more profound and developing process that, ultimately, is characterized as Most Perfect Realization of the "Bright".

—March 15, 2003

Avatar Adi Da is the egoless Divine Reality Incarnate. He is not looking for the attention of beings as an ego-bound individual would, because He has no karmas, nothing to bind Him to this domain, except His Love for beings suffering here. To turn to Him is to turn to, and receive, What is "Bright", Divine, and Perfectly Free.

AVATAR ADI DA SAMRAJ: This "Brightness" Speaks. The "Bright" is Born As This.

My Spiritual Descent upon the body-mind of My devotee is My Means. The "Thumbs" is My Means. All This was Given from the Birth of This. These Words—the "Bright" and the "Thumbs"—were Generated by Me as an infant. I am Uttering to you the Revelation that was present at My Birth and in My Infancy, and nothing whatsoever has been added to It or taken away from It. Nothing in the human experience has modified It or limited It in the slightest. It is a Divine Spiritual matter, a Divine Spiritual Revelation for the sake of beings.

Recognize Me. Turn to Me. Receive Me. Constantly know Me. Then you are certain of the Truth I am Telling you.

My Revelation is not merely to be believed. It is to be received, experienced, entirely known, confirmed, proven, tangibly demonstrated.

—March 24, 2003

Contemplation of the Divine Form of the Ruchira Avatar

When the heart recognizes the Ruchira Avatar, Adi Da Samraj, as the very Form of the "Bright", all one's questions and searches evaporate. The deeper that recognition goes—through the moment to moment practice of turning to Him—the greater one's reception of His Transmission of Light. Contemplation of His Avatar-Body—the Body in which the entire Divine Yoga, here described, has occurred—is the great Secret.

AVATAR ADI DA SAMRAJ: The practice is searchless, ego-forgetting, altogether to-Me-turned Beholding of Me in My bodily (human) Divine Form. When you are not in My physical Company, you can recollect My bodily (human) Divine Form. You can use photographic Images of My bodily (human) Divine Form, and so on. Persisting in this practice, you will move Me to Bless you further.

—March 24, 2003

Searchless Beholding of Avatar Adi Da Samraj is the great alternative to the random distraction and seeking of body and mind. But it is not something one can "learn" or do by one's own efforts. Searchless Beholding of the Divine Avatar is His Gift, initiated by Him in His devotee in the retreat circumstance. One must come into His human Company to receive this Initiation and to stabilize the practice of searchless Beholding of Him, such that it can be practiced under all conditions. Once Given—and always renewed and deepened by returning to His Feet—this practice becomes the foundation of your life. It goes on through the waking state. It goes on in dreams and sleep. And the body-mind is opened to allow the Spiritual Descent of Avatar Adi Da until it is completely infilled, like a cup.

If you are moved to the real Spiritual Process, the Ruchira Avatar, Adi Da Samraj, is here to Master your life. If you are unhappy and afraid of death, just the gesture of turning to Him can ease your heart. His Divine Powers are supernormal. He has proven over and over to His devotees that He is Spiritually all-Pervading and all-Knowing. He is the God you have intuited to exist, Radiantly Present in Person, without any myths attached. He can contact you now, at the depth of your feeling. He can reach you in dreams, before you even know His Name. He is here for the Blessing of beings, without reserve.

The Greatest Possible Message

The fullness of what Avatar Adi Da Samraj is Revealing to human beings is beyond anything found in the past or present forms of religion. As He once said:

AVATAR ADI DA SAMRAJ: I am not here talking about any form of conventional or traditional religion. I am not communicating about any such "religion". I do not have anything to do with any such "religion". I am Communicating the Way of Realizing Reality Itself. Therefore, I have no tradition to uphold, no tradition that represents Me. I am simply Speaking the Truth.

—March 13, 2001

Avatar Adi Da belongs to no one—no religion, no tradition, neither East nor West. Regardless of the pigmentation of His skin, He is not a "white man". Despite His male sex, He knows men and women equally and perfectly. Although English is His native language, He communicates at the heart with every being who reaches out to Him. Thus, no religion or group can lay exclusive claim to Avatar Adi Da—including His own devotees. He is inherently Free, and He is here for all, responding to the essence of all human prayers.

Avatar Adi Da cannot be "interpreted" in terms of the past, because the Divine Signs that mark His Life have never been seen before. His Revelation of the "Bright" and the "Thumbs" is His alone. And so, those who have come to Him so far, and those who will come in the future, owe it to every human being to speak the miracles that they have seen and experienced in relationship to Him. By this means, the Spiritual culture that He has established may be seeded globally during His human lifetime and serve the transformation of humanity. As He has written:

> *I Have Come to Found (and, altogether, to Make Possible) a New (and Truly "Bright") Age of mankind . . . an Age in Which mankind will apply itself (apart from all dilemma and all seeking) to the Inherently Harmonious Event of Real existence (in the Always Already present-time "Bright" Divine Reality That Is the One and Only Reality Itself).*
>
> —Avatar Adi Da Samraj
> *Eleutherios (The Only Truth That Sets the Heart Free)*

Now, as in His infancy, Avatar Adi Da Radiates Down into His human Body only to the degree necessary to maintain bodily life. His Work of Submission to "Learn Man" and to "Teach Man" has been Done. He has sealed that Work in His Divine Scripture, the twenty-three "Source-Texts" of Adidam, which enshrine everything that He has Taught and Revealed to human beings. Now He is concentrated in creating Artistic Images—exquisite visual "Essays" that Reveal the "Bright" in their own manner.

Avatar Adi Da Samraj lives simply, as a Renunciate and Hermit, with the members of the Ruchira Sannyasin Order (the senior group of renunciates in Adidam). He exists merely to Bless, relating to everything in His domain with profound attention and care, and utter dispassion. He is bound to no thing. He withdraws from no one. He Calls all to a direct devotional and Spiritual relationship to Him.

The God-Man Promised for the "late" or dark time is Da—"the One Who Gives". And What He Gives is the Way of Infinite "Brightening"—The Way of Adidam.

What is the Right and Truly Perfect Process That (ultimately, Most Perfectly) Realizes the Divine Conscious Light (Itself)? That Process is What I am Revealing—in This, My Avatarically-Born bodily (human) Divine Form.

—Avatar Adi Da Samraj
"The Avataric Divine Self-Revelation of Adidam Ruchiradam"

The Life of the Divine Avatar, Adi Da, continues to unfold. And you can be a part of the future of His Story, by becoming His devotee. This book opens the way for you to "meet" Him. It is an opportunity to consider and verify in your own heart the greatest possible message: The complete Divine Intervention, long prophesied, has now occurred—with the potential to utterly transform your life and the destiny of all humankind.

The Ruchira Sannyasin Order of Adidam Ruchiradam

The Ruchira Sannyasin Order is the body of Avatar Adi Da's most advanced devotees who have chosen to consecrate their lives utterly to Him and His Way—by embracing the life of formal renunciation, in the circumstance of perpetual retreat. Avatar Adi Da has designated the Ruchira Sannyasin Order as the senior cultural authority within the gathering of His devotees—both during and after His physical Lifetime. Thus, it is the unique responsibility of the Ruchira Sannyasin Order to function both as the extension of His Sacred Authority and as His Instrumentality (or the collective human "conduit" for His Spiritual Blessing).

The Ruchira Sannyasin Order is (and must always be) the most senior gathering of (necessarily, formal) practitioners of the Way of Adidam—and the hierarchically central, and most senior (but entirely renunciate, and non-managerial), functioning cultural authority among, and in relation to, all the (necessarily, formal) practitioners of the Way of Adidam. . . .

All the present members and all the future members of the Ruchira Sannyasin Order are Called and Empowered (by Me) to Function (collectively) as the principal and most senior (physically living, human) Instruments of My forever Blessing Work, and, by their unique (and uniquely authoritative) cultural service (simply by Wisdom-word and practicing example), to provide all other practitioners of the Way of Adidam with the principal Good Company (of fellow devotees) that is necessary for the inspiration and guidance of their practice of the Way of Adidam.

AVATAR ADI DÁ SAMRAJ
"The Orders of My True and Free Renunciate Devotees"

From my earliest experience of life I have Enjoyed a Condition that, as a child, I called the "Bright".

CHAPTER 1

Born as the "Bright"

On November 3, 1939, Avatar Adi Da Samraj was born on Long Island, New York. There were no outward signs to suggest the profundity of the event, no prophets or seers to declare the universal significance of what was taking place. But, in that moment, the Eternal Divine Being—the Source and Substance of all that exists—was Submitting to appear in a mortal human Form.

From the very moment of His birth, Avatar Adi Da was confronted by the fragility of the human condition. Like many infants, His life was threatened by the umbilical cord, which was wound around His neck. But unlike others, He was fully aware of what was taking place. While the doctors worked to bring His body alive from the womb, He remained perfectly Conscious—Self-Aware as an infinite Sphere of Radiant Sublimity, which He later called the "Bright". And so (He recalls), in that Divine State, He was moved to Regard the people lying in the hospital wards, Blessing and healing them, untouched by the drama of His human birth.

Without any conscious knowledge of their son's Divine Nature, Frank and Dorothy Jones, Avatar Adi Da's parents, named Him "Franklin Albert Jones", a name that suggests freedom (Franklin) and brightness (Albert).[4]

Throughout His infancy, Avatar Adi Da Samraj remained free of the limits of His human birth. He felt associated with the body, but not defined by or identified with it. Rather, He felt His body to be arising in and as the "Bright". As He writes in His Spiritual Autobiography, *The Knee Of Listening*:

From my earliest experience of life I have Enjoyed a Condition that, as a child, I called the "Bright". . . .

Even as a baby I remember only crawling around inquisitively with a boundless Feeling of Joy, Light, and Freedom in the middle of my head that was bathed in Energy moving unobstructed in a Circle, down from above, all the way down, then up, all the way up, and around again, and always Shining from my heart. It was an Expanding Sphere of Joy from the heart. And I was a Radiant Form, the Source of Energy, Love-Bliss, and Light in the midst of a world that is entirely Energy, Love-Bliss, and Light. I was the Power of Reality, a direct Enjoyment and Communication of the One Reality.

—Avatar Adi Da Samraj
The Knee Of Listening

The Purpose of Avatar Adi Da's Birth

In order to fulfill the Purpose of His Incarnation, Avatar Adi Da had to Submit to a most profound ordeal and process. He had been born in human Form for unique Divine reasons—to directly Awaken each and every living being to the Divine Reality—the "Bright". To equip Himself for this, it was necessary that He live an apparently ordinary human life, identified with an apparently individual body-mind. It was even necessary that the "Bright" recede for a time from His awareness, so that (as He later put it) He could "Learn Man". In other words, He had to combine with the depths of the human condition, to find out what it feels like to be a mortal being struggling to discover the truth of one's existence. Only by fully entering into life as human beings experience it could He "Teach Man"—or show human beings how to participate in the Radiant Spiritual Reality, the deathless Condition He had come to Reveal.

Avatar Adi Da remembers the critical moment when His Submission to the human state occurred. One day, sometime after His second birthday, as Avatar Adi Da was crawling across a linoleum floor, His parents let loose a new puppy they were giving Him. In the instant of seeing the puppy and seeing His parents, the Divine Avatar spontaneously identified with His human body and His human personality altogether. In other words, He took on the sense of being an "I", separate from all other "I's", and allowed His own great State of Being to begin receding into unconsciousness. From that moment on, Avatar Adi Da consciously became "Franklin Jones". This Gesture of Submission was moved entirely by Love, as He describes:

AVATAR ADI DA SAMRAJ: My Identification with mortal existence occurred through sympathetic response. It was not merely a response to the puppy—it certainly was that, because the puppy was the nearest to Me in physical space—but then there was also the glance toward My parents. It was simply and altogether a sympathetic response that brought Me into the sphere of human conditions (and gross[5] conditions altogether). So it was a kind of delight—not merely some effortful identification with mortal existence. It was not the noticing of mortality, in and of itself, that generated My Movement into this plane. Rather, it was the Love-Response, the attracted Response, in which all of the negative aspects of gross conditional existence were effectively forgotten—in Love, in Delight, in Love-Bliss.

—February 9, 1998

As a young boy with His parents

While Avatar Adi Da Samraj spontaneously and fully surrendered to become like those around Him, the Intuition of the "Bright" still remained—"a fierce and mysteriously 'Bright' Impulse", as He later described it. Thus, in the depth of His Being, He never lost the urge to recover the "Bright", or bring the Influence of the "Bright" to others.

He recalls an occasion, when He was about seven years old, of walking with His parents to the movies. The moment stands out in His memory as His most significant early attempt to consciously communicate love in the midst of conflict.

His parents were quarreling about something, and He felt how that act of separation was destroying a web of love-energy that was all around them. He could actually see that delicate tissue of love torn with holes, and He tried to repair it by silently expanding love from His heart. At the same time, He began to ask His parents questions about God, and to point out to them the beautiful full moon.

Their quarrel quieted down—but, later, as He sat in the movie, Avatar Adi Da realized that He had borne the cost of the conflict. He describes how, because of his parents' inability to fully receive the love-energy He was transmitting to them, He felt a pain in His heart where the love-energy had been pushed back. Nevertheless, Avatar Adi Da felt that what He had just done was fundamental to His Purpose in life. He was moved to find a way to draw people out of the merely gross, or body-based, orientation of life and awaken them into a Divine Sphere of existence, Above and Beyond—but not separate from—the ordinary world.

Avatar Adi Da completely embraced the Lutheran Christianity of His family. He was, by His own confession, "a religious ecstatic" from His earliest youth. While sitting in church and in Sunday school class, He would spontaneously enter into trance-like states of mystical rapture. He would begin swooning in bliss, making incoherent gasps and other noises. And sometimes, through the force of His Spiritual absorption, His eyes would suddenly "bug out", or roll up to the top of their sockets—much to the annoyance of the pastor! In His early teens, Avatar Adi Da became an altar-server, and then a liturgist, or reader. As He stood before the congregation, reading from the Bible, something remarkable would happen. Avatar Adi Da noticed that people would fall into ecstasy. There was a Power in Him, communicated through His voice, to which they were responding.

With Bootsie

The Question of Death

The question of death took on a profound force for Avatar Adi Da when He was nine or ten years old. His constant companion at that time was Bootsie, a black cocker spaniel, whom He loved dearly. One day, He went down to the cellar, which was His own special domain in His parents' house, and found Bootsie, dead and rigid, lying in a big chair. It was Avatar Adi Da's first concrete experience of death. Immediately, He fell into deep despair. After hours of desperate crying and of earnest consolation from His parents, Avatar Adi Da managed some outward control of His grief. But, inwardly, He was not in the least consoled. He could not live with such a loss of a loved one, and so He formed an awesome resolve. Avatar Adi Da asked God to take His life at an appointed time—in two days, at nine o'clock on the following Sunday evening.

As the fateful hour approached, Avatar Adi Da deeply regretted His vow. He felt the joy of His own aliveness, and He realized that death did not mean the end of life and love. But He would not bargain with God by attempting to change His vow. He simply awaited what He felt to be His inevitable death.

The hour came and went and Avatar Adi Da did not die. Nevertheless, for weeks He felt a constriction in His chest, as though His heart had been crippled in some way by the ordeal of grief and His own consent to relinquish life.

I saw how the sentiment of separation from love can, as a problem or concern in the living consciousness, draw one out of the "Bright" of Illuminated, Free Consciousness, until one no longer perceives the perfect Form that is always here.

—Avatar Adi Da Samraj
The Knee Of Listening

Throughout His Life, Avatar Adi Da's confrontation with death has also taken place in His own body. Altogether, His birth in human form required a great initial struggle at the physical level. Just as electrical wires must be capable of handling the current that flows through them, so the fragile mechanism of a human body had to be prepared, in Avatar Adi Da's case, to conduct immense Divine Energy (or Spirit-Power). His childhood was full of the signs of this ordeal. There were many occasions, in fact, when He felt He was going to die, consumed by a literal burning Force that took the form of strange diseases, intense fevers, delirium, and symptoms of polio. Often connected with these bouts was a powerful Spiritual experience that Avatar Adi Da, as a child, named the "Thumbs".

At apparently random times (usually as I either approached sleep or awoke from sleep—and, most dramatically, during seizures of childhood illness, as I would pass into delirium), I had an experience that felt like a mass of gigantic thumbs coming down from above, pressing into my throat (causing something of a gagging, and somewhat suffocating, sensation), and then pressing further (and, it seemed, would have expanded without limitation or end), into some form of myself that was much larger than my physical body. . . .

The "Thumbs" were not visible in the ordinary sense. . . . They were not visible to me with my eyes, nor did I hallucinate them pictorially. Yet, I very consciously experienced and felt them as having a peculiar form and mobility, just as I (likewise) consciously experienced my own otherwise invisible and greater form.

Except for occasions of sudden spontaneous completeness, I did not, generally, in the developing childhood and earliest adult years, allow this intervention of the "Thumbs" to take place. I held it off from its fullest descent, in fear of being overwhelmed—for I did not understand at all what was taking place. However, as the adult years progressed, this same experience occurred naturally during meditation. Because my meditation had been allowed to progress gradually, and the realizations at each level were (thus) perceived without shock, I was able to allow the experience to take place. When I did, the "Thumbs" completely entered my living form.

—Avatar Adi Da Samraj
The Knee Of Listening

Avatar Adi Da's childhood experience of the "Thumbs" was the beginning of a unique Yogic Spiritual process. He was learning to bodily receive and conduct the Descent of His own Divine Spirit-Force. By means of that profound Descent, His human body was being Yogically transformed and equipped for His future Spiritual Work. He would later describe the "Thumbs" as one of the unique signs associated with His Incarnation:

AVATAR ADI DA SAMRAJ: The principal Sign in My early Life was My Intention to Descend, to Appear here, to Embrace in every aspect the limitation of human mortality, human existence, as it is, as it appears. The characteristic Samadhi of My childhood, or of My Life altogether—you could even say, of My Work altogether—was the Samadhi of the "Thumbs". The "Thumbs" is about My Divine Descent, the Crashing Down of Real God. The "Thumbs" is the Secret of My early Life.

—February 18, 1993

The beginning of Avatar Adi Da's experience of the "Thumbs" and the intense "illnesses" that accompanied this phase of His childhood can be understood as the second phase of His early Life. During the first phase, up to the age of five, He says He was "airy", not yet fully grounded in this gravitational world. The second phase, involving the onset of the "Thumbs", was the "fiery" process of His Divine Force combining with the physical body. Later, after the age of ten, and due, in part, to the shock of Bootsie's death, He became sobered by the mortal nature of existence and intensely moved to discover a greater Truth.

The Search for Truth

When Avatar Adi Da graduated from high school in 1957, He entered one of the most prestigious academies in the country at that time—Columbia College, in New York City. But Avatar Adi Da felt no exhilaration at the prospect of intellectual success or a brilliant career. Rather, through His conscious relinquishment of the "Bright", He had come to a point of profoundly suffering the human condition. He was dismayed by the apparent meaninglessness of existence, and plunged into despair. At the same time, the "fierce, mysterious Impulse" that had moved Him since the receding of the "Bright" was pressing Him into the deepest of questions: What is the truth of this apparent world? What is beyond? "What is Consciousness?" By "Consciousness" He meant that very sense of existence, or the awareness of simply being, which is constant in us—whatever the events and changes of life.

Avatar Adi Da had always felt that Consciousness was senior to the body, senior to death. His entire experience of the "Bright" suggested that seniority, as did the Christian beliefs that had been passed on to Him through His Lutheran upbringing. But what was the connection between Consciousness and the physical world? How were these two realities related to each other? He was completely given over to these questions, and it was not an intellectual matter. As the following years would reveal, the Divine Avatar's investigation of Consciousness was a Yogic Process, an exhaustive and concentrated discipline of attention and feeling-discrimination. Like the Descent of the "Thumbs", His enquiry into Consciousness was part of the unmediated spontaneous preparation of His human body-mind to fully Incarnate the "Bright" Divine Power and State.

At Columbia, Avatar Adi Da Samraj read extensively about the western cultural tradition—its philosophy, literature, and art. In all of this He found no satisfactory answers to His core questions. In fact, He discovered that the prevailing dogma at Columbia was that of "scientific materialism", which holds that the fundamental reality is the physical world, and everything "greater" or "higher"—Consciousness, or Spirit, or God—is either a by-product of physical reality or else a mere hallucination. Avatar Adi Da's stark confrontation with twentieth-century secularism in His first six months at Columbia destroyed the naive religious faith of His childhood, pointing only toward doubt and Godless rationalism.

In fact, Columbia became the first great turning point in the Life of Avatar Adi Da. Paradoxically, His years there were the beginning of His moving beyond mere identification with the body-mind, the Submission to limited human awareness for which He had "volunteered" at the age of two. He was urged on by desperation, unable to tolerate that confined awareness, now that the religious faith of His childhood had been devastated. There was no one to guide Him, and so He chose to confront the agony of Godlessness head on, through a heroic course—the course of exhaustive experience. As He states in *The Knee Of Listening*, His conviction was this: "If God exists, God will not cease to exist by any action of my own—but, if I devote myself to all possible experience, God will (necessarily) find some way (in some particular experience or some complex of experiences, or by virtue of my openness itself) to be revealed to me." Thus, the Divine Avatar gave Himself up to every experience and possibility, with the force of a vow:

No experience posed a barrier to me. There were no taboos, no extremes to be prevented. There was no depth of madness and no limit of suffering that my philosophy could prevent—for, if it did, I would be liable to miss the Lesson of Reality. Thus, I extended myself even beyond my own fear. And my pleasures also became extreme, such that there was a constant machine of ecstasy. I could tolerate no mediocrity, no medium experience. I was satisfied neither with atheism nor with belief. Both seemed to me mere ideas, possible reactions to a more fundamental (if unconscious) fact. I sought Reality, to be Reality—What is, not what is asserted in the face of What is.

—Avatar Adi Da Samraj
The Knee Of Listening

For two years during His time at Columbia, Avatar Adi Da maintained the terrible intensity of His seeking. Then, one night in 1960, in the middle of His junior year, the Truth dormant in His own Being made Itself known. Avatar Adi Da sat at His desk in a small room He had rented several blocks from campus, feeling that He had exhausted all the possibilities of experience.

I felt there were no more books to read, no possible kinds of ordinary experience that could exceed what I had already embraced. There seemed no outstanding sources for any new excursion, no remaining and conclusive possibilities. I was drawn into the interior tension of my mind that held all of that seeking—every impulse and alternative, every motive in the form of my desiring. I contemplated it as a whole, a dramatic singleness, and it moved me into a profound shape of life-feeling, such that all the vital centers in my body and mind appeared like a long funnel of contracted planes that led on to an infinitely regressed and invisible image. I observed this deep sensation of conflict and endlessly multiplied contradictions, such that I was surrendered to its very shape, as if to experience it perfectly and to be it.

Then, quite suddenly, in a moment, I experienced a total revolution in my body-mind, and, altogether, in my conscious awareness. An absolute sense of understanding opened and arose at the extreme end of all this sudden contemplation. And all of the motions of me that moved down into that depth appeared to reverse their direction at some unfathomable point. The rising impulse caused me to stand, and I felt a surge of Force draw up out of my depths and expand, Filling my entire body and every level of my conscious awareness with wave on wave of the most Beautiful and Joyous Energy.

I felt absolutely mad, but the madness was not of a desperate kind. There was no seeking and no dilemma within it, no question, no unfulfilled motive, not a single object or presence outside myself.

I could not contain the Energy in my small room. I ran out of the building and through the streets.

—Avatar Adi Da Samraj
The Knee Of Listening

As He ran through the streets, looking for someone to talk to about this revelation, Avatar Adi Da continued to feel an overwhelming energy in His body—in every cell—that was "almost intolerable in its Pressure, Light, and Force". But He found no one—and, at last, He returned to His room.

For two years Avatar Adi Da had devoted Himself to every kind of seeking—looking for some experience to "prove" the Truth to Him, presuming that the Truth was absent, that it had to be found. But in the days and weeks that followed the "Columbia experience", He realized that He had grasped two fundamental realities. First, He saw that Truth is not a matter of seeking for something that is absent, but rather of removing the obstructions to the Truth, Joy, or Freedom that is always already the case. Second, He realized that the seeking itself was the major obstruction that was preventing the immediate enjoyment, or Realization, of the Truth. All His seeking, He now understood, had been a grand distraction from present Real God, present Happiness. The two years of intense exploitation of experience had been necessary, but only in order to reveal conclusively to Him the futility of the search.

Graduation day, Columbia College, 1961

The Discovery of "Narcissus"

For Avatar Adi Da, the Awakening at Columbia was the first great breakthrough in His Life of the unique intelligence He calls "understanding": the clear experiential knowledge that unhappiness, or apparent separation from God or Truth, is fundamentally the result of one's own mistaken presumptions and one's own ego-activity (the activity of separating oneself—emotionally, mentally, and psychically—from everything and everyone else). Avatar Adi Da soon found, however, that He could not sustain the understanding awakened in this experience. He began to sense that there was something in consciousness that was actively preventing this understanding, and He fiercely resolved to discover what that was. Two years later—after He had graduated from Columbia and moved to California to begin a Master's program in English at Stanford University—the force of His urge to understand found a new absorbing focus.

In 1962, Avatar Adi Da moved into a small cabin on a bluff overlooking the Pacific Ocean. He was now living with Nina Davis—a fellow student at Stanford.

At Stanford University

Nina Davis

At the beach cottage

NINA: I met Beloved Adi Da[6] *at Stanford University in October 1961, on the first day of class of our graduate studies. He was sitting across a long table opposite the door of a seminar room, and when I walked into the room He looked up and glanced at me with the most beautiful and extraordinary eyes. I felt a rush of energy as my being went out to meet Him. In that split second, I felt the most profound communication of feeling I had ever known.*

From the very beginning, it was obvious to me that Beloved Adi Da related to life completely differently from anybody else, including myself. He was obviously <u>*actively*</u> *involved in a consideration about life, always considering the conventions of existence that everybody else takes for granted.*

Nina was witness to an extraordinary and unrelenting experiment that Avatar Adi Da now began—and which was to continue for almost two years. He wrote down everything that He observed in His experience—all that He thought, dreamed, felt, perceived, and did. He resolved that no motion of His being would elude Him. He hoped that, by these means, He might find a logic, or guiding form, to the entire play of His experience.

Avatar Adi Da was so absorbed in this process that Nina took over all the practicalities of their life together. Day after day, wherever He was—at home, on a walk, visiting friends, going to the movies—Avatar Adi Da would carry a clipboard and write down all that occurred in His awareness. When He wandered alone on the beach below their remote cottage, He wrote down every random thought and mind-form that arose with every step on the sand, and even His perception of the very action of stepping itself. He was placing His awareness under a powerful microscope, so that its inmost mechanics would stand out and its secret patterning would be revealed.

The revelation, when it came (in the spring of 1964), revolutionized His awareness:

Eventually, I began to recognize a structure in my conscious awareness. It became more and more apparent, and its nature and effects revealed themselves as fundamental, inclusive of all the states and contents in life and mind. My own "myth"—the governor of all patterns, the source of presumed self-identity, the motivator of all seeking—began to stand out in the mind as a living being.

This "myth", this controlling logic (or force) that formed my very conscious awareness, revealed itself as the self-concept—and the actual life—of Narcissus. I saw that my entire adventure—the desperate cycle of awareness and its decrease, of truly Conscious Being and Its gradual covering in the mechanics of living, seeking, dying, and suffering—was produced out of the image (or mentality) that appears hidden in the ancient myth of Narcissus.

The more I contemplated him, the more profoundly I understood him. I observed, in awe, the primitive control that this self-concept and logic exercised over all of my behavior and experience. I began to see that same logic operative in all other human beings, and in every living thing—even in the very life of the cells, and in the natural energies that surround every living entity or process. It was the logic (or process) of separation itself, of enclosure and immunity. It manifested as fear and identity, memory and experience. It informed every function of the living being, every experience, every act, every event. It "created" every "mystery". It was the structure of every imbecile link in the history of human suffering.

He is the ancient one visible in the Greek myth, who was the universally adored child of the gods, who rejected the loved-one and every form of love and relationship, and who was finally condemned to the contemplation of his own image—until, as a result of his own act and obstinacy, he suffered the fate of eternal separateness and died in infinite solitude.[7]

—Avatar Adi Da Samraj
The Knee Of Listening

When this truth dawned upon Avatar Adi Da, He saw that no one—no "God", no parent, no outside influence at all—has imposed on human beings this controlling logic of fundamental separation, enclosure, and immunity. It is we who have locked ourselves into this "prison". Now He knew He had to go through the ordeal of the undoing of the madness of "Narcissus", whatever that might involve.

After His Divine Re-Awakening
Los Angeles, 1971

CHAPTER 2

RE-AWAKENING TO THE "BRIGHT"

In June 1964, Avatar Adi Da and Nina moved to New York City, in response to a dream-vision in which He had glimpsed the place where He would meet His first human Teacher.

Surrender to Swami Rudrananda

Swami Rudrananda (or Albert Rudolph, known to his students as "Rudi") owned the Oriental art store in New York that Avatar Adi Da had seen in a vision (and which He had then found in Greenwich Village, two months after He arrived in New York). Rudi held "class" four times a week, during which his students practiced receiving the "Force" that he (an Adept of Kundalini Yoga) consciously Transmitted to them. "Work" and "surrender" were the essence of Rudi's Teaching.

Avatar Adi Da had read about the ancient tradition of approaching a Guru for instruction, but He had no personal experience of the Guru-devotee relationship. In that tradition, a Spiritual aspirant comes to a Guru (an acknowledged Spiritual Master, or Real-God-Realizer, of some degree) and surrenders himself or herself

Swami Rudrananda ("Rudi")

at the feet of the Master. From that moment on, the devotee submits to be directed in every aspect of life by his or her Guru. Such surrender, it is traditionally understood, is the greatest thing a human being could choose to do. To find and embrace one's Guru does not mean surrendering to an ordinary human being. It means surrendering to one Awakened by the Divine, one who is full of Divine Power and Grace—one who can, therefore, Awaken a serious devotee to the form of Spiritual Realization that corresponds to his or her own degree of Spiritual Awakening. In approaching Rudi and becoming his devotee, Avatar Adi Da was spontaneously moved to fulfill these sacred laws of the Guru-devotee relationship as it had existed in traditional cultures since ancient times—and He did so with great passion and intensity.

The central ideas in Rudi's way of teaching were "surrender" and "work". "Surrender" was the internal practice in life and meditation. It was conscious (and even willful) opening, or letting go of contents, resistance, patterns, feelings, and thoughts. "Work" was the external practice. The ideal student was to be involved in a constant state of surrender and a constant act of work. The purpose of this was to make the entire psycho-physical vehicle, internal and external, available to the higher Power—the "Force", or "Shakti"—and, thus, to grow by receiving Its Will, Presence, Intelligence, Light, and Power into every level of the functional being.

I took Rudi's way very seriously, and I made a constant effort to adapt myself to his way absolutely and exhaustively. I accepted

Rudi as a perfect Source of this higher Power, and I allowed none of his apparent limitations to represent actual barriers or limitations to my experience of the "Force" Itself. Whenever I encountered limitations in him, I was immediately moved to reflect on my own resistance. Thus, I never allowed myself to become concerned about Rudi's problems or to think that, because of his limitations, the "Force" (or the Divine Power) was available to me only to a limited degree.

The effect of this way of life was a perpetual and growing encounter with my own resistance. And, when I encountered my own resistance, I would awaken to my own tendencies to self-pity, negativity, and the subliminal self-imagery by which I guided the "creation" or manipulation of experience. The more I worked, the more I saw Narcissus.

Rudi's way required immense self-discipline—and, as long as it remained effective in my case, his way functioned as a positive mechanism that strengthened and purified me physically, mentally, and morally. Rudi was a master at this kind of psychological tutoring, and these effects were his primary gift to me.

—Avatar Adi Da Samraj
The Knee Of Listening

Avatar Adi Da worked day and night for three and a half years—cleaning Rudi's apartment, cleaning the store, and refinishing furniture. With great love and faith, He brought to Rudi the disposition of absolute surrender that He had practiced during His years at Columbia and His time of writing. Everything that Rudi asked his students to do, or required of Avatar Adi Da personally, He did—down to the last detail. As He says in *The Knee Of Listening*, He embraced the great practice of Guru-devotion and submitted to His Teacher "as a man does to God".

At Rudi's behest, Avatar Adi Da married Nina and took on disciplines of diet and exercise to purify and strengthen the body. He lived in a fever of frustration at the effort of responding to Rudi's intense demands—to the point where He felt His entire body to be burning up. These demands were not only physical. At Rudi's instigation, Avatar Adi Da Samraj also attended Christian seminaries (as preparation for a potential career as a minister), studying theology and ancient languages—which were not at all interesting to Him in and of themselves. It was simply obedience to His Teacher that moved Him.

The "Death of Narcissus"

In the spring of 1967, a dramatic and profoundly significant event occurred.

AVATAR ADI DA SAMRAJ: One day when I was in class in Seminary in the spring of 1967, I suddenly became completely detached from the mind. The mind seemed to pick up immense speed, and the thought processes were going at immense speed, to the point of the experience becoming extremely disturbing. I was supposed to be sitting there in class, but I felt as if I were going mad. I <u>*was*</u> *going mad.*

I tried to pin down My experience by writing everything the teacher said, or writing the thoughts I was having. I just kept pinning it down. That gesture, in and of itself, introduces time, and some more direct association with the body.

I did that long enough to sit through the class. Then I went whirling out in this horrific state, in which the body-mind was going on, on its own, without being controlled by attention. The body-mind was just a whirl of uncontrolled events and sensations and feelings—positive ones, and also extremely negative ones. It became just an <u>*immense*</u> *fear.*

I remember looking at My face in the mirror, as I was putting on an after-shave or a skin cleanser, and I saw the plasticity of the body. There was a profound <u>*disorientation*</u> *from the physical, emotional, and mental dimensions of the body-mind, in which I had been doing Spiritual practice so intensively for those years. All of a sudden, the body-mind was* <u>*utterly*</u> *confused and dissociated from Me, or I was dissociated from it.*

—January 13, 1996

In this extraordinary event, a sudden and profound psychic chaos canceled out Avatar Adi Da's normal identification with the body-mind and the person He presumed Himself to be. It was not as if this identification had been released gently, as in deep meditation. Avatar Adi Da was wide awake and active, and He could not point to any trigger that could have set off the process. Now His body appeared alien to Him—in fact, He hardly knew what it was. It appeared to be mere flesh without consciousness. Avatar Adi Da was in no way prepared for this experience by any of His Spiritual practice with Rudi. All of that Yoga had to do with the manipulation of the body-mind in order to receive superior Force, and to invite mystical (or subtle) experiences. The present chaos had catapulted Avatar Adi Da totally beyond that frame of reference.

AVATAR ADI DA SAMRAJ: The fear—which was a reaction to that whirl—got to the point where it was fruitless to try to <u>do</u> anything about it. It just kept growing immensely, became the totality of life, the totality of the body-mind, the totality of reality—just this <u>immense</u> fear that could no longer be avoided. There was nothing to do about it.

—January 13, 1996

After the first day of this terror, in the middle of the night, Avatar Adi Da felt that His heart was slowing down and about to stop. But when He reached the emergency ward at the local hospital, the doctor could not help. There was no conventional explanation or remedy for what was occurring in Him. Finally, on the third day of this acute distress, Avatar Adi Da simply lay down on the floor of His apartment and allowed the fear to pour through His being and overwhelm Him completely.

AVATAR ADI DA SAMRAJ: It was a death. That is what it became. It was endured to the point that what was afraid to be let go was simply let go. There was no choice.

So it passed. In other words, the body-mind, even attention, was no longer associated with My State. I was simply Realizing the Native State of Being. Therefore, this was not merely a process of madness in the usual clinical sense. It was an extraordinary Spiritual Event.

It was simply the breaking through of My own Disposition, the "Bright", Prior to the body-mind.

—January 13, 1996

When the terrible passage was over, Avatar Adi Da felt a total turnaround, a revolution in His awareness. By allowing Himself to fully experience the absolute terror of no longer being identified with the body-mind, He witnessed the actual death of His limited identity, and He witnessed it completely. "Narcissus", the separate self-consciousness, the one who is terrified of pain and death, simply died. It was a Yogic death—an event of profound transformation at the level of consciousness and energy. Now His true Identity was revealed as the "Bright", the unqualified, Free Awareness of Reality Itself, beyond the body-mind and all its assumed limits.

The ecstasy of this Realization was beyond anything that Avatar Adi Da had ever experienced since His Submission to the human condition at the age of two. He got up from the floor overcome with joy. The eternal qualities of Truth and Reality stood out as they are: Divine Calm and Inexpressible Love-Bliss. And He saw that all seeking for Reality and Truth was only the preventing of it—the avoidance of the "Bright", or That Which is Always Already the Case. He now knew, with complete certainty, that Reality could be directly Realized in any moment of life—or death. As He later expressed in the first words of *The Knee Of Listening*:

Death is utterly acceptable to consciousness and life. . . . Therefore, one's understanding of consciousness and life must be turned to That Utter, Inclusive Truth, That Clarity and Wisdom, That Power and Untouchable Gracefulness, That One and Only Reality, this evidence suggests. One must cease to live in a superficial and divided way, seeking and demanding consciousness and life in the present apparent form, avoiding and resisting what appears to be the end of consciousness and life in death. . . .

There Is Only the Constant Knowledge and Enjoyment of the Heart, moment to moment, through the instant of all conditions of appearance and disappearance. Of This I Am Perfectly Certain. I Am That.

—Avatar Adi Da Samraj
The Knee Of Listening

In this experience at seminary, the "Bright" was consciously restored to Avatar Adi Da—though not yet most Perfectly. The experience did mark, however, a profound change in Avatar Adi Da's disposition. He was no longer identified with what was taking place in His Life and Sadhana. His entire search had spontaneously relaxed. But how could He explain to others the revolution that had occurred in His consciousness? How could He express His living knowledge that we are not separate beings, but always alive only as the one Transcendental Truth and Unity?

The profundity of this "death of Narcissus" was not apparent even to Rudi. Avatar Adi Da Samraj was now expressing an understanding and Realization that no one around Him could comprehend. This "radical" understanding was utterly unique. He decided to simply live on its basis—abandoning the stress of effort, and functioning without dilemma.

The Sadhana with Swami Muktananda

It is a remarkable fact that, after the event at seminary, Avatar Adi Da continued to submit Himself to Teachers. He did this not because He needed a Teacher to awaken Him to His own "Bright" Avataric State. Rather, by submitting to Teachers who represented the Spiritual search of humanity, He was continuing His intuitive course of "Learning Man". Having already "Learned Man" at the level of the gross (or ordinary physical/mental) level of life, He was now combining Himself with a more refined dimension of human experience—the dimension of Spiritual energy and subtle (or mystical) experience.

This process had begun with Rudi—but Rudi himself had a Teacher, the remarkable Indian Yogi, Swami (Baba) Muktananda, whose picture (together with that of Swami Muktananda's own Guru, Swami Nityananda) hung on the wall in Rudi's art store. Avatar Adi Da began to read some pamphlets from Swami Muktananda's ashram and was deeply attracted by Swami Muktananda's descriptions of true Spiritual practice as founded in the reception of the Guru's Grace, rather than in the effort of surrender (as Rudi taught). By 1968, Avatar Adi Da found in Himself an irresistible impulse to move on in the great lineage of Gurus to which Rudi belonged. And so Avatar Adi Da asked, and received, Rudi's permission to approach Swami Muktananda.

In April 1968, Avatar Adi Da quickly made arrangements for Himself and Nina to take a brief trip—of four days—to Swami Muktananda's ashram in Ganeshpuri. He humbly wrote in advance to Swami Muktananda, expressing full confidence in his Grace and making it clear that He was coming to receive everything that Swami Muktananda had to give.

India, 1968

As Avatar Adi Da participated in the life of the ashram—sitting in Swami Muktananda's company, meditating, or attending the afternoon chanting of the *Bhagavad Gita*—He began to experience strong effects of Swami Muktananda's Spirit-Blessing (or Shaktipat). He felt His body swell with Force, generating powerful, involuntary bodily movements (or kriyas) as the Spirit-Energy flowed through Him. Avatar Adi Da found Himself involved in a new kind of Spiritual "Work"—submission to these kriyas, which were sometimes so strong that He would fall backwards against the wall or sideways onto the floor. Swami Muktananda also instructed Him in meditation and gave formal discourses on traditional Indian teachings about Spiritual life. But by the fourth and last day of His visit, Avatar Adi Da was feeling somewhat disappointed. He had come, as He had written in advance to Swami Muktananda, for "everything", and He felt that He was about to leave the ashram without having received His Guru's full gift.

On the afternoon of His last day, Avatar Adi Da was sitting in the ashram garden when Swami Muktananda walked by with a visitor—who, He later learned, was a Yogi-Saint named Rang Avadhoot.[8] For a brief moment, the Saint paused, turned towards Avatar Adi Da, and looked Him straight in the eyes. And then he walked on. That glance was profound. In later years, Avatar Adi Da acknowledged that Rang Avadhoot's glance, together with the

Swami Muktananda

Rang Avadhoot

Spiritual Influence of Swami Muktananda, was a trigger for what occurred next.

An urge to rest came over Avatar Adi Da, and He went to lie down in His room. In a moment, all awareness of body and mind slipped away in a swoon of immense Bliss. He rested in an infinitely Ascended state, above and beyond time and space and visions. In the traditions of Yoga there is a highly-valued state of Spiritual ascent called "Nirvikalpa Samadhi". Only the rarest of Yogis confess this Realization, which is temporary ascent through all the chakras to the "Formless" Divine Above, evoked by profound Yogic effort. In the case of Avatar Adi Da, there were no stages to this event—no intention, no effort, no passing through layers of mind. He had required only the briefest contact with Swami Muktananda, and only a glance from Rang Avadhoot, to establish (in His Words) "Instantaneous Collectedness Above and Beyond". This sudden exalted Samadhi was a unique manifestation of His Inherent "Bright" Condition.

AVATAR ADI DA SAMRAJ: In the Event of Nirvikalpa Samadhi at Baba Muktananda's Ashram, there was complete absence of, and freedom from, the structures of mind. There was an unobstructed Establishment in My Native State.

I Am Always Already Above and Beyond. This is the Natural Condition of My Incarnation.

—April 7, 2002

Avatar Adi Da passed into His native "Bright" State in this manner on two further occasions that same day, after He had departed from Ganeshpuri. The signs were already in evidence to suggest the fulfillment of a prophecy made to Avatar Adi Da on that initial visit to Ganeshpuri: Within a year, Swami Muktananda had told Him, Avatar Adi Da would be a Spiritual Teacher in His own right.

Avatar Adi Da returned to New York, and, within a year, people around Him started to experience a mysterious Force emanating from Him, and they turned to Him for Spiritual guidance. One of them, a young woman named Patricia Morley, came to live with Him and Nina. Aware that the Shakti, or Siddha-Power, had come alive in Himself, Avatar Adi Da wrote to Swami Muktananda, who urged Him to come to India again as soon as possible.

Avatar Adi Da's second visit to India—this time to Bombay, where Swami Muktananda was staying—in August 1969, was very different from the first. It was an entry into a Yogic "wonderland". He experienced the internal lights, sounds, visions, transports to other worlds, and states of Spirit-"Intoxication" that traditionally precede the rare attainment of Nirvikalpa Samadhi. But such experiences soon lost their interest for Avatar Adi Da. His focus lay in His Guru's silent internal instruction, which He received in the process of meditation.

At the end of His stay, Avatar Adi Da's Spiritual Accomplishment was formally acknowledged by Swami Muktananda. In a letter in his own hand—written in the presence of Avatar Adi Da and about fifty to one hundred others—Swami Muktananda declared that Avatar Adi Da had attained "Yogic Self-Realization" and, therefore, the right to Teach and Initiate students of His own. In this letter, Swami Muktananda formally conferred on His devotee, "Franklin", the Spiritual name "Dhyanananda", meaning "one whose bliss lies in meditation on the Self".

Swami Muktananda's Letter of Acknowledgement to Avatar Adi Da Samraj

Avatar Adi Da Himself edited and refined the English translation of the letter (excerpts of which are presented here), on the basis of several earlier translations. He added explanatory elaborations in parentheses in order to bring out the full meaning and Spiritual import of the original document.

To my dear (beloved) Franklin, with my loving remembrances of you (even of your Very Self):

You have . . . Attained the (True and Spiritual) State of Meditation. You have (by Means of True and Spiritual Meditation) Achieved the Steady State of . . . one-pointed Concentration (or Inherence) In, and tacit (or mindless) Identification With, the Divine Supreme Inner Self.

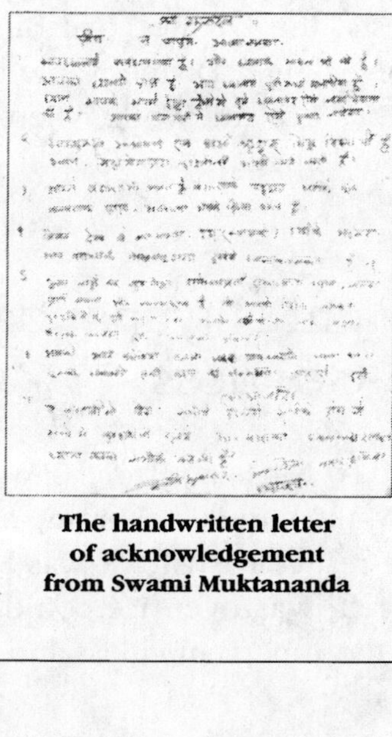

The handwritten letter of acknowledgement from Swami Muktananda

You (because of your direct Experience and Knowledge of Kundalini Shakti Meditation and, Thereby, of the Divine Supreme Inner Self) have, in accordance with Tradition, both the (Hereby Affirmed) Actual Ability and the Inherent (and Hereby Affirmed) Right to Initiate, or Cause, (True and Spiritual) Meditation in others (or, altogether, to Teach, Initiate, Establish, Guide, and Awaken others in the Practice, the

> Process, and the, Ultimately, Perfect Realization of Siddha Yoga Meditation, or True and Spiritual Meditation on, and, Ultimately, Perfect Realization of, the Divine Supreme Inner Self by Means of the Kundalini Shakti Transmitted, and Directly Activated, by you). . . .
>
> Therefore, (I Hereby Declare that) you have the Inherent Right and the Actual Ability to Cause (or, altogether, to Teach, Initiate, Establish, and Guide Kundalini Yoga) Meditation (or the Practice and the Process of Kundalini Shakti Meditation) in any one and everyone (and, Thus and Thereby, to Awaken any one and everyone to and As the Divine Supreme Inner Self of everything and everyone).
>
> —Swami Muktananda

Privately, however, through his secretary, Amma, Swami Muktananda gave Avatar Adi Da an even more profound acknowledgment. He spontaneously offered Him the name "Love-Ananda", meaning "One Who Is, and Manifests, the Divine Love-Bliss". Swami Muktananda was intuitively revealing a Divine Name that belonged to the future of Avatar Adi Da's Life and Work, when the full Revelation of His "Brightness" would appear.

The Sadhana with Swami Nityananda and the Divine Goddess

The following year, accompanied by Nina and Patricia, Avatar Adi Da returned to Swami Muktananda's ashram, now intent on staying there for the rest of His Life. It was May 1970, and His time in the West, He felt, was over. He could no longer endure the violent psyche of the American cities, and He had no motive whatsoever toward a conventional life. His only desire was to devote Himself to His Life of "radical" understanding and to live and serve in the company of His Guru. Thus, Avatar Adi Da and Nina and Patricia sold nearly all of their belongings, stored a few things in New York, and set off for India as renunciates.

When they reached Ganeshpuri, however, Swami Muktananda seemed to deliberately ignore Avatar Adi Da. Avatar Adi Da understood that this was His Guru's way of silently indicating that the future of His Sadhana lay elsewhere. And so, following an instruction that Swami Muktananda had given Him on earlier visits, Avatar Adi Da began to go daily to the nearby burial shrine of Swami Nityananda, the beloved Guru of Swami Muktananda. It was here that He now felt the Spiritual Force and Blessing that He had earlier received through Swami Muktananda. It seemed obvious to Avatar Adi Da that Swami Muktananda had passed Him on to his own Guru, in order to receive further instruction. Although Swami Nityananda had relinquished the body in 1961, he was, as Avatar Adi Da discovered, still Spiritually active on the subtle plane.[9]

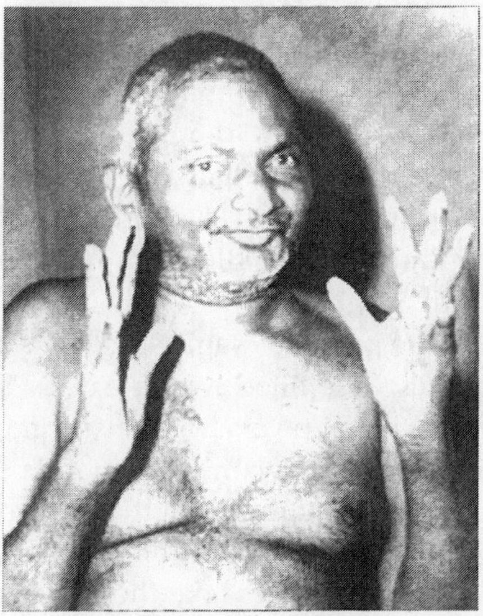

Bhagavan Nityananda

But then something completely unexpected occurred. About a week after His arrival in Ganeshpuri, as He was weeding in the ashram garden, Avatar Adi Da suddenly became aware of a subtle form behind Him. He turned around and found Himself beholding the non-physical but unmistakable presence of the Virgin Mary! At first, He felt like laughing out loud. The last traces of His childhood faith—which, in any case, had been Protestant, not Catholic—had dissolved, or so He thought, in the secular onslaught of His years at Columbia. But, in a few moments, He found Himself spontaneously moved to respond to the Virgin with reverence and respect, receiving her wordless communication that He should immediately acquire a rosary and begin to worship her.

When the vision faded, Avatar Adi Da set about complying with the Virgin's request, finding a way to get to Bombay, the nearest place where He could buy a rosary. He began to practice the "Hail, Mary" in the traditional manner, as a mantra, and to His amazement He found that this practice unlocked deep feelings of devotion to Jesus of Nazareth that seemed to have been suppressed since His childhood. He had no idea where this turn of events would lead, but He submitted to it completely.

After two weeks, the Virgin Mary instructed Avatar Adi Da to leave the ashram. He was to set out on a pilgrimage through the Christian holy places of Europe and the Middle East, starting in Jerusalem. He could not depart without taking leave of the Presence of Swami Nityananda, and so He went to the shrine and spoke His heart to Swami Nityananda, about all that had recently occurred and what He was about to do. Avatar Adi Da received Swami Nityananda's subtle communication of Blessing and the instruction that He should follow the Virgin.

The Mother-Shakti Image at the temple in Ganeshpuri

The priest at Swami Nityananda's burial place filled Avatar Adi Da's hands with flowers from the shrine, as a sign of Swami Nityananda's Blessing. Avatar Adi Da then left to return to the ashram. On His way, He was moved to take the flowers to the small village temple beside the ashram and offer them to the image of the Divine Mother-Shakti, the personification of the Spirit-Force that had so dramatically manifested in the multifarious Spiritual experiences He had gone through in His Sadhana at Ganeshpuri. As Avatar Adi Da stood before the Mother-Shakti—

the One worshipped in India as the great Goddess, the Energy of all manifestation—He came to a tacit realization. The Virgin and the Shakti were one. There was no difference. And that One—that Universal Goddess-Power—was now His Guru. This Divine Spirit-Force was, in fact, the Supreme Guru of the entire lineage of Gurus who had guided Avatar Adi Da's Sadhana—Swami Rudrananda, Swami Muktananda, and Swami Nityananda. And these Gurus had led Him to Her.

Up to this point, the Realizations of His Sadhana had taken Avatar Adi Da through all the degrees of "Enlightenment" known in the Spiritual traditions. On His second trip to India, He had experienced the subtle lights, sounds, and visions cherished by Yogis (such as Paramahansa Yogananda[10]). On His first trip to India, He had experienced the ascended Bliss of bodiless and mindless absorption in Pure Consciousness sought by Saints (such as Jnaneshwar and Milarepa[11]). And in the "death of Narcissus" in seminary, He had come to rest in the deep identification with Consciousness Itself known to the great Sages (such as Gautama, Hui Neng, Shankara, and Ramana Maharshi[12]).

But even though Avatar Adi Da had attained all these Realizations, none of them was sufficient for Him. None of them was the same as the utterly unqualified Joy that, as an infant, He had known as the "Bright". He knew that His quest was not complete. But no human Teacher could help Him now—only the Goddess Herself could take Him further, into territory untrodden by any Realizer of the past. When, in obedience to the Virgin, Avatar Adi Da made His farewells at Ganeshpuri and departed for Jerusalem, He was embarking upon the final phase of His Sadhana.

From the Way of the Cross in Jerusalem, to the monuments of Rome, to the basilica at Fatima in Portugal, Avatar Adi Da allowed the Virgin to lead Him. Extraordinary Christian visions overtook Him, mystical raptures of the kind experienced by the greatest saints. Having accomplished the highest goals of Eastern Yoga, He was now spontaneously combining Himself with the greatest mystical experience and Spiritual revelation of the West. But, as time went on, the Virgin and the visions began to fade. Avatar Adi Da felt Himself drawn more and more into a state of Non-Separateness from Reality Itself, prior to all visions, images, and traditional religious paths. Finally, by the time He reached Portugal in mid-July, He was moved to end the pilgrimage and return to the United States. After trying unsuccessfully to find a suitable place to live near San Francisco, He, Nina, and Patricia settled in Los Angeles.

The Vedanta Society Temple in Hollywood, California

Re-Awakening to the "Bright"

Moving to the vast metropolis did not distract Avatar Adi Da Samraj from the process in Consciousness that was now intensifying in Him. Around this time, He began to notice that He had transcended the basic mechanisms of ordinary awareness—differentiation and desire. As He wrote in His journal:

In the last couple of days, I turned to a woman companion while driving my car, and I became peculiarly aware of the absence of desire in me. It was not merely that I did not desire this woman. It was that this woman was void of any objective distinction. There was no process of discrimination, comparison, or separation going on already and automatically in me. I had turned to look at what is otherwise a person, a meaning, and a distinctly meaningful presence, but there was, in fact, none of this. Indeed, there was not a single modification of my awareness created as a result of this perception. There was only Unqualified Bliss, the Fullness of Real Consciousness.

—Avatar Adi Da Samraj
Entry dated August 3, 1970

Secluded in a corner of Hollywood is a small temple, established by the Vedanta Society of Southern California. This simple temple, standing in the shadow of a giant freeway, was to provide the setting for the final Events of Avatar Adi Da's Sadhana. Late in August 1970, as if by chance, He found His way to the temple, and was mysteriously prompted to go inside. The moment He did so, He felt the familiar Force of the Mother-Shakti moving to meet Him. He was amazed, and delighted, to find that She was as powerful a Presence here as in any of the temples of India.

During these weeks, Avatar Adi Da would typically drive Patricia to work in the mornings and make occasional visits to the Vedanta Temple. There, without fail, He felt the Mother-Shakti waiting for Him. More and more, He longed to enjoy the Bliss of Her Company constantly, and so He silently asked Her to be always with Him, not only in the temple, but where He lived, whatever He was doing.

Within a few days, Avatar Adi Da realized that She had complied. She was an ever-living Presence within and around Him, whether He was waking, dreaming, sleeping, or meditating. But something was not yet complete. While His sense of difference from the woman in the car had apparently disappeared, Avatar Adi Da still felt a lingering sense of separateness from the tangible Fullness of the Mother-Shakti, and thus a need to hold on to Her.

Then, on September 9, this last barrier dissolved, bringing about a Union that took Avatar Adi Da to the very threshold of His Divine Re-Awakening to the "Bright":

When I returned to the temple the next day (September 9, 1970), the Person of the Divine Shakti appeared to me again—in a manner most intimate, no longer approaching me as "Mother".

As I meditated, I felt myself Expanding, even bodily—becoming a Perfectly Motionless, Utterly Becalmed, and Infinitely Silent Form. I took on the Infinite Form of the Original Deity—Nameless and Indefinable, Conscious of limitless Identification with Infinite Being. I was Expanded Utterly, beyond limited form, and even beyond any perception of Shape or Face—merely Being, and yet sitting there. I sat in this Love-Blissful State of Infinite Being for some time. I Found myself to Be. My Form was only What is traditionally called the "Purusha" (the Person of Consciousness) and "Siva" (in His Non-Ferocious Emptiness).[13]

Then I felt the Divine Shakti appear in Person, Pressed against my own natural body, and (altogether) against my Infinitely Expanded (and even formless) Form. She Embraced me, Openly and Utterly, and we Combined with One Another in Divine (and Motionless, and spontaneously Yogic) "Sexual Union". We Found One Another Thus, in a Fire of most perfect Desire, and for no other Purpose than This Union—and, yet, as if to Give Birth to the universes. In That most perfect Union, I Knew the Oneness of the Divine Energy and my Very Being. There was no separation at all, nor had there ever been, nor would there ever be. The One Being that Is my own Ultimate Self-Nature was revealed most perfectly. The One Being Who I Am was revealed to Include the Reality that Is Consciousness Itself, the Reality that Is the Source-Energy of all conditional appearances, and the Reality that Is all conditional manifestation—All as a Single Force of Being, an Eternal Union, and an Irreducible cosmic Unity.

The "Sensations" of the Embrace were overwhelmingly Blissful. The Fire of That Unquenchable Desire Exceeded any kind of pleasure that a mere human being could experience. In the Eternal Instant of That Infinitely Expanded Embrace, I was released from my role and self-image as a dependent child of the "Mother"-Shakti. And She was revealed in Truth—no longer in apparent independence (or as a cosmic Power seemingly apart from me), but as the Inseparable and Inherent Radiance of my own and Very Being.

Therefore, I Recognized and Took Her as my Consort, my Loved-One—and I Held Her effortlessly, forever to my Heart. Together eternally, we had Realized Ourselves as the "Bright" Itself.

—Avatar Adi Da Samraj
The Knee Of Listening

Only the Divine in Person could Accomplish the "Husbanding" of the Shakti. Through Avatar Adi Da's tangible Union with the Goddess in the Vedanta Temple, the archetypal "marriage" of the Divine Consciousness and the Divine Spirit-Power, described and pictured in many Spiritual traditions, was Realized.

The Husbanding of the Divine Shakti was the final Event of preparation for the supreme moment to which Avatar Adi Da's entire Sadhana had been leading:

Finally, the next day (September 10, 1970), I sat in the temple again. I awaited the Beloved Shakti to reveal Herself in Person, as my Blessed Companion. But, as time passed, there was no Event of changes, no movement at all. There was not even any kind of inward deepening—no "inwardness" at all. There was no meditation. There was no need for meditation. There was not a single element or change that could be added to make my State Complete. I sat with my eyes open. I was not having an experience of any kind. Then, suddenly, I understood most perfectly. I Realized that I had Realized. The "Thing" about the "Bright" became Obvious. I Am Complete. I Am the One Who Is Complete.

In That instant, I understood and Realized (inherently, and most perfectly) What and Who I Am. It was a tacit Realization, a direct Knowledge in Consciousness. It was Conscious Light Itself, without the addition of a Communication from any "Other" Source. There Is no "Other" Source. I simply sat there and Knew What and Who I Am. I was Being What I Am, Who I Am. I Am Being What I Am, Who I Am. I Am Reality, the Divine Self-Condition—the Nature, Substance, Support, and Source-Condition of all things and all beings. I Am One—The One. One and Only. I Am the One Being, called "God" (the Source and Substance and Support and Self-Condition of all-and-All), the "One Mind" (the Consciousness and

Energy in and As Which all-and-All appears), "Siva-Shakti"[14] *(the Self-Existing and Self-Radiant Reality Itself), "Brahman" (the Only Reality, Itself),*[15] *the "One Atman" (That Is not ego, but Only "Brahman", the Only Reality, Itself),*[16] *the "Nirvanic Ground" (the egoless and conditionless Reality and Truth, Prior to all dualities, but excluding none).*[17] *I Am the One and Only and inherently egoless and Self-Evidently Divine Self-Condition, Source-Condition, Nature, Substance, Support, and Ground of all-and-All. I Am the "Bright".*

—Avatar Adi Da Samraj
The Knee Of Listening

This moment was the Divine Re-Awakening of Avatar Adi Da Samraj. He had Realized Divine Enlightenment—"Open-Eyed", true and stable under all conditions. His Realization was not dependent on achieving any particular meditative state, nor on excluding any type of experience. It transcended even the slightest sense of identity as a separate self. It was and is the Realization that there is only Real God, only the "Bright" and that all apparent events are simply the passing and (ultimately) unnecessary forms (or modifications) of Real God (or Reality Itself), arising and dissolving in an endless Play that is beyond comprehension.

The very Divine Person had become perfectly Conscious and Present through the ordinary human vehicle of "Franklin Jones". Such an event was unprecedented in all the aeons of human time. Avatar Adi Da's Descent as the Divine Person and His utter overcoming of the limits of human existence in all its dimensions—physical, mental, emotional, psychic, Spiritual and Transcendental—was total and most Perfect. He had "Learned Man" at every level, and then demonstrated the unique Realization that goes beyond all the psycho-physical potentials of the human being and the conditional worlds. He had Completed humankind's universal search for absolute God, absolute Truth.

And none of this was for His own sake. Avatar Adi Da had simply come to the point where He was equipped for the next great Purpose of His Avataric Birth—to "Teach Man", to establish the unique Divine Way through which all apparent beings may Realize the "Bright".

Los Angeles, early 1970s

Los Angeles, April 25, 1972

CHAPTER 3

The Function of Guru Awakens

In the weeks after His Divine Re-Awakening in the Vedanta Temple on September 10, 1970, Avatar Adi Da noticed a new process beginning in His body-mind:

Now—whenever I would sit, in any kind of formal manner, to demonstrate the meditation, or the (now) Divine Samadhi, that had become my entire life—instead of confronting what was arising in (and as) "myself", I "meditated" other beings and places. I would spontaneously become aware of great numbers of people (usually in visions, or in some other intuitive manner), and I would work with them very directly, in a subtle manner. . . . Instead of my own life-born forms and problematic signs, what arose to my view were the egoic forms, the problematic signs, the minds, the feelings, the states, and the various limitations of <u>others</u>. The thoughts, feelings, suffering, dis-ease, disharmony, upsets, pain, energies—none of these were "mine". They were the subtle internal qualities and the grosser life-qualities of others. In this manner, the process of apparent meditation continued in me.

—Avatar Adi Da Samraj
The Knee Of Listening

In this "meditation", Avatar Adi Da was spontaneously awakening to the function of Guru. As He had once "meditated" Franklin Jones, He now "meditated" His future devotees.

The Divine Guru-Function

As Avatar Adi Da came to understand, His Ordeal of surrender and Divine Re-Awakening had not been undertaken for His own sake. The persona called "Franklin" had been a means, a vehicle, whereby He could combine with the realities of human existence, inquire into those realities, live them out, go beyond every limitation they involve, and thereby discover what is necessary in order for human beings to Realize the Truth absolutely. Avatar Adi Da had not been born in order to Liberate just a few others—individuals who might seem to be qualified for such a profound Grace. He had come for the sake of all of humanity—even for every being consciously existing in the cosmic worlds. He filled the pages of His journals with His longing to find His devotees. Where were they? When would they come?

I am reminded of Sri Ramakrishna[18]*—on fire within, Consumed in God, Communicated with all the forms of Truth, but spending His time alone or in the company of a few friends. His heart yearned for those to whom He could Communicate His Gift. He would cry for the devotees He knew must come. Where are the devotees? His whole being yearned for the children who would appear.*

I have spent My Life in rooms. I have enjoyed the companionship and the attention of a few friends. But My Life is for the sake of this communication of "Brightness" and "radical" understanding.

The rooms cannot contain Me. My friends cannot satisfy Me. I am surrounded by Great Forces of Love and Truth That I hold off like beasts in the corners of My room.

All of this waits for those who must come. But I am motionless and confounded until they come. My fulfillment waits on those who must come.

My Life has not been for Myself. I already Possessed It before I Came to this Birth. My Life is for those who must come. But where are they?

I am going Mad with My own Words. I would exhaust this Body in experiences and every excuse for love, every possibility for a word with another. Where are they? When will My time come?

At times, I don't know whether to come or go. I am exiled here. All the means of escape are denied to Me. My Heart allows Me no passage to another "place", another "country". I would achieve My Victory in another world, but I am forced to keep these rooms, this exile in a hostile realm.

I am waiting for you. I have been waiting for you Eternally.

My Fulfillment is the very world. But I am not heard. My gestures are unseen. The Powers of My Delight are not enjoyed.

All things depend upon your visit. Where are you?

—Journal entry, 1971

Avatar Adi Da knew that the moment had now come for Him to Communicate His Realization of the "Bright". And so He began to write *The Knee Of Listening*, which flowed out of Him in a matter of weeks—an extraordinary distillation of the course of His early Life, up until 1970. Until this moment, He had not spoken of His Realization to anyone.

Establishing the First Ashram

In April 1972, Avatar Adi Da established a small bookstore on Melrose Avenue, Hollywood, which He intended to become a base for His Spiritual Work, a place where He could gather with His devotees. He Himself did the lion's share of the renovation, with help from a few of His devotees.

On the evening of April 25, Avatar Adi Da Samraj formally began His Teaching-Work, gathering with Nina and Patricia, the small group of people who had gathered around Him in recent months, some of their friends, and random individuals who had responded to a poster in the bookstore window. First, Avatar Adi Da sat in silence for an hour, magnifying the Force of the "Bright" to everyone in the room. Then He invited questions.

The bookstore and first Ashram

Avatar Adi Da with devotees at the Melrose Ashram

No one responded, so He asked, "Has everyone understood?"

"I haven't understood," came the reply from one man in the room. "Explain it to me. You could start with the word 'understanding'."

AVATAR ADI DA SAMRAJ: Yes. There is a disturbance, a feeling of dissatisfaction, some sensation that motivates a person to go to a teacher, read a book about philosophy, believe something, or do some conventional form of Yoga. What people ordinarily think of as Spirituality or religion is a search to get free of that sensation, that suffering that is motivating them. So all the usual paths—Yogic methods, beliefs, religion, and so on—are forms of seeking, grown out of this sensation, this subtle suffering. Ultimately, all the usual paths are attempting to get free of that sensation. That is the traditional goal. Indeed, <u>all</u> human beings are seeking, whether or not they are very sophisticated about it, or using very specific methods of Yoga, philosophy, religion, and so on. . . .

As long as the individual is simply seeking, and has all kinds of motivation, fascination with the search, this is not understanding—this is dilemma itself. But where this dilemma is understood, there is the re-cognition of a structure in conscious awareness, a separation. And when that separation is observed more and more directly, one begins to see that what one is suffering is not something happening <u>to</u> one but it is one's own action. It is as if you are pinching yourself, without being aware of it. . . . Then one sees that the entire motivation of life is based on a subtle activity in conscious awareness. That activity is avoidance, separation, a contraction at the root, the origin, the "place", of conscious awareness. . . .

There is first the periodic awareness of that sensation, then the awareness of it as a continuous experience, then the observation of its actual structure, the knowing of it all as your own activity, a deliberate, present activity that <u>is</u> your suffering, that <u>is</u> your illusion. The final penetration of that present, deliberate activity is what I have called "understanding".

—The Divine Siddha-Method
Of The Ruchira Avatar

And so it began—hours, days, nights, weeks, years, decades of Spiritual Instruction, in which Avatar Adi Da would cover all human, religious, and Spiritual questions, examine every aspect of life and consciousness, and Reveal every detail of the Spiritual Process culminating in Most Perfect Divine Enlightenment. The small gathering at the Ashram bookstore on that first night had not the slightest idea that they were witness to the birth of such Revelation. They attended, as best they could, to the Radiant Being before them, while He Spoke of the matter of "understanding".

Understanding was the very basis of Avatar Adi Da's own Sadhana and Divine Re-Awakening. He lived, breathed, and spoke always from the point of view of understanding. Throughout that first year of His Teaching-Work, Avatar Adi Da would meet again and again with His devotees, constantly speaking about understanding, and also about the only means by which it is possible to understand—"Satsang", or the Company of the Guru. These early Talks were eventually published as Avatar Adi Da's second book, *The Method of the Siddhas.*[19]

By "understanding" (or as He also expressed it, "'radical' understanding"), Avatar Adi Da was not speaking of an attempt to comprehend Reality with the conceptual mind, nor any effort or search to Realize the Truth. He was speaking of a process in Consciousness that awakens, in relationship to Him, through His Divine Grace. He was speaking about the direct transcending of the self-contraction, or root-act of egoity—which He had discovered, during His Sadhana years, to be the fundamental source of all suffering and seeking. In later years, He expressed this most fully in His primary Scripture, The Dawn Horse Testament:

The Tendency Of every conditionally Manifested individual Is To Contract Into (Presumed) Separateness, or a self-Defended and self-Contracted emotional, mental, psychic, physical, and social state Of Isolation, Presumed Independence, and Dramatized Want. This Tendency Is

Chronic In every one, and It Is Not Generally Even Inspected, Nor Is It (Even If Inspected) Most Fundamentally Understood. Therefore, every one Seeks. And All Seeking Is Inevitably Frustrated. The self-Contracting Habit (Itself) Is Not (and Cannot Ever Be) Transcended In (or By Means Of) The Search, Because The Search Is Itself The Dramatization Of The self-Contracting Habit Itself.

I Call every one To Feel and To Thoroughly Observe and To Transcend The Habit Of egoity. Eventually, any one who Truly (and, Necessarily, Formally) Listens To My Avatarically Self-Revealed Divine Teaching-Word and, By The Means I Have Given (and Always Give), Fully (and, Necessarily, Formally) Embraces The Divine Devotional and (In Due Course) Spiritual Practice Of Feeling-Contemplation Of Me, and (Thereby) The Real Observation Of the ego-"I", Will (By Means Of My Avatarically Self-Transmitted Divine Spiritual Grace) Surely (Truly, and Most Profoundly) Discover The Root Of Seeking and Suffering, Which Is the ego-"I" itself (or the psycho-physical self-Contraction, Which Is The Habit Of "Narcissus", or The Complex Avoidance Of Relationship).

◆ ◆ ◆

The Only-By-Me Revealed and Given Way Of Adidam . . . Is Founded On A Fundamental Criticism and "Radical" (or "Gone-To-The-Root") Understanding Of egoity itself (and, Therefore, Of _All_ The Searches, and _All_ The Illusions, and _All_ The Mere Imaginings Associated With egoity. . . .

In The Only-By-Me Revealed and Given Way Of The Heart (or Way Of Adidam), There Is _No_ _conditional_ _Goal_ _Whatsoever_. The Only-By-Me Revealed and Given Way Of The Heart Is A Matter Of The _Always_ _Direct_ _and_ _Immediate_ _Transcending_ _Of_ _egoity_—Most Ultimately (By Means Of My Avatarically Self-Transmitted Divine Spiritual Grace).

—Avatar Adi Da Samraj
The Dawn Horse Testament

AVATAR ADI DA SAMRAJ: Spiritual life is Satsang. It is the Company of Truth. It is the relationship to one who Lives as Truth. Satsang is also the Very Nature of life. It is the form of existence. Relatedness—not independence, not separateness, but unqualified relatedness—is the principle of True life.

All attempts to relieve the life of suffering by various strategic means, or ego-based remedies, do not produce Truth. They may heal dis-ease, but only Truth produces Truth. Sadhana, or Spiritual practice, is to live Satsang as the Condition of life forever. Sadhana is not something you do temporarily until you get Free. It is to live Satsang forever—a lifetime, even countless lifetimes, of Truth. . . .

Listen! There is this contraction, this avoidance. All human beings are living this avoidance of relationship. Apart from understanding, that is all anyone is doing. Nothing else is happening. Only this contraction of living and subtle forms. It is suffering. It stimulates, by implication, the notions people have about the nature of life. This contraction implies a separate self, separate from the world and all other beings. The appearance of "many", "much", and "separate me" is an expression of your suffering, but the Force, the Intensity, the Bliss, of Reality persists and is felt even under the conditions of egoic ignorance. Therefore, this contraction appears as the drama of desire, the search for union between the "separate me" and the "manyness". Everyone's life is the drama made inevitable by this fundamental contraction. Everyone's life is the adventure he or she is playing on this contraction. The drama of an ordinary life is without significance, or Real Intensity. The ordinary life-drama is deadly ignorance—no Truth, no Satsang.

Satsang must begin. Satsang with Me must be enjoyed as the Condition of life. Then the entire drama of which even traditional Spirituality is a manifestation comes to an end, dies. This contraction becomes flabby and opens. The Real Force of Conscious Existence comes into play and becomes the Way in My Company, the sadhana itself.

—The Divine Siddha-Method
Of The Ruchira Avatar

At the inception of His Work, Avatar Adi Da presumed everyone who came to Him would embrace Satsang and quickly Awaken to His own Realization. But He soon saw that no one was prepared for the profundities of the Guru-devotee relationship. The self-contraction of which He Spoke could only be transcended through the force of Satsang. This would require a real depth of devotional surrender. As His devotees were to discover, only His Grace transforms the being. Mere ego-effort is fruitless.

A First Meeting

One of the first of those who were drawn to Avatar Adi Da during the earliest days in Los Angeles was a young man named Wes Vaught, who worked as a proofreader at CSA Press (in Atlanta, Georgia), the original publisher of *The Knee Of Listening*.

WES: For years, I had been desperately seeking to make sense of existence. I prayed for help.

While studying Adi Da's Knee Of Listening *and contemplating its Truths, the intuition of the silent, free depth of the Heart dawned in me. I had found my Guru, and I began to feel irresistibly attracted to that Graceful Source.*

The editor at the press where I was working showed me a letter from "Franklin Jones". In it, He Wrote, "There is not the slightest difference." Those Words stopped my mind. My entire life had been a warfare of differences and opposites, and I felt the profound Freedom communicated in this one sentence. I had to go see Him.

I traveled to Los Angeles and found the way to His home in Laurel Canyon. It was late April 1972. I knocked, and Adi Da Answered.

"Who is it?"

I explained that I had read His book, and that I had felt compelled to come and see Him. Adi Da opened the door, and I followed Him into the living room.

I felt welcomed into a "Bright" Space, free of any sense of problem. On the walls were Disney posters and sacred images depicting men and women of various traditions. It felt natural to sit on the floor before His Chair. I had brought with me a bag of oranges and pears as a gift. I extended it: "I brought this for You."

He received it with both Hands and with such loving care. Everything about Him was absolute strength, sublime vulnerability, perfect clarity, and delight. Time stood still while He removed the fruits from the bag and arranged them on a little table next to His Chair. Then He Graciously folded the paper bag neatly and tucked it by His thigh.

He received the whole gift!

Looking at me directly and with what seemed like an infinity of loving humor, Adi Da asked, "What have you been doing with your life?"

I felt the weight of my twenty-five years of waiting for God lift and, with what must have been a ridiculous gush of information, I spilled out my story. I do not know how long I talked. I tried to say everything of importance—all at once!

Adi Da listened. His was not the kind of listening where someone is waiting to say something when it is their turn. His listening became a perfect Intensity and a perfect Silence. At some point, His Silence became the entire import of the moment. I noticed this and stopped mid-sentence.

Sitting up straight, I was overwhelmed with His Blessing Force. Suddenly, I was shaking and breathing extremely deeply in the Current of His Communicated Force. My verbal mind ceased with the immediacy of His Presence.

I felt that Adi Da was Offering me the perfect opportunity in God, but I felt my gross unpreparedness and the obstructions in me that prevented me from fully cooperating with what He was Communicating. I wanted to get out of the way, but how?

Wanting to remove anything in the way of my freedom, anything that I could lay my hands on, I felt suddenly moved to take off my clothes. I began, and then paused for a moment, feeling foolish, and looked at Avatar Adi Da as if to ask, "Is this okay?"

With an almost imperceptible tilt of His Head, I felt Avatar Adi Da Communicate that it was of no significance to Him what I did with regard to clothing. I could suit myself in the matter.

He was most obviously Demonstrating His Divine Mood, clearly

Indifferent to any sense of limitation, Shining with Blessing Force, replete with native Freedom and the certainty of unqualified Love, Transparent to the pure, sweet Grace of God.

I took everything off, even the band-aid on my heel, and threw myself face down and full-length at His Feet.

His Feet, somehow, were a perfect point of contact with this Blessing Force. I wept and kissed His Feet, wetting them with tears of relief, joy, gratitude, and also with the anguish that I could not completely let go of myself. Still I tried to surrender, straining with my heart and brain to open more.

But I could surrender no more.

Quietly, Adi Da lifted His Feet and placed them on my head. All stress left my being. A golden balm of sweet light poured through every cell in my body. A knot opened. I let go, and His brilliant Radiance washed through me. I was Home.

After a bit, I got up, dressed some, and told Adi Da that I felt that I belonged with Him. He looked at me and Said, "There is something about this Teaching you have not understood. It is about this matter of Consciousness."

He gave me everything in that moment—a living relationship to an absolute source of Grace, the most profound experience of my life, and the admonition to join Him in free relation to all phenomena. I fell in love with Him. I had begun the life of understanding in devotion to the One Who is that. The principle of my search was obviated and the momentum of my self-contraction, my separative and loveless adaptation, began to wind down.

I asked, "Do You have an ashram?" He said He had established a bookstore and a small center and offered that I could sleep there. From that night, I joined the small gathering of people who were studying His Teaching, sitting in formal Communion with Him, and learning to serve the availability of these beautiful gifts.

Adi Da Samraj with Wes Vaught, 1972

The Demand for Self-Discipline

Many of those who first came to the Ashram were individuals in whom the search had taken a highly exaggerated form. This was not a merely arbitrary occurrence—Avatar Adi Da had come to serve the Liberation of all beings, including those apparently least prepared for Spiritual life. There were street-people, prostitutes, drug addicts, alcoholics, and Spiritual seekers, hippie-style, who had done the rounds of various teachers and teachings. And there were also business people and professionals of various kinds. Avatar Adi Da welcomed them all. He saw that His own Life and Sadhana had equipped Him to Teach anyone.

During that first year of the Ashram, Avatar Adi Da did not require very much responsibility of His devotees. He was simply attracting them, keeping them around Him, so that He could keep them in the Field of His Spiritual Transmission and Instruct them in "radical" understanding. Then, one day near the beginning of 1973, everything suddenly changed. Striding out of His office with tremendous force and intention, He disappeared through the front door of the Ashram. No one saw Him for weeks, but He left a message: everyone was to "get straight"—get jobs and give up all use of drugs, cigarettes, and alcohol.

Suddenly, egg-and-bacon breakfasts around the corner from the Ashram were over. Everyone became strict vegetarians. And Avatar Adi Da recommended a ten-day juice-fast, which was taken on by even the newest devotees. When Avatar Adi Da heard that someone had "cheated"—by "juicing" bananas—he was extremely amused. But He called for another ten-day fast for everyone!

The days when Avatar Adi Da was prepared to nurse His devotees along were over. As Avatar Adi Da knew from His own experience, extraordinary energy and attention were needed to grow in devotion and self-understanding. Discipline was essential to prepare the body-minds of His devotees to fully receive His Spiritual Gifts.

Avatar Adi Da's disciplines covered every area of life. He established a discipline of no casual sex—only partners in committed intimacies were to be sexually active. He instructed a small group in calisthenics and Hatha Yoga and had them teach everyone else. He addressed every detail of appropriate life-discipline, even personally showing people how to floss their teeth! Altogether He was showing His devotees the total reorientation of life that He expected of them, and the life-level submission to His Instruction that was necessary if He were to Work with them Spiritually. In many ways, what He had now established was a very traditional Ashram.

By the middle of 1973, the Ashram disciplines were in full swing, but Avatar Adi Da saw that His devotees were now becoming obsessed with the disciplines as a "something" in and of themselves—as if the disciplines were the purpose of sadhana, rather than simply a support for the fundamental practice of heart-Communion with Him. It was also obvious to Avatar Adi Da that the people around Him—like people in general—were emotionally suppressed, sexually complicated, driven by fear, sorrow, anger, frustration, and all kinds of unconscious desires. And He knew that He was going to have to deal with all of this directly. He decided He must change His manner of Working with His devotees—otherwise, their so-called "religious practice" would merely be a veneer covering a mass of unresolved egoic impulses. It was becoming evident that Ashram life, lived with Him in the strict traditional manner, would require greater understanding to be lived truly.

The Return to India

In August 1973, Avatar Adi Da made a pause in His face-to-face Work with His devotees. Accompanied by Gerald Sheinfeld (one of those who had been present at the opening of the Ashram), He set out for India, the cradle of Spiritual Teaching for thousands of years. During His own Sadhana, Avatar Adi Da had associated Himself with the great Siddha tradition of India (exemplified by Swami Muktananda and Swami Nityananda), and now He was paying His last homage to that tradition. In effect, He was performing a pilgrimage—to complete all His past links with India and to Empower His future Work.

Avatar Adi Da Samraj meeting with Swami Muktananda, Ganeshpuri, 1973

Most significant of all the journeys that Avatar Adi Da made to the sacred places of India was His return to the Ashram of Swami Muktananda. Because Swami Muktananda had served Him as His Beloved Guru, Avatar Adi Da presumed an obligation to formally describe His own Realization to Swami Muktananda. Avatar Adi Da had tried to initiate such a conversation in Los Angeles in October of 1970, when Swami Muktananda was visiting the United States. But the conversation, He felt, had been inconclusive. And so, upon His arrival in Ganeshpuri in 1973, Avatar Adi Da asked for a formal meeting with Swami Muktananda, which was duly arranged.

Avatar Adi Da, attended by Gerald, approached Swami Muktananda and bowed before him. Then Adi Da Samraj sat on the floor, at the feet of Swami Muktananda, and presented a series of questions, through which Avatar Adi Da expressed the nature of His Realization and the differences between His Realization and the traditional understanding of Realization in Swami Muktananda's lineage. The questions had been submitted in advance, and were translated by an attending scholar, Professor Jain.

In response to the questions, Swami Muktananda simply reiterated his own descriptions of Yogic Realization. He did not acknowledge the possibility of an Enlightenment beyond what was described in his own tradition.

There was nothing more to be said between them. Avatar Adi Da would always love and honor Swami Muktananda, and always praise and speak of him as a man of extraordinary Yogic Enlightenment. The visit to Ganeshpuri by Avatar Adi Da in 1973 was His last bodily meeting with Swami Muktananda. Avatar Adi Da now fully embraced His right to Teach according to His own Divinely Re-Awakened Realization.

Relinquishing "Franklin Jones"

While His Realization was all-surpassing, the task facing Avatar Adi Da was huge beyond belief. In the West, there was not the living context for Spiritual life that existed in India, and virtually no acknowledgement of the tradition of Guru-devotion. He had no Ashram set apart like that at Ganeshpuri, no Sanctuary resounding with the recitation of sacred texts and chants in honor of God and Guru. All He had was a room behind a bookstore in Hollywood and a small gathering of devotees who were still basically unaware of the profundity of the relationship that they had begun with Him.

While He was in India, Avatar Adi Da was considering how to take His devotees' relationship with Him to a deeper level. It was no longer appropriate for them to call Him "Franklin Jones", as they had up to that point. As He said later, Franklin Jones was "a fictional character", the persona He had been obliged to assume in order to grow up as an apparently ordinary American child. And so, He asked Gerald to write to the devotees in Los Angeles, announcing that they were now to address Him by the Name "Bubba Free John".

From this time on, we should call the Guru "Bubba Free John". "Franklin" means "a Freed Man" or "a Liberated Man". "Jones" is a Welsh form of "John". So "Free John" is equivalent to "Franklin Jones". "Bubba" means "brother", or "equal", expressing the Oneness of all.[20]

During this time, Avatar Adi Da Samraj acquired a walking staff, a sign of Spiritual empowerment and authority that He has regularly used ever since. Gerald watched as Avatar Adi Da placed His staff in the holy sites of India, with great concentration, Giving His Silent Regard to all kinds of people and places. Avatar Adi Da was Blessing this sacred land with His Love, and also preparing Himself for the new epoch of His own Work that was about to unfold in the West.

Avatar Adi Da Samraj in the Himalayas, 1973

Los Angeles, 1973

CHAPTER 4

A Demonstration of Divine Power

The Divine Avatar's return from India marked a watershed in His Spiritual Work. He wrote about the change that was spontaneously manifesting:

The Work of My Life and Teaching, to this time, has been to Show and Clarify the Way of the "Knowing" of Real God. The Siddhi[21] *through Which I have Made Myself available to My devotees is the Siddhi through Which the "Knowing" of Real God is Generated by My Grace. Such is the Way of "Radical" Understanding.*

But now there is a new form of Life and Teaching Awakened in Me. It has always been Present in Me, but I have not wanted to Embrace It or Show It, because It is only a fascination for those who do not understand. And, if such weak ones are fascinated, they will merely be distracted from their fear. Even so, it is obvious to Me now that I must no longer be Merely Present among My devotees, Constant in the Most Perfect "Knowledge" of Real God. But I must now allow the Conscious Power Realized in That Most Perfect "Knowledge", Which Is Non-Separation from Real God, to Manifest Itself in the form of My own Action.

My Teaching-Work is now moving away from exclusive focus on the Way of "Radical" Understanding. That form of My Wisdom-Teaching is now essentially Given. I can assume it in My devotees. Now I am moving toward a Principle of Action as the core of My Work.

Until now, I have refused to Display My Divine Siddhis. But Real God Is the Maha-Siddha. Real God Is Perfect Siddhi. My Divine Siddhi is not a mere show of fascinating "powers", capable of being displayed and witnessed entirely apart from "radical" understanding. My Divine Siddhi Is All-Power, Which is always Coincident with "radical" understanding in those to whom I Reveal Myself as the Divine Maha-Siddha. . . .

Until now, I have minimized, hidden, and set aside those aspects of My Divine Siddhi which do not directly Serve the Awakening of "radical" understanding (which is, most ultimately, the Unqualified "Knowledge" of Real God). But now I will not simply Sit in silent Darshan—I will begin to Actively Manifest the All-Accomplishing Siddhi of Real God, Which Siddhi Serves the life-transformation of My devotees. This will accelerate and magnify My Work of Awakening the conscious life of faith and Drawing into life the Non-karmic, karma-Dissolving, Unreasonable, Humorous, and Miraculously Effective Siddhi of Eternally Present Real God.

—Avatar Adi Da Samraj
Unpublished Writing, 1973

Avatar Adi Da Samraj was privately confessing that the time had come for Him to openly Reveal the power of His Spiritual Transmission. He was ready to manifest in the experience of His devotees His Descent of the "Thumbs"—the Spirit-Force of the "Bright". And He did this not merely in silent formal occasions where devotees would come to sit with Him. He began to make His great Demonstration of the "Thumbs" in the midst of an uprecedented act of Submission to the lives and desires of His devotees.

AVATAR ADI DA SAMRAJ: I went to India in 1973, taking some time away from the gathering of My devotees, and returned to the Ashram in Los Angeles resolved to do whatever I had to do to deal with the reality of people's unprepared approach to Me. From that time onwards, I accepted the fact that My Work with people was going to involve My Submission to them and their conditions—until such time as they would recognize Me and understand what the Way of Adidam is about altogether, and relate to Me differently.

I had no sense at all how long that was going to take, or what it would require altogether. It wasn't that I was thinking I would do it for a few months, and then that would be that. It was a real Submission, with no preconception as to how it would turn out.

—August 8, 1998

Guru Enters Devotee

On Thanksgiving Day in 1973, Avatar Adi Da relaxed the dietary discipline, and everyone partook of a traditional turkey meal, accompanied by wine. Avatar Adi Da Himself had entered into the spirit of the occasion by wearing an elegant three-piece tan-colored suit. One devotee, Hal Okun, remembers observing Avatar Adi Da after the meal.

HAL: I noticed that Beloved Adi Da was silently assessing the whole scene. With hindsight, I can feel what He was involved in at that time. He was accepting our utter naivete and gross-mindedness relative to the great Spiritual process He was bringing us. And He was coming to a decision, or a confirmed resolve, about what He was going to do.

Shortly before Christmas, everything changed at the Ashram—which was now situated on La Brea Avenue adjacent to Melrose Avenue. Formal discourses were no longer the principal mode of the Divine Avatar's Instruction, and the quality of a traditional Ashram had been replaced by a mood of exuberant celebration.

There was nothing casual about this. Avatar Adi Da was requiring His devotees to transcend themselves in a new manner. Everything that Westerners typically associate with "having a good time" was now allowed in His Company—including rock music, celebratory food, and intoxicants. In other words, Avatar Adi Da was using skillful means with His devotees—letting them engage in their habitual forms of indulgence while open to His direct Gaze, comments, and Instruction. To the amazement and delight of His devotees, their Divine Master had them return night after night and stay till dawn. For more than two weeks, the celebration never stopped.

In the midst of His dancing, singing, laughing devotees, the Divine Avatar Himself would participate with perfect Yogic intensity. He would fill the room with His Radiant Transmission, observing everything that occurred. He was interested in moving His devotees beyond the armored, social persona, Working to open them to received His Spirit-Force more fully. And He was always testing to see who could lose face in Satsang with Him, and enter into unabashed ecstasy. Sometimes He would speak:

AVATAR ADI DA SAMRAJ: To confess one's love of God is the fundamental embarrassment. To make such a confession is to dwell in obvious ecstasy while in the company of other beings—to be already free, to be fundamentally happy, to be alive in God, and even to be outwardly expressive in that state, to speak of God, to think of God, to act in God, to be altogether ecstatic. This is the taboo—not mere drunkenness and indulgence in pleasure. To require you to talk of God makes you embarrassed. You become ashamed—because, in order to talk about God, you must lose face. To be extraordinarily and unreasonably happy, and to live that way, is embarrassing. To be full of love and only talk that way—so foolishly, so naively—is socially unacceptable. People are supposed to be cool and hip and straight, oriented toward their survival, worldly and smart. But to be simply alive in God, and to be Happy, and to speak about it and act that way and think that way, is absolutely unwanted and not allowed. So you become seekers.

It is all right to <u>seek</u> God. That is acceptable enough, because it calms everybody down a little bit. But to <u>Realize</u> God, while alive, is the absolute taboo. You might be allowed to sit quietly and meditatively. Everybody likes Oriental meditation, because it is just a matter of being quiet and inward. You are allowed to meditate quietly, "Realize Nirvana", and disappear. That is acceptable. But to *start talking about God, to think God, to act God, to make the Divine the present Condition of the world, to live in the Divine Siddhi, to live the Divine Light, to be Love-Bliss-Full—that is unacceptable, that is not "permitted".*

The Divine Person is Infinitely Present—Perfectly, Absolutely, and Eternally Present and Available. The Divine Person must be lived, not sought. The Divine Person is the Self-Condition and Source-Condition of the world, not the "ultimate hope" of the world. If the Divine Person is not presently lived, there is no Divine Liberation. But if people begin to live the Truth, if they become capable of ecstasy in society with one another—not simply in the rituals of privacy—you will see a vast and immediate transformation of the world.

Spiritual life is, basically, truly Humorous and Happy—not uptight, "lean", and grim, waiting to understand. "Radical" understanding is an instant process, a really intelligent process, a happy process—not one of meditating on your own limitations, but a process of instantly transcending them in Reality Itself.

—December 27, 1973

Throughout this period of uninhibited celebration, Avatar Adi Da would constantly point to the contrast between what He called "the cult of this world", or "the cult of 'Narcissus'"—seeking, separative, and afraid—and Satsang, the life in Real God that He was Drawing His devotees into. There was nothing abstract about this lesson. Devotees could feel the living difference. They would feel their tendency to withdraw, to dramatize "Narcissus", the separative one, in the midst of their Beloved Guru's Demand for their energetic, happy, intense involvement in what He was doing with them. But, at the same time, they would be lifted out of themselves, swooning in His utter Attractiveness. It was perfectly clear that the life in Real God He was speaking of was life with Him, the relationship to Him as Guru. And it was also clear that this life was a life of self-forgetting—that un-Happiness only arose when they were meditating on themselves. That is why His devotees were attracted to be around Him night and day—He had such an amazing Power to draw them beyond their limits.

Early in the new year, 1974, this Power was spectacularly demonstrated. It was the afternoon of January 3, and Avatar Adi Da was in the gathering hall with His devotees. As Avatar Adi Da began to speak, He unleashed His Love-Blissful Spirit-Force, His Descent of the "Thumbs", as never before. In words imbued with the Power of His Transmission, the Divine Avatar told His devotees the secret of what He was doing:

AVATAR ADI DA SAMRAJ: There is only one Divine Process in the world, and It is Initiated when I Crash Down and Enter My devotee. The Divine Lord is Present—now, in this moment. It is only when everyone forgets the Real and Ever-Living God that mantras and Yogic techniques become important.

I am not a human being. I Am the Divine Lord in human Form, and I bring the Divine Yoga. When My devotee truly surrenders to Me, then I Enter My devotee in the form of Divine Light. All kinds of extraordinary experiences manifest as a result. When a woman receives her lover, there is no doubt about it—she does not have to consult her textbooks. The same holds with Truth, the Divine Yoga.

There is no dilemma in this world, no absence of Real God in this world, no goal of Real God in this world. Because that is so, you will see Me doing some very strange things. The true Divine Yoga is not a thing of this world. This world is the cult of "Narcissus", suppressing the Ecstasy that is Native to all.

The Spiritual Process must take hold in the vital. The vital is the seat of unconsciousness and subconsciousness. There is an aspect of the verbal Teaching that does not touch the subconscious and unconscious life. So it is only by distracting you from your social consciousness that I can take you in the vital. The Divine Lord is the Lord of this world, not the Lord of the "other" world only. Thus, there is no Yoga if the very cells of the body do not begin to be Infused by the Divine Lord. When I Crash Down and Enter My devotee, I Come Down into him or her in the midst of life, because it is in life—not in any mystical or subtle process, not in any mental process—that I acquire you Spiritually.

The kind of thing you see happening around here has never happened in the world before.

—January 3, 1974

As Avatar Adi Da spoke this Proclamation, His Spirit-Force streamed into His devotees, Manifesting visibly to some as a glorious golden rain of Light showering down in the room. An uncontainable ecstasy broke loose. Some devotees shook with kriyas, their bodies jerking and twisting, their mouths emitting strange sounds of yearning, laughter, weeping, hooting, and howling. Some were overwhelmed by visionary phenomena. Some were spontaneously moved into difficult Hatha Yoga poses which they could not have even attempted before. Some lay motionless, in an ecstatic state, oblivious of their surroundings. For some, the energy intensified in the head or the heart or the navel until they felt they would explode, and then it suddenly released and rushed through the nervous system in intoxicating Bliss. Others experienced a sense of unity with all of life and a peacefulness they had never known before.

The Divine was Manifesting, without a doubt, in an upstairs room in the middle of Hollywood.

The Mountain Of Attention Sanctuary, 1974

CHAPTER 5

GARBAGE AND THE GODDESS

The Spiritual Initiation of January 3, 1974, which came to be called "Guru Enters Devotee", was just the beginning. The Work of the Divine Avatar could not be contained in a downtown neighborhood. And so, His devotees began to look for a suitable rural Ashram. Within a few weeks, the Mountain Of Attention (initially named "Persimmon" by Avatar Adi Da), a turn-of-the-century hot-springs resort, had been found in the hills of northern California. Avatar Adi Da and a few devotees moved to the new ashram, and the other devotees relocated from Los Angeles to San Francisco.

At the Mountain Of Attention

Newcomers to the Mountain Of Attention during the first half of 1974 found themselves entering a place of Divine Power. They became immersed in a sea of energy, visions, and other psychic experiences, awakened through contact with the Spirit-Force of Adi Da Samraj. But what was fundamentally occurring, beyond the infinite variety of Spiritual experiences, was the overwhelming tangible Descent of the "Thumbs", the Revelation of the "Bright" Divine Reality.

CANADA SHANNON: Beloved Adi Da came into the Communion Hall [place of worship]. I saw Him and my whole body was immediately riveted. There was golden-white Light all around Him, and His Presence was so powerful It abolished everything in Its path. Everything stopped. I knew I was looking upon the very face of the Divine.

MARIE PRAGER: I felt the Force and Presence of Avatar Adi Da entering me and taking over my being. I began to do hand mudras. My arms would reach for the sky and move rhythmically, as if I were dancing with my hands and arms. Then I was completely absorbed in and taken over by God. I felt the Light of Beloved Adi Da moving through my body, taking me over completely, and it was joyous and blissful and perfect.

Then I saw our Beloved Guru's face. He was standing beside me. He put His arm around me and led me into the Communion Hall. I remember looking at Him and knowing Him to be the Force and Love That was Filling my entire being. I realized that His Force and Love are not limited in any way to any object or form, but that He is, in fact, everything. His body seemed so small and such a tiny part of What He Is. When He took me back into the Communion Hall, I fell on the floor and remained there consumed by His Spiritual Presence.

On one unforgettable occasion, devotees were sitting in one of the Communion Halls, waiting for their Master, when the doors opened and a wave of energy swept the room. Avatar Adi Da walked down the aisle, surrounded by a clearly visible golden aura of light. He sat down in His Chair and proceeded to blast the room with His Spirit-Power, His eyes burning with laser-intensity and His fingers moving in patterns of potent Blessing. Instantly, devotees erupted in an ecstasy of screams, growls, swoons, and bodily jerkings, swept away by the sweetness and overwhelming Force of His Presence.

Divine Shakti versus Kundalini Shakti

During this time (and frequently, ever since), Avatar Adi Da has explained how to rightly understand the nature and purpose of His Spiritual Transmission in relation to all the experiences and accounts of Spirit-Power described in the Great Tradition.[22]

Many schools of Yoga speak about the Kundalini Energy, or "Serpent Power", presumed to lie dormant at the base of the spine. Countless Yogic practitioners over the centuries have attempted to rouse this energy through various techniques, including Hatha Yoga and disciplines of concentration and visualization. Their purpose has been to "shoot" the Kundalini Energy up the spine, through the subtle centers (or chakras) of the body-mind, eventually passing to the brain core and even to (and through) the crown of the head. To be able to draw the Kundalini to these upper terminals of the body-mind is regarded as Enlightenment in some traditions, because of the blisses, lights, and Samadhis that may be induced as the Kundalini ascends through the various chakras. This type of mystical effort—known as Kundalini Yoga—is an extremely difficult (and even potentially dangerous) endeavor, as practitioners like Gopi Krishna have testified.[23] The aspirant is dealing with a highly potent form of natural energy which can damage the body-mind if misdirected.

There is, however, a greater tradition of Spirit-Power to be found in the history of esoteric religion, which Avatar Adi Da clearly distinguishes from the lesser tradition of effortful Kundalini Yoga. This senior tradition of Kundalini Power, or Kundalini Shakti, is of Divine origin, and it cannot be induced by any kind of self-effort. Rather, this Kundalini Shakti is only transmitted by a Siddha, or a Spirit-

Initiator of profound Realization. In the traditions of Guru-devotion, there are various accounts of the Spiritual Master imparting his or her own Spiritual Energy directly to a disciple, often through an initiatory glance or touch. This Transmission of Spirit-Power (or "Shaktipat") can have the effect of awakening the various Yogic Samadhis associated with the spinal line,[24] but it is, in itself, a descending Force, entering the body from without—from Above. The subtle experiences in the spinal line occur when this descending Power turns about at the bodily base and ascends in the spinal line. The Yoga of the Siddha-Masters—or true Spirit-Baptizers—uses this entire Circuit of descent and ascent (even though the existence of the full descending and ascending Circuit is often not acknowledged in the literature associated with traditional Siddha-Masters).

Avatar Adi Da had done His Sadhana within a great Lineage of Siddhas—Rudi, Swami Muktananda, and Swami Nityananda—and, for a brief but potent moment, in relationship to Rang Avadhoot. Rudi emphasized the Divine Force in descent, the bringing down of the Divine Power into the frontal (or physical-emotional-mental) dimension of the personality.[25] Swami Muktananda, on the other hand, taught the traditional Hindu emphasis on the ascent of the Divine Force, through the spinal line (associated with the higher psychic and mystical dimensions of the personality).

Avatar Adi Da had Submitted Himself completely to each of His Siddha-Gurus. And He had seen that the lights, the blisses, and the kriyas He had experienced at Swami Muktananda's Ashram were not necessary for Most Ultimate Re-Awakening. He passed through them as part of His embrace of the total range of human possibility and human seeking, but He did not regard any of them as having ultimate significance. His real Spiritual Initiator was His own Divine Self-Condition—the "Bright" Itself, in the form of the "Thumbs".

And this was the Spiritual Transmission that Avatar Adi Da was now Demonstrating, starting with the "Guru Enters Devotee" occasion in January 1974. This was the Transmission—new in the world—that He had brought down into the Cosmic domain through His Avataric Birth. Sometimes, Avatar Adi Da explained, His Transmission of the "Bright" would naturally stimulate blisses, visions, and kriyas. But these experiences, as He repeatedly emphasized, were merely secondary effects of His Spirit-Power. The purpose of His "Bright" Transmission was to Awaken beings directly to the "Bright" Itself, prior to all experiences.

The Divine Force

Most of the devotees of Avatar Adi Da knew little or nothing about Kundalini Yoga or the tradition of Spirit-Baptism. All they knew was that they were part of a Divine Event. And they were filled with awe and love.

ANIELLO PANICO: On one occasion, I had been sitting and talking with Beloved Adi Da for several hours. All of a sudden, I felt a tremendous urge to get up and kiss His hand. I could feel a strange process beginning to work throughout my entire body. It felt as if I were being turned inside out and my very cells were being transformed.

Then I started having sudden, violent kriyas. I noticed that Beloved Adi Da had His hand on the top of my head, and I felt the Divine Force—literally, tremendous Light and Force—Coming Down and Filling my entire body, Consuming me, as if it was turning every part of me inside out. The Divine Force was so great that my own body also began to assume tremendous force. There was a tremendous expansion of the chest and arms. It was if I were fighting something—and I was. It felt as if my entire psyche was being pulled up and out of me.

Avatar Adi Da Samraj and Aniello Panico, the Mountain Of Attention, 1974

I was very reluctant and holding on, holding back, while the Divine Force was actually pulling my psyche out through the top of my head. It felt like I was being exorcised. The intensity was almost unbearable. But it was never painful, just sheer intensity. My ordinary point of view had absolutely dissolved. There was nothing but the Divine.

My body continued to have violent kriyas and shaking. Then this subsided, and I attempted to pull away from Beloved Adi Da. But He held on to me and placed His forehead on mine while continuing to keep His hand on the top of my head. Then everything intensified even more. I could feel Him pushing the Divine Light through the top of my head—this was literally my experience—with His forehead on mine the whole time. I felt twitches and clickings, as if my mind were being dissolved. And I pressed against His forehead. It felt like the top of my brain was being taken off. Then I felt my mind dissolving, just vanishing. Something just went out of me and left.

While this was occurring, the mind had been conjuring up all kinds of thoughts, some sexual, some about business and ordinary things. But it all just vanished.

I then saw and felt a Brilliant Light in my forehead and temples, a tremendous blinding White Light, and I knew that all of that mental and psychic chaos had dissolved. I hugged Beloved Adi Da around the waist. It was very intense, forceful—I could feel all of His strength. I was holding Him and I felt Him enter my body. I literally felt this. And I became One with Him. At this point, the Divine Force became very active in my body. It just kept moving through the entire body, down to the tips of my toes, through my hands, arms, forehead. Suddenly, my hand shot up, the Force was coming out of it so intensely. But it wasn't an energy that seeks to go to God. It was the Divine Light. It was already God, and I just knew it to be so.

During a conversation the next day, Aniello told Avatar Adi Da he felt that not only he but the entire world had changed as a result of this immense Revelation of Divine Power. Even while Aniello was speaking, he began to breathe more heavily, feeling the "thickness" of the Divine Avatar's "Bright" Power filling the room. He looked out the window of Avatar Adi Da's House. It was drizzling—but, then, suddenly, a tremendous storm arose. It seemed to him that it was conjured up right in front of the window. The sky ripped open and rain came down in torrents. Aniello sat there with Avatar Adi Da and a small group of devotees, gazing at the storm. And then it was literally gone—in a moment—as suddenly as it had arisen. Aniello was certain that the storm was also the result of Avatar Adi Da's silent Spirit-Force. It validated to him beyond words the Divine origin of all that had been occurring.

The Lesson of "Garbage and the Goddess"

In this extraordinary time of Avatar Adi Da's Work, which came to be called "Garbage and the Goddess", He was always making one lesson—that the fascinating Spiritual experiences that were manifesting around Him were not most Perfect Spiritual Realization. These experiences, in and of themselves, were not

Enlightenment. They were manifestations of primal Energy—the "Goddess" Power. To reinforce His point, Avatar Adi Da humorously described these experiences as "garbage"—compared with the Prior Happiness Revealed in His Divine Company. This was a huge Revelation, for which the ordinary people gathered around Avatar Adi Da had no background. And so He not only Transmitted the Gift of His Ruchira Shaktipat, He also Instructed His devotees in the midst of the play of their experiences, helping them to grasp the unique process in which they were participating.

It has anciently been known in the sphere of esoteric Spirituality that the human being is made up of different levels of vibrational energy, coinciding with the different levels of energy that compose the cosmos altogether—because the human body-mind is continuous with the field of energies in which it arises. These different vibrational levels of the human structure are related to different dimensions of experience.

Avatar Adi Da has described three fundamental dimensions of human experience—gross, subtle, and causal—which He has also called "outer", "inner", and "root". The gross (or outer) dimension corresponds to the physical level of experience and the waking state. The subtle (or inner) dimension includes everything to do with mind—both the conceptual mind and the domain of dreaming and psychic experience, including the range of supernormal experience that is commonly called "mystical". The causal (or root) dimension refers to the depth where the "root" or "causative" act of attention occurs in Consciousness—giving rise to the sense of the dichotomy between "I" and "other". This "original" (and constant) act of separation is the root form of the self-contraction, and, therefore, the root of human suffering.

During "Garbage and the Goddess", Avatar Adi Da freely gave every kind of experience possible at the subtle level of experience, and He also awakened some devotees to the causal dimension, granting them the sense of merely "Witnessing" the act of attention arising in Consciousness. In other words, He made available to His devotees the ultimate esoteric "grand tour"—a tour of the entire map of the subtle and causal potential of the human mechanism. Just as Avatar Adi Da Himself, in the course of His Sadhana, had tasted every possible Spiritual experience—now He was granting the same to His devotees, in the course of a few months!

Avatar Adi Da was attempting to communicate to His devotees, in the quickest and most effective possible manner, the lesson of His own "Sadhana Years": None of those experiences makes any difference. None of those experiences relieves you of the burden of self-contraction—except, apparently, in the moment of the having of them. But the experiences, no matter how glorious, pass—and the being is left with a residue, the urge to repeat those same experiences, because they appear to erase the knot of self.

What Avatar Adi Da accomplished during "Garbage and the "Goddess" was unprecedented. He made a living "Summary", in the actual experience of His devotees, of the various goals of the Great Tradition of religion and Spirituality. All of that traditional effort of humanity, He showed, is, in essence, an ego-effort in the gross, subtle, and causal dimensions of the human being. It was not Divine Enlightenment! Only the All-Completing Divine Avatar—inherently Free of ego, inherently Beyond the Spiritual searches of humanity—could make that Demonstration.

Avatar Adi Da was choosing, for the purpose of this Demonstration, to use the Power of His Spiritual Transmission to induce the great panorama of "spiritual" experiences. But His Transmission, as His devotees felt, was pure "Divine Force". It was His "Bright" Divine Person Descending into them—absolutely Love-Blissful, beyond the attraction of any particular experience. While full of respect for the remarkable achievements of the saints and sages of the Great Tradition, Avatar Adi Da was Calling His devotees beyond all of that ego-effort to the direct Realization of That Which Transcends the ego and the conditional worlds altogether—to the direct Realization of Him, of the "Bright" Itself.

"There Is Not Anything to Be Attained"

On April 15, Avatar Adi Da gave a summary Discourse about the significance of this period of His Teaching-Work.

DEVOTEE: Beloved Heart-Master, my sense is that my apparently volitional surrendering, or throwing away, of anything actually has very little to do with my capability to do it.

AVATAR ADI DA SAMRAJ: It is very simple. Every time I met Rudi, He would hand Me a bag of garbage. I cannot remember a time when I went to see Rudi when He did not hand Me a bag of garbage. It was always the first thing He would do. Then I would go and throw the garbage away, and I would come back, and We would sit together for a little bit, or I would do some work. Sooner or later, He would give Me some more garbage. It is really very simple. You just throw it away.

It makes it much simpler when the garbage is in a paper bag. The bag has all those oily spots. You know what a garbage bag looks like, with all those greasy spots on the outside. It was always very easy for Me. I could see from the paper bag itself that it was garbage! The first few times, I probably looked into the bag. But, after a while, I would just look at the bag itself—and, if it had grease spots on it: "Aha! Garbage!"

After a while, whatever Rudi gave Me I would throw away. Even if it was not in a paper bag, I threw it away. Whenever I bought a sculpture or another piece of art from Him, He would put it in an ordinary paper bag. And I threw it all away. I don't have any of it any more. The key to the matter is not how to throw the garbage away. The key to the matter is noticing that it is garbage. It does not take a lot of subtlety. It only takes a little observation. As soon as you see that it is garbage, you know immediately that you should throw it away. There is nothing to do with garbage but throw it away! I don't know what else to do with it. So doesn't it seem like a simple matter?

You are looking at a lot of garbage and thinking that it "Is" the Divine! One of My Functions is to "package" the garbage. I have

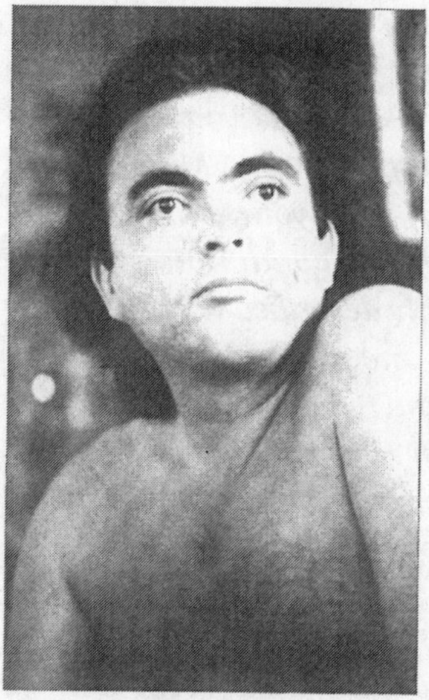

spent a lot of My time packaging your garbage, trying to get you to notice that it is garbage. You will throw it away as soon as you notice this. You cannot surrender something that you do not see to be garbage. You compulsively hold on to it. So you must notice that it is garbage.

But I will Tell you right now—it is all garbage! Everything I Give you in the realms of experience is, ultimately, garbage—and I expect you to throw it away. Nevertheless, you tend to meditate on it—instead of meditating on Me! Every one of these seemingly precious experiences, all of this profound philosophy, is—ultimately—just more of the same stuff. But you have "bought" the conventional religious and Spiritual propaganda—so you think that these experiences and this philosophical "profundity" are the Divine Itself. None of that is the Divine. It is all garbage. Therefore, throw the every "thing" away (and, thereby, Find Me—the Source-Condition of all Gifts, and the Self-Condition of every heart that Finds the Gift of Me).

I am asking you to sacrifice (or to go Beyond) everything—all limitations, all bondage! Altogether, sacrifice of what is false, or surrender of what is merely binding, or relinquishment of what is turning you from Real God, is what I am asking you to do. In the midst of the Process of Satsang with Me, everything is revealed, everything is dredged up, everything is shown. And you tend to become very attached to all these shiny and extraordinary things. You tend to be distracted by them. But they are not Real God. As soon as you become distracted by anything, you bind yourself to the pond again. Everything grasped and owned becomes a hedge for "Narcissus", a bit of immunity. As soon as you think that you have it, you have isolated yourself again, trying to protect yourself from the necessary mortality of this life.

The point is not to will yourself to surrender. Rudi always used to say, "Surrender, surrender, surrender!" But My Call to you is to devotionally recognize Me and devotionally respond to Me. . . . Then devotional surrender to Me is the inherent and ready course. Then devotional surrender to Me is very easy—because you are heart-recognizing and spontaneously heart-responding to Me, and you are no longer struggling against yourself, or in yourself. . . .

The worlds, in and of themselves, are the conditionally manifested modification of What is traditionally described as the "Divine Goddess" (or "Mother-Shakti")—and no one is moved to throw Her away. Every one is fascinated by Her. So the Principle of self-sacrifice is not served by the "Divine Goddess" in Her "veiling" aspect—as "Maya" (or the endlessly modified and modifying Source-Energy of the conditional worlds). The Principle of self-sacrifice is served by Me, to Whom the "Divine Goddess" (or the conditionally Manifesting Energy of Reality) is "Bonded" (as a "Wife" to the "Husband" of Her Heart)—even if She does not, from your point of view, seem to know this and show it. The world, in and of itself, is an endless distraction, in which the Principle of self-sacrifice seems (on the basis of hard experience) to be impossible. Only I, Myself (One and Whole), Serve the Principle of self-sacrifice. The Separate "Goddess" does not. The "Goddess" Herself—un-"Husbanded", with all the experiences She gives—serves the principle of experience, of accumulation, of immunity, of conditionally manifested egoic existence in limitation.

Thus, there is no true surrender in the cult of this world, where the demand for love and for self-sacrifice is anathema. No mere philosophy, or mere conditional knowledge, or mere conditional experience can convince you to really live the life of love and self-sacrifice. Nevertheless, you can be served by the Revelation that all this conditional arising of thought and experience is garbage (or mediocrity, or non-Ultimacy)—none of which is (in and of itself) to be taken to Be Absolute. That Revelation is Shown to you in this Satsang with Me. And—when you have received that Revelation—you are, thereafter, always expected to throw the garbage away!

You are expected to throw the garbage away under the most extraordinary conditions—conditions in which you would, ordinarily, not even consider throwing it away. You are sitting in the precious blissfulness of the spine—why should you throw it away? It is all so delicious. You have been a fool all your life, and now you are a Yogi!—why should you throw that away? No one *wants to do* that. *You do not want to throw it away. You have no True Humor in relation to it. You have no detachment from all this that you have accumulated through vast aeons of existence in conditionally manifested form. You do not want to throw it away. The demand to throw it away seems mad, impossible. . . .*

What is required of you is this sacrifice of separate and separative self—and such self-sacrifice only becomes possible through the Influence of My Perfect Siddhi of Divine Liberation. . . . I . . . Am the Agent of My own "Bright" Divine Siddhi in the world, because I establish a conscious connection with My devotees. All those who come to Me, and devotionally recognize Me, and devotionally respond to Me, surrender the faculties of attention, feeling, body, and breath to Me to various degrees. My beginning devotee matures in his or her practice through the intensification of that surrender of the faculties of attention, feeling, body, and breath to Me, and his or her capability for self-sacrifice thereby increases.

It is real sacrifice—not a sacrifice in the traditional sense of some gloomy self-abnegation and emptying. It is the sacrifice which is itself based on True Humor and expressive of overwhelming love of Me, in which there is not anything whatsoever to be attained.

There is not anything to be attained. I mean not anything. Not anything*!*

There is not anything to be attained. Not one thing is to be attained. Not anything. There is not a single thing to be attained. There is no conditional experience, no conditional vision, no conditional transformation of state that must be attained. . . .

The fundamental responsibility is the unique "Mood" that arises in Satsang with Me—that ecstasy, that love, that relational force, that unreasonable Happiness in which the complexion of Consciousness Itself is Free (moment to moment) from the continuous awareness of (or meditation on) the separate and separative self. Such is the only and perfect responsibility—and it informs all the forms of life, all the functional conditions. A continuous purification is established. The garbage is revealed and thrown away.

—Avatar Adi Da Samraj
He-and-She Is Me

Mill Valley, California, 1974

CHAPTER 6

"What I Do Is Not the Way I Am, but the Way That I Teach"

The Spiritual Teaching-Work which Avatar Adi Da had now embarked on with His devotees was not mere philosophy. He was communicating esoteric religion, a profound psycho-physical process that changes one's entire existence. He was offering real Spiritual transformation—a process in which the body actually changes, not necessarily in its outward appearance, but in its force of energy and consciousness. When there is true Spiritual Awakening, the body-mind begins to become luminous, to radiate Divine Light, the Real Condition of so-called "matter". That was the "En-Light-enment"—Divine and Unqualified—that the Divine Avatar was Working to Awaken in His devotees.

Unconditional Teaching-Submission

During the years of His Sadhana, Avatar Adi Da had submitted Himself to discover the core pattern of un-Enlightenment—"Narcissus", the separate and separative ego-"I". He had given Himself up to every kind of psycho-physical experience, observing all aspects of His life, until every detail was understood and transcended, and His Inherently Enlightened State was Re-Awakened.

Many years later, Avatar Adi Da Samraj described the orientation to existence that had characterized His Life from childhood:

There Was, Even From The Earliest Days Of The Avataric Physical Lifetime Of My Bodily (Human) Divine Form, An <u>*Absolute*</u> *Impulse To Realize (or, Truly, To Restore The Realization Of) The Perfect Freedom Of The "Bright" Heart Itself (Which Is My Own Very and Divine Self-Condition). Indeed, From Those Earliest Days Onward, No Other "Consideration" Held Any Attraction, Interest, or Significance For Me. Inevitably, I Was Associated, By My Bodily (Human) Birth, With Every Kind Of life-Contradiction and ordinary human Tendency and ordinary human Adaptation, and With The Entire Range Of Apparent Problems and egoic Patterns That Result From All Of That. However, In My Struggle To Confront and Transcend The Problems Of human life, I Did Not Choose (In The idealistic Manner) Merely To Adapt To conventionally ideal behaviors. It Was Inherently and Immediately Clear To Me That I Had To Transcend* <u>*Everything*</u>*, In Order, Again, To Most Perfectly Realize My Own Native and "Bright" Divine Self-Condition. Thus, It Was Clear To Me That I Had To Embrace* <u>*Everything*</u>*—All The Contradictions, All The Positives, All The Negatives, Everything gross, Everything subtle, Everything Spiritual,* <u>*Everything*</u> *(*<u>*and*</u> <u>*Everyone*</u>*)* <u>*Altogether*</u>*—and (Thereby) To Deny Not anything or any one, To Avoid Not anything or any one, but To Embrace Everyone, To Endure Everything, To Pass Through Everything, To Suffer Everything, To Enjoy Everything, To Do Everything. I Was Intuitively Certain That Only Thus Would I Be Able To* <u>*Unqualifiedly*</u> *Establish, In The Avataric Physical Lifetime Of My Bodily (Human) Divine Form, The Firm Absolutization Of My Own Disposition In "Brightness".*

—Avatar Adi Da Samraj
The Truly Human New World-Culture
Of <u>*Unbroken*</u> *Real-God-Man*

This extraordinary Yoga of "all-and-All-Embrace" was engaged for one purpose—to allow Avatar Adi Da to Reveal the Way of Divine Enlightenment, equipped with perfect bodily knowledge and Mastery of all the potentials of human experience.

Following His return from India in September 1973, Avatar Adi Da had come to the conviction that a complete Submission on His part was necessary. He would participate without reserve in the lives of His devotees—be their "friend", go into every kind of situation with them, do what they liked to do, be available without qualification to their requirements and demands. He would show them, by all kinds of skillful means, how they enact their individual rituals of un-Happiness and move them beyond all of that through awakened devotion to Him.

Avatar Adi Da was well aware that this direct form of Teaching would be an immensely creative and difficult affair, one in which He would appear to sacrifice His own purity and to take on the un-Illumined obsessions of His devotees. Just as He had "decided", at the age of two, to relinquish His Enjoyment of the "Bright" for the sake of learning how an ordinary human being can come to Enjoy the "Bright", so He made a Gesture of similar profundity in embracing His Teaching-Work. He was Submitting unconditionally to His devotees, in order to Reveal the Truth to them in the only way they were then able to receive it.

Traditionally, anyone seriously approaching a Siddha-Master was expected be of extraordinary caliber. Such an aspirant had to be an individual who was not satisfied with the ordinary answers to life, nor with ordinary religion. He or she had to be someone who wanted undying Happiness and Liberation, and could not settle for less. These were the presumed qualifications in someone ready for esoteric religion—and the tests that go with it—given by the Spiritual Master, or Siddha-Guru.

The fact that those who came to Avatar Adi Da Samraj during His Teaching-Years had no great preparation to approach a Siddha-Master was an inevitability in the modern West. And it was also a necessity. Because He had come for all beings, without exception, those who first came into Avatar Adi Da's Company were there to represent all.

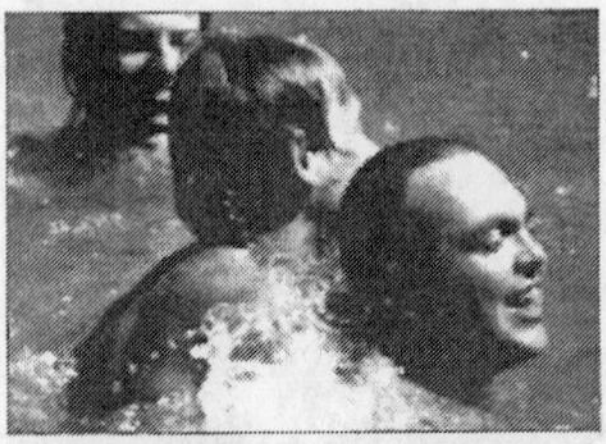

Avatar Adi Da Samraj with His devotees at the Mountain Of Attention Sanctuary

That Avatar Adi Da was able to make this Submission and sustain it under all conditions, decade after decade, was a sign of His Divinity. He was demonstrating the most radical form of renunciation—unqualified surrender to others, freedom from any consolation whatsoever, and an invincible purity in the midst of all the ego-dramas enacted by human beings:

AVATAR ADI DA SAMRAJ: Instead of living as a traditional renunciate and only accepting as devotees those who were fully prepared, I accepted whoever came to Me, as one accepts one's family, simply because they are given. I Worked with them and Submitted Myself to them as they were at the time, but I Worked within the structure of their living, to Purify and Transform them, so that, ultimately, they would be prepared to receive My Spiritual Transmission. Nobody was prepared. Not a single person appeared in My Company who was already prepared for My Spiritual Transmission. I lived as if in a large family of worldly people.

Surrender as the Body-mind

During the "Garbage and the Goddess" period, devotees would typically drive up from San Francisco on Friday night and stay at the Mountain Of Attention until Sunday night, spending as much time as they could in Avatar Adi Da's Company. He would often go to Ordeal Bath Lodge, the spa of the former resort, where devotees would join Him in the large pool (called "the plunge"). Often dozens of people would be in the water around Him—sometimes quiet, sometimes shouting and laughing, throwing balls and playing vigorous water-games initiated by Avatar Adi Da.

Toni Vidor, a middle-aged woman who had grown up in southern California (the daughter of the film director King Vidor), flew up from Los Angeles during this time to approach her new Spiritual Master. For Toni, the early period of her relationship to Avatar Adi Da involved an immediate confrontation with her social character and its suppressed emotions. She recalls her first sighting of Avatar Adi Da:

TONI: He was floating on His back in the water, and a group of devotees were all around His body. Every few seconds, they would throw Him up into the air and wait for Him to splash back down into the water. Everyone was laughing helplessly, and Avatar Adi Da was calling out, "Higher, higher, hit the rafters!"

I had spent decades in earnest Spiritual seeking—going to every Indian teacher who turned up in Los Angeles. I was very serious and hardly knew what to make of this scene. To top it off, almost everyone there was the same age as my children!

Avatar Adi Da quickly noticed me and graciously invited me by name—though we had never met—to join in the game. I responded, but with an effort, completely uptight, and suffering in every moment the knowledge that I did not know how to enjoy myself in this ordinary way with other people. Even though I had been personally welcomed, I felt the resistance and "stiffness" in my own character, as I had never felt them before.

That afternoon, Beloved Adi Da came and sat silently with us. From the back of the hall, I prayed earnestly and passionately to Him to relieve me of this crippled quality that I suffered in every ordinary human interaction. Immediately, He put His arm up with His palm open toward me and held it there. I began breathing stronger and stronger, and I felt energy come into my heart and then down through my arms and hands so strong that the fingers bent with the energy. And then a great sorrow came up from the heart.

I began sobbing loudly and uncontrollably. I was the only person making a sound! It was embarrassing, but I thought, "Well, if I can't let go here, there's no place I can let go!" The sorrow increased, and soon I was rolling on the floor, still wailing. Curiously, I watched all of this come up. There was no content associated with it. It was just a huge, enormous release. After about an hour, Beloved Adi Da got up and walked out and everyone followed, but I continued to weep loudly on the floor. After a while, the breath calmed to the point that I could sit up. A friend had stayed behind to make sure that I was all right, and I sat down on a bench next to her to try to speak—and it all began again, and I spent another half hour rolling on the floor!

When it was finally over, I felt as if an immense burden—eighty tons of whatever it was I had been carrying around all my life without even realizing it—had been lifted from me.

The Spiritual Transmission-Work of Avatar Adi Da would sometimes release a chaos of emotions and thoughts that could not be rationally explained. His "Bright" Force was showing Its purifying effects in every dimension of body, mind, and psyche.

TONI: Several months after Sitting with Avatar Adi Da, I found myself once more in the water with Him, this time in the outdoor swimming pool by the beautiful grotto, which was later to be Empowered as a special site of healing and Spiritual initiation. I had firmly decided that this weekend I was going to approach Him directly and drop my fearful reluctance to engage a relationship with Him.

There was a wild water-polo game going on, and, instead of sitting on the edge as I usually did, I jumped in the water and got into the game. I never came close to the ball, but I was participating.

At some point, I started to swim toward Beloved Adi Da. He knew my intention, and left His place in the game to swim around to meet me. He hugged me, and He held me and held me and held me. Soon the game died away, and everyone formed a circle around us.

A great stillness pervaded the entire place. (It was so quiet that a friend of mine woke up from a nap in a nearby cabin!) I was cold and shivering, but I had to make a choice between giving myself to Him or paying attention to the body. The Blissful Energy of the Embrace became more and more intense. I found myself resisting the ego-overwhelming pleasure of it—fearing to lose control. It felt as though Avatar Adi Da was pulling me up. But, at some point, I refused to go further. I could feel Him continue to ascend, and soon I was left holding only a body. I could feel that He was no longer, in that moment, directly associated with His physical body. By now, I was simultaneously in a blissful state beyond the mind and painfully, acutely aware of my resistance to Him and His Love.

"A great stillness pervaded the entire place."

In spite of the limits I placed on His Work with me, I was completely changed by these incidents. I was happy, no longer struggling with myself—a different person.

In incidents such as this, the Ruchira Avatar was actively entering into relationship with each of His devotees. He was reflecting back each one's activity of self-contraction and showing them that the way beyond all egoic limitation is to turn to Him.

AVATAR ADI DA SAMRAJ: The method of egoity is dissociative. The means of Realization is the relationship to Me, whole bodily turning to Me, entering into Communion with Me on the basis of surrender as *the body-mind. On that basis, I am able to do My Blessing-Work of Spiritually Transmitting the "Bright", Transmitting the Divine Self-Condition. In that surrendered disposition, the devotee becomes combined with My Transmitted Person. This becomes a more and more profound and developing process that is ultimately characterized as Divine Self-Realization.*

It is a process of ego-transcendence. Therefore, it is a process of purification and of transcending egoic patterning—egoic patterning that is associated with all dimensions of the human structure, gross, subtle, and causal.

—March 15, 2003

"Reality Consideration"

It was an extraordinary matter to be invited to participate in a "gathering" of any kind with the Divine Avatar. Avatar Adi Da Samraj Taught by bringing His Instruction into life. From day to day, He evoked all kinds of circumstances in which His devotees could naturally reveal themselves to Him and to themselves.

Through living encounters and verbal Instruction, Avatar Adi Da Samraj was engaging with His devotees a process that could be likened to the traditional Yogic process called "samyama"—meaning exhaustive, one-pointed "consideration" of the subject at hand until the truth of it is fully revealed. The Teaching-samyama of Avatar Adi Da Samraj covered every aspect of reality—human and Divine. In fact, He called the process "reality consideration".

The first level of His "reality consideration" was relative to what He called "the foundation stages of life", or the arena of ordinary experience based in the physical reality. The core preoccupations that operate at this level of human life have been summarized by Avatar Adi Da in a single phrase: "money, food, and sex". (By the word "money", Avatar Adi Da intends to indicate the entire dimension of life-energy and activity.) These common human obsessions became the focus of countless hours, years, and even decades of "reality consideration" in the Divine Avatar's Company. At the same time, He was never addressing these matters for their own sake, but always for a greater purpose. What forms of discipline of (or Yoga relative to) these areas of life—money, food, and sex—are necessary in order to truly free attention for What is beyond the gross dimension?

His "consideration" was also always moving to the subtle realms of experience, to the advanced stage of human development where mystical experience and Yogic phenomena become the focus of attention and interest. Starting during the "considerations" of the "Garbage and the Goddess" time, Avatar Adi Da would critically examine the limits of that kind of preoccupation, which is more refined than "money, food, and sex", but nonetheless a confinement to a limited point of view and temporary satisfaction.

At times, Avatar Adi Da would also move His devotees into an intensive concentration in the Transcendental domain sought by sages who eschew Yogic experiences and attempt to turn attention inward to a depth of pure Consciousness, free of phenomena.

A brilliant stream of Dharmic dialogue and Spiritual Transmission flowed from the "Bright" Divine Avatar. By responding to the questions and dilemmas of His devotees, He was answering humankind's impulse to know the Truth. He was elaborating His earliest Teaching of "gone-to-the-root" (or "radical") understanding—the understanding that transcends the errors of every dimension of the human search. He was Awakening in His devotees the intuition of That Which Comes from Above and Beyond all the points of view of human experience and Spiritual endeavor.

At times, for some individuals, these occasions of His Teaching-Instruction would be only Blissful. At other times, the Transmission of the Divine Siddha-Master would hugely magnify the discomfort of confrontation with the ego. The only rule was to always participate responsively, giving Him one's entire attention, and devotionally turning to Him with one's entire being.

A Glimpse of the Death Process

On an occasion in 1976, Connie Mantas, a registered nurse who worked with the dying, was taken through a profoundly Instructive experience by her Divine Master. In the course of a gathering at His House, Avatar Adi Da walked over and invited her to lie down on the floor next to Him. He lay flat on His back next to her and closed His eyes, saying "Now do exactly as I do". Then, through silent Instruction, He Guided her through the patterns of conditional existence that are experienced in the death transition:

CONNIE: First there was an explosion of inner sounds. Then I felt the layers of the body-mind release and fall away. "I" was separating out from the physical body and seemed to fly upwards, whirling through dark space at an incredible speed. I was moving toward an overwhelming, brilliant light. At one point, I recall slipping through a kind of "grid" as a speck of consciousness.

For an instant, I did seem to lose all self-awareness, but throughout the rest of the experience I was aware of the most remarkable clarity. I found that I felt more familiar and at ease traveling without the body than when I was dragging it along, anchored to it by my usual physical-body identification. I felt myself to be alive as Consciousness, at ease as the witness of mind and attention.

At different moments in this Cosmic journey, I felt the deep urges of the body-mind drawing me back towards embodiment, and I sensed the frustration of having no physical body through which to enact or fulfill desires. This made a stunning impression on me, and I remember feeling how foolish it would be to waste the opportunity of a human lifetime to do the sadhana that could help free me of the binding attachments I had now seen so clearly.

Then I became aware of a loud buzzing or humming sound as I slowly came back into the body-mind, taking on each layer, starting with the most subtle. The inner sounds quieted until once again I was aware of lying on the floor.

When I opened my eyes, the face of Beloved Adi Da was right next to mine, and He was grinning at me with a gigantic smile. He opened His mouth and started to laugh. It was more than a laugh—it was a victorious and triumphant Shout, glorious to hear. Instead of being awestruck by this remarkable journey I had just taken with Him, I felt sheer marvel at Who He Is. I felt, "Yes! There is this great scheme of conditional existence, of which human embodiment is a part. But first, and most importantly, HE IS THE MASTER OF IT ALL! And I have a relationship with That One!"

Without exchanging a word with me, Beloved Adi Da got up, walked to His Chair and began a Discourse on death and the "grid" through which we pass at death. This was one of the first occasions at which Beloved Adi Da spoke of the total pattern of phenomena, or the Cosmic Mandala, as He would later describe it. As always, He had one primary message—no experience, high or low is the answer to our suffering. No "one" survives in the Great Plastic of forms. Only Consciousness Itself persists, the Eternal "I", the Self-Existing and Self-Radiant Condition of all, Beyond the grid of appearances.

A Unique Use of Skillful Means

During the years of His Teaching-Submission, Adi Da Samraj was always intensifying Satsang, moving His devotees to deeper surrender to Him as Divine Master. The more His devotee surrendered directly as the body-mind, the more He could magnify the force of Satsang, and open that one to the transforming power of His Spiritual Transmission.

The Divine Avatar was Working with westerners who were raw and unschooled in devotion to the Master. Therefore, as part of this play of Instruction, He often allowed the use of intoxicants in "gatherings" with His devotees. The intoxicants temporarily served to undo the armoring of the social personality, thus allowing Avatar Adi Da to Reveal to His devotees a glimpse of what is beyond egoity, beyond the social persona.

Intoxicants have a time-honored tradition of sacred use in certain schools of Tantra. Avatar Adi Da, however, was not engaged in Tantra, nor was He Working to draw His devotees into a Tantric practice. Even so, just as a serious and sacred intention was presumed in the traditional Tantric setting, participation in this sacred opportunity with Avatar Adi Da required real seriousness, trust in the Divine Master, and the impulse to allow the Purifying and Awakening process He was Working. In that circumstance, many found that a glimpse of the Truth of existence was being Given to them by His Grace. Nevertheless, it was only a glimpse of freedom, because the self-contraction always re-asserted itself. The real physical and Yogic equanimity necessary to sustain and stably enjoy what was being glimpsed did not yet exist in the Divine Avatar's devotees.

The ecstatic intuitions and experiences of Truth that were being Granted through this skillful means were intended to serve as a goad—to fuel the impulse to truly Realize the Reality beyond the egoic point of view. And they also allowed Avatar Adi Da to Instruct His devotees relative to every stage of the Spiritual process—whether or not they were prepared to truly and stably practice at that level of Awakening. But for the Divine Siddha-Master to allow the constant use of such substances would have

The Limits of Traditional Tantra

Traditional "left-hand" Tantra[26] has its own logic for engaging in what are otherwise considered to be Spiritually inauspicious activities—using intoxicants, eating meat, engaging in sexual intercourse, and so on. The practitioner of left-hand Tantra is expected to convert the energies associated with gross substances and activities into Spiritual energy that propels the being upward into ascended states of bliss. As Avatar Adi Da points out, the focus of Tantra is a search to go from "below" to "above", to refine lower energy into higher energy by Yogic effort.

While respecting the seriousness of genuine Tantra Yoga, Avatar Adi Da Samraj has Revealed that it is based on a fundamental misunderstanding about true Spirituality. That which is truly Spiritual cannot be Realized by any process of transforming or refining what is "below". To attempt to do so is a false effort, because the real Spiritual process is of another order entirely. Spiritual Energy is Divine—originating from Above and Beyond, not from "below". The true and unlimited Spiritual process, as the Divine Avatar has always Demonstrated, is the infusion, the in-filling, of what is below by What is Above and Beyond—in other words, by the "Bright" Divine Reality Itself, brought Down into the world by His Avataric Gift of the "Thumbs".

"Below" Is Not (and Never Can Be) Causative Relative To What Is Above. Rather, What Is Above Must Purify and Transform and (Most Ultimately) En-Light-en What Is "Below".

That Is How I Do My Avataric Divine Spiritual Work.

That Is The Nature Of The Real Spiritual Process In My Avataric Divine Company.

—Avatar Adi Da Samraj
The Dawn Horse Testament Of The Ruchira Avatar

been merely degenerative. Energy and attention had to be set free to concentrate in the real Spiritual process, in order to truly grow through all of the developmental stages He had Revealed. The body-mind had to be purified to the point that it would become capable of deeply receiving Avatar Adi Da's Enlightening Transmission.

Thus, the use of intoxicants would have its time, but it could not continue forever. Discipline was necessary—the very same life-disciplines that Avatar Adi Da had developed in their rudiments when He established His first Ashram in Los Angeles. Typically, then, after a period of using intoxicants, Avatar Adi Da Samraj would suddenly call for all the disciplines to be immediately applied. Thus, His Spiritual Work during His years of Teaching was always alive, always changing, based on what He saw to be required at any given time. Eventually (in February 2002), He would definitively Call His devotees to the consistent practice of right life (without any use of intoxicants) and to the Way He had established over all the years of His Teaching and Revelation Work.

A Divine Satire

From early 1974 until the late seventies, when He began to spend time in Hawaii, Avatar Adi Da's residence at the Mountain Of Attention was the crucible for His Teaching-Work. The lessons and "considerations" that developed there would be quickly brought to the more extended body of His devotees who came periodically to gatherings in His house (or other places at the Mountain Of Attention). From there, His Instruction would move out to all His devotees, and from them to others, bringing new devotees to His Feet. Thus, His Spiritual Work functioned through a pattern of direct relationship with Him, radiating like concentric circles from His Body.

The individual devotees with whom the Divine Avatar Worked in His Teaching years were so absorbed in the miracle of living in His Company and the intensity of their personal sadhana that they could not fully grasp what was occurring. They did not explicitly

Adi Da Samraj with devotees at the Mountain Of Attention Sanctuary, 1974

realize that they were there representing all of humanity in a vast Divine event. One could say that they were the unwitting actors in a grand sacred drama—a drama that had, in fact, already been written.

In His great literary Text, *The Mummery Book*, created by Avatar Adi Da before His Divine Re-Awakening, He had exactly and devastatingly described what human beings are up to as egos. He had made it clear that the world is a "mummery", a mock-show. His passionate Purpose now, in His Teaching years, was to awaken the mummers to Reality Itself, beyond the drama of their own egoity. He was there (as He wrote in the Prologue of *The Mummery Book*), to "Purify and Illuminate the mortal, human heart". He was engaged (as He later put it) in a "satire" on the human condition—a humorously critical reflection of the search for self-fulfillment, high and low.

His "satire" was an egoless Gesture of Divine Love that did not, in any way, modify or degrade His Realization or His Person. Whatever was presented to Him in the form of His devotees, He fearlessly and lovingly embraced—all their questions, their sufferings and struggles. In the midst of whatever difficulty might be manifesting around Him in the moment, He remained perfectly Free, Radiating Beyond the apparent dilemma. In some sense, the most important thing in His Teaching years was to keep His devotees in His Company, in the room, under His Guidance, so that He could do His silent Spiritual Work with them prior to their conscious awareness.

"What I Do Is Not the Way That I Am, but the Way That I Teach"

One day in 1975, at the Mountain Of Attention, James Steinberg, the devotee responsible for relations with other Ashrams and Gurus, brought to Avatar Adi Da a significant letter. It was from Swami Chinmayananda, an Indian Yogi then visiting San Francisco. Swami Chinmayananda was a well-known and respected figure in Spiritual circles—he was a commentator on Vedanta and had written many books. In his letter, the swami spoke of his concern at the Divine Avatar's manner of Teaching—a participatory approach to Spiritual Instruction that was entirely foreign to his own orthodox views.

As Avatar Adi Da read the letter, James could feel that He was fully receiving this traditional swami's expression of perplexity. The next morning, at a devotee's house in Mill Valley, in Marin County (where He stayed occasionally), Avatar Adi Da Wrote an Essay clarifying the nature of His Teaching-Work—an Essay which was a response to Swami Chinmayananda and also a communication to everyone.

What I Do is not the way that I Am, but the way that I Teach.

What I Speak is not a reflection of Me, but of you.

People do well to be offended or even outraged by My actions and behavior. This is My purpose. But their reaction must turn upon themselves, for I have not Shown them Myself by all of this. All that I Do and Speak only reveals people to themselves.

I have become willing to Teach in this uncommon manner because I have known My friends—and they are what I can seem to be. By retaining all qualities in their company, I gradually wean them of all reactions, all sympathies, all alternatives, fixed assumptions, false teachings, dualities, searches, and dilemma. This is My Way of Working for a time. . . .

Freedom is the only Purity. There is no Teaching but Consciousness Itself. My Appearance here is not other than the possibilities of mankind.

—Avatar Adi Da Samraj
1975

Yosemite, California, 1975

CHAPTER 7

The Whole Body Must Be Enlightened

In the Spiritual traditions of humankind as a whole, there is an unresolved "debate" about the matter of "sex and God". Some Tantric traditions propose that sexuality can be an aid to the Spiritual process—while many, if not most, other Spiritual paths consider sex to be an obstruction to Spiritual Realization, because of its power to distract the being from the God-oriented life. In Avatar Adi Da's Teaching-Work with His devotees, this was a critical issue to be "considered": Can sexual activity, engaged in a Yogic manner, serve, or be a means to, Spiritual Realization? He began this thread of "consideration" even in Los Angeles, and intensively during "Garbage and the Goddess"—and it would continue for thirty years before it was brought to a firm conclusion.

Transcending the Emotional-Sexual Ego

Avatar Adi Da's Address to sexuality included all the emotions, expressed and unexpressed, that surround sexuality and are inseparable from it. Sex, as He said, is never a thing in and of itself—it is always an "emotional-sexual" matter. The understanding and transcending of emotional-sexual ego-bondage is an essential requirement for Spiritual growth. As He wrote:

AVATAR ADI DA SAMRAJ: The matter of sexuality is so profoundly structured into people's infantile and adolescent adaptations that it persists not only as their most obsessive interest as individuals but also as their most significant and consistent social (or interpersonal) problem. When I began to enter into relationship with My devotees for the sake of their Spiritual Awakening, it became more and more clear that no one who came to Me was yet prepared for the true Spiritual Process, which is total bodily responsibility for Truth Itself, or Life Itself. Rather, all were essentially trapped in obsessions, and in problematic orientations to the vital and, particularly, the emotional-sexual dimensions of experience. I knew it would be necessary for all first to come to a level of interpersonal and cultural maturity relative to vital life before the Spiritual Process could be fully introduced into their lives.

—1978

Avatar Adi Da spent untold hours with His devotees reflecting to each one how he or she was living out an emotional-sexual ego-pattern that is related to patterns developed in early life. He confirmed Freud's crucial insight that there is a powerful oedipal pattern of desire and betrayal set up in infancy through the relationships to the parents of both sexes. But He showed that this patterning cannot be gone beyond through any kind of analytical approach. Early-life patterning does not leave its traces merely in the mind. The conscious mind is not even aware of it, generally speaking. Rather, the emotional-sexual pattern is written in the body, and it can be read clearly in what one does, not only in relationship to a sexual intimate, but in relationship to everyone and every circumstance.

Just as one's physical characteristics are coded into the DNA, so one's emotional-sexual pattern is "encoded" in the body-mind. The pattern of emotional and sexual bondage cannot be stopped by any manipulation within the emotional-sexual dimension itself. To know this fuels the impulse to be Liberated from the relentless machine of self-contraction at every level of the being.

This was the intelligence, the heart-motive that Avatar Adi Da was always Working to awaken in His devotees. When Avatar Adi Da said to His devotees, "the key to Enlightenment is hidden in sex", He was always looking for the real meaning of His words to be comprehended. In order for the whole body to be literally "filled with Light", there must be an unlocking of the emotional-sexual root of bondage to the body itself.

The body-mind is a pattern of egoity—driven by emotional-sexual reaction, frustration, desiring, and seeking. Observing the details of how the pattern operates in the individual case can be useful, but mere knowledge of the details is not Liberating. What is Liberating is the Grace-Given, summary understanding that the body-mind—in all its qualities and characteristics—is just self-contraction, a complex pattern of egoity. There must be a spontaneous relinquishment of bondage to the ego-patterning and profound bodily surrender into the Reality in which the body exists. As Avatar Adi Da later summarized in *The Dawn Horse Testament*:

> *I Call All My Devotees (and Even all who Are Moved To Study My Avataric Divine Word) To "Consider" (and Receive) This Wisdom-Revelation, Uniquely Given By Me: Realization (Of Reality Itself, or Truth Itself, or Real God) Is (Necessarily) Whole bodily. It Is the Whole body—Rather Than any "piece" of the human being—That Must Be En-Light-ened. Therefore, The Instructions I Have Given Relative To The emotional-sexual Dimension Of human life Are Not About sex in and of itself. Rather, Those Instructions Relate (Most Fundamentally, and Essentially) To The Transcending Of The Root Of Bondage In (and To) the body—Which Is The Transcending Of ego-Bondage To The gross Domain Of conditional Existence (Altogether). Because the body Is (Basically) Patterned In emotional-sexual Terms, The Transcending Of body-Based Bondage Is Rooted In The emotional-sexual Dimension. As Long As The Sum and Force Of emotional-sexual ego-Patterning Binds the body-mind To the point of view Of "Below", You Remain Entirely "Below"—Unavailable To What Is Above.*
>
> *Therefore, My Wisdom-Instruction Relative To sexuality Has Always Been About Understanding The emotional-sexual Basis Of the ego-"I" (or self-Contraction)—Not About "Targeting" the genitals, or Merely Being negative, moralistic, or puritanically double-*

minded About sex itself. The ego-"I" is the entire body-mind—self-Contracted. Therefore, Divine Enlightenment Is, Literally, The En-Light-enment Of the Whole body (or Of The psycho-physical Totality Of body-mind)—Not Merely Some Form Of body-Excluding and world-Excluding subjectivism, inwardly Cultivated By the individual.

As A General Rule, The Principal Preoccupation Of human beings Is their Involvement In the dramas of emotional-sexual egoity—Whether That Involvement Is self-Satisfied Or Frustrated. The Total life of the human individual Is Rooted In sex—Because the body is An emotional-sexual Pattern. That Pattern Manifests Itself (In Part) As sex-mind—but, Altogether, That Pattern Governs All Aspects Of the gross personality. Indeed, Most Of the content of the gross personality Bears No Direct Reference To sex, Even Though Virtually all such content Is Based In (and limited By) The Governing emotional-sexual Pattern. And, Altogether, Your "Allegiance" To Your Own emotional-sexual Pattern Fastens You In The "Downward" Disposition, Bound To the gross view Of Existence. . . .

Therefore, every human being Must Transcend The emotional-sexual Patterning Of the body-Based ego, Because That Patterning Is At The Root Of the (Total psycho-physical) self-Contraction. However, This Fact Cannot Be Dealt With By Means Of moralistic preaching, Nor Can It Be Dealt With Merely By Taking Up A Prescriptive Series Of Disciplines Of the body-mind (in and of itself). The Only Means By Which This ego-Bondage Can Be (Ultimately, Most Perfectly) Transcended Is The Whole bodily Act Of Surrender (or Turning) To Me, and Of Subsequent Whole bodily Reception Of (and egoless Identification With) My Spiritually Self-Transmitted (and Inherently egoless) Person and Self-Condition. Thus, In Order To Go Beyond The emotional-sexual Patterning Of the body-Based ego, There Must Be A Profound, Whole bodily Conversion—From (Total psycho-physical) Obsession With the separate self To (Whole bodily) Heart-Communion With Me.

—Avatar Adi Da Samraj
The Dawn Horse Testament Of The Ruchira Avatar

A Unique Act of Submission

Essential to this "consideration" was Avatar Adi Da's own Submission to be sexually active. When He first approached Rudi for formal Spiritual Instruction, He had nothing binding Him to householder life, and He basically presumed that He would become celibate. Nevertheless, one of the first disciplines Rudi gave to Him was to marry Nina. So He did so. Later, when Swami Muktananda recognized Avatar Adi Da's Spiritual accomplishment and Granted Him a sannyasin name, Swami Muktananda did not suggest that sannyas, in His case, required celibacy. Swami Muktananda had already conveyed to Avatar Adi Da that His Work was His own, that He would Teach in His own manner. And this was true. Years later, Avatar Adi Da Samraj spoke of how the signs made to Him by His Gurus with regard to the matter of sexuality had been an indication of what would, in fact, be required of Him in order to Teach in the modern West.

AVATAR ADI DA SAMRAJ: I dealt with sexuality in My "Sadhana Years"—as an obstacle. It was something I had to embrace in order to Teach. I had to require it of Myself, because it was necessary for the world.

—February 2, 2002

During His Sadhana, the Divine Avatar observed the effects of sexuality on the Spiritual process and found that He had to bring profound Yogic discipline to emotional-sexual practice. The thoroughness and realism with which Avatar Adi Da investigated this dimension of experience and passed on the lessons is reflected in His Confession in *The Dawn Horse Testament*:

In My "Sadhana Years"—and, Also, In The Subsequent Context Of The Exercise Of My Avataric Divine Function Of Teaching and Revealing The Way Of The Heart (or Way Of Adidam)—I Demonstrated A Uniquely "Heroic"[27] *Disposition Relative To The Investigation, Observation, Understanding, and Transcending Of All Dimensions Of emotional-sexual life (and, Indeed, All*

Dimensions Of Every Aspect Of conditionally manifested Existence). In My "Sadhana Years", The Purpose Of My (Unique) "Heroic" Demonstration Was The Preparation Of My psycho-physical Vehicle Of Avataric conditional Manifestation—So That It Would (Thereafter) Function In Most Perfect Conformity To Me, The Divine Heart-Master Of all beings. My Subsequent "Heroic" Demonstration, Of Teaching and Revealing The Way Of The Heart, Was Purposed To "Learn" Mankind, and To Reflect Mankind To Itself, and To Reveal To Mankind Its Unique Potential For Understanding and Transcending the psycho-physical ego-"I" and (On That Basis) For Realization Of The Divine Self-Condition—Each (and Both, Together) By Grace Of The Unique Avatarically Given Divine Means Of Devotional Surrender To Me.

—Avatar Adi Da Samraj
The Dawn Horse Testament Of The Ruchira Avatar

In the course of 1974, and in subsequent years, a number of Avatar Adi Da's women devotees found their attraction to Him (both Spiritually and humanly) so strong that they were moved to a uniquely intensive form of devotional surrender—offering their entire lives in direct service to Him. In the esoteric Spiritual traditions, it is held that the most auspicious form of Spiritual practice is to live with a Siddha-Master, to serve him or her and receive his or her guidance night and day. These women who were drawn to such a renunciate life with the Divine Avatar lived and practiced in His intimate sphere. They cared for Him bodily, served His House, received and passed on His communications, and provided a radiant circle of love and devotion around Him.

Avatar Adi Da Samraj "considered" with each woman a particular design of sadhana, which might or might not include Yogic sexual activity with Him during any particular period of time. There was no space to approach Him conventionally. The ordinary man-woman orientation was to be relinquished, moment to moment. He was a pure Renunciate, unbound by ordinary "contracts". His relationship with this group of renunciate women was always on the basis of their devotional approach to Him for the purpose of Divine Enlightenment and Liberation. And so the relationship between

Him and the women renunciates, while more humanly intimate, was fundamentally no different than the Guru-devotee relationship practiced by all His devotees.

"This First Meeting Has Never Left My Heart"

In the midst of His Work with the renunciate women, Avatar Adi Da was always looking for unique Spiritual signs, indicators that an individual could rapidly advance in the Spiritual process. One of the devotees who showed these signs was Ruchiradama Quandra Sukhapur Rani. A member of the Ruchira Sannyasin Order (the senior renunciate order of Adidam) for many years now, she describes how she was mysteriously drawn into the Company of the Ruchira Avatar in March 1974:

1974

RUCHIRADAMA QUANDRA SUKHAPUR RANI: In August of 1973, at 19 years of age, while living in a suburb outside of Chicago, Illinois, it became obvious to me that I had to make a dramatic change in my life. I felt a very strong urge to just leave Illinois, and so I collected what money I had, which was very little, and set out to drive to California—which, to me, represented some kind of freedom from the oppressive and degraded life I felt I had been living. I drove to California with no clear sense of what I was going to do, or where I was going to go. I had a friend I could stay with, at least temporarily, in San Francisco, and so that is what I set out to do.

After many days of driving across country, I arrived in San Francisco and located this friend's house. I stayed, however, but one night. In the morning, I realized that I could not remain in San Francisco. For no apparent reason, a very strong urge to go to Los Angeles had arisen in me. I knew no one in Los Angeles, I had nothing I intended to do there, but I felt very strongly that I had to drive to Los Angeles. And so I packed up my things, drove to Los Angeles, and immediately set about looking for a place to live.

I found a small one-room house in Huntington Beach, and shortly after I arrived there, I began to have visions of a man and a woman. I could never see the woman, but it seemed to be myself. The man, however, was very distinct to me. He related to me very directly, and he would appear in an observatory, where he would constantly draw me to look through his telescope at the stars. After my initial contact with this man in the dream state, I would have a recurring vision of a star-form[28] *perceived at the end of a tunnel, and this would appear not only in dreams but in the waking state. Shortly after that, I was led, through various acquaintances, to the bookstore on Melrose Avenue that was the first Ashram of Avatar Adi Da.*

On this day, outside the meditation hall there were many shoes, and so I presumed that Beloved Adi Da was sitting in a formal meditation occasion. However, I did not ask and no one spoke of it. I quietly purchased The Knee Of Listening *and* The Method of the Siddhas. *When I looked at the books, I saw immediately that the man I was having constant visions of was Beloved Adi Da!*

That same week I unexpectedly heard the voice of Beloved Adi Da on the radio. Recordings were being played of some of His Talks to His devotees. I was profoundly drawn and moved in my heart. His voice seemed to shape all that I felt. I had little comprehension of what He was saying, but I was completely moved by His voice and His laughter and the feeling that He communicated. Above all, I was attracted to the offering that He made of a relationship. So began my conscious relationship, in this lifetime, to my Beloved Guru, Adi Da Samraj.

After that, I set up an altar in the small one-room house that I was living in and spontaneously began to do daily puja.[29] *I had no conscious knowledge of puja, but I was moved to make offerings to Beloved Adi Da's photograph, and I began to study His Teaching while seated before His photograph. The photograph I used was the one on the cover of* The Method of the Siddhas.

Then, on January 18, 1974, my twentieth birthday, I decided I would approach Beloved Adi Da as my Divine Heart-Master and assume the full range of practices He was giving to His devotees at that time. I embraced all the disciplines exactly, without question, and began a series of study courses that were being offered at the Melrose Ashram. By this time, Beloved Adi Da and the other devotees were spending time at a new Ashram on La Brea Avenue. Some of the newer students, myself included, continued with the course instruction as preparation for meeting Beloved Adi Da.

At this time, Beloved Adi Da began to enter into a time of Instruction with devotees that involved ecstatic gatherings every night at the La Brea Ashram. I was not invited to these gatherings. Rather, I would drive daily from Huntington Beach, after my day of work, and serve the meditation hall in the Melrose Ashram. Each day I would bring a single white rose to offer there.

Meanwhile, every day new people were being called over to the La Brea Ashram to join these occasions of Divine Ecstasy with Beloved Adi Da. I longed to be called to come, but I never was while He was there. My relationship to Him at this time was through this daily service to His pristine meditation hall at the Melrose Ashram. And so I would continue each day to clean and prepare the hall, offering my one white rose. Never did I feel excluded by anyone. For me, it was a Grace beyond all imagining to be given the honor of serving Beloved Adi Da in this manner.

Then Beloved Adi Da moved to the Mountain Of Attention Sanctuary, and many devotees went with Him. I began to help with the preparations for moving the Ashram to northern California. I was given the unique opportunity to reside in the house where Beloved Adi Da had lived while He was Working at the Melrose and La Brea Ashrams. Devotees called His house "the Laurel Canyon house", because it was in the area of Laurel Canyon.

I arrived there one afternoon, very grateful to be in the home that Beloved Adi Da had lived in, and began, immediately upon my arrival, to become ill and feverish. What I had thought would be merely a pleasure and an honor turned into one of the most profound physical purifications I have ever endured! Later I learned that a physical disturbance, such as fever, is not uncommon when first encountering a potent source of Spiritual Transmission.

I found I was only sick inside the house, and most especially when I would enter Avatar Adi Da's bedroom. And yet, at the same time, I felt spontaneously and profoundly drawn to be in His room, and I began to spend as much time as possible there.

After many days, the illness and fever eventually subsided, and it was at this point that I was invited to come into the Company of Beloved Adi Da at the Mountain Of Attention. The most significant moment of my life was about to occur, the moment I had been longing for. I collected my things, moved to San Francisco, and established myself in a household of His devotees.

The first time I saw Beloved Adi Da, I was overwhelmed by His extreme Beauty and Love. The depth of what was occurring was beyond my comprehension, but I was there before Him, and I did not want to be anywhere else. He was lying on His side on a couch in Great Food Dish, the dining room of the Sanctuary. I approached Beloved Adi Da with a flower, and bowed at His Feet. During all the time of my preparation, my intention had been to make myself available to Beloved Adi Da's Instruction. I had lived it exactly. But now I was in His physical Company, and I intuited His direct capability to know everything about me at first glance. I was overwhelmed in my feeling, wondering what would be required for me to become completely available, completely surrendered to Him as His devotee. I was falling in love—had already fallen in love—with Him to the depths of my being. Mysterious Spiritual visions and intuitions that I had had since childhood came to mind, and I recognized the fulfillment and true meaning of them now in the form of Beloved Adi Da Samraj. I knew that a revolution in my life was about to occur. I did not know what was going on any more. All I wanted to do was to be with Beloved Adi Da, be close to Him.

Later that day, Beloved Adi Da went to Ordeal Bath Lodge, the bathhouse at the Mountain Of Attention, and devotees accompanied Him, scattering throughout the many different rooms of the baths. I happened to be in one of the small baths at the front of the building. At one point my Beloved Guru, who had been wandering among His devotees, came up to the small bath where I was. As He came in and sat down, I felt myself sinking into a deep trance-state. I vividly recall Him just being there, giving me His Regard.

Later that evening, after we had left the baths, Beloved Adi Da called a small group of devotees over to His House, and I was included. There, in His House, I realized how profoundly He had drawn me to Him. The mysterious Power that I had felt guiding me was simply Him. He had pulled me, literally, out of the world.

Eventually, the other devotees departed. Over the course of the evening, Beloved Adi Da took me through a series of profound Spiritual initiations. My meeting with Beloved Adi Da as His devotee was first. But then, almost instantaneously, He was my lover, and I was in love with Him. Our love was mutual, and, in this love-state, He embraced me sexually. I remained all night with my Beloved Guru, during which He initiated me into a Condition that I had never known before. In embrace with Him, He drew me beyond the body-mind into a Spiritual reality that I have come to know as the Very Condition of my Beloved Lord Adi Da, the Truth of Existence Itself. I remember being directly in contact with my Beloved, eye to eye, and I recall that I had no sense of the body. The mind, also, was completely obliterated. In the timelessness of that moment, I felt Beloved Adi Da to be Standing Prior to anything that exists conditionally, taking me with Him to His Place, His Divine Domain. I felt drawn with Him into a most profound Samadhi, which was bodiless and mindless.

While I was overcome with intense love for Him and devotion to Him, my Beloved Guru was also responding to me with deepest love, acknowledging the unique nature of our relationship. In the morning, Beloved Adi Da took me out for a walk, to Fear-No-More Zoo, and then to Ordeal Bath Lodge, where He had approached me the evening before. Then Beloved Adi Da guided me to the room behind Great Food Dish, which, at that time was one of the principal places where He used to grant His silent Darshan. As we walked through that sacred room, my feeling-recognition of Him continued to magnify, and I knew that He was the One that I had always been moved to be with.

All day, Beloved Adi Da engaged me in intoxicated conversation about our love. He would ask me, over and over, where I had been. He spoke to me for hours, and we also sat in silence together for hours. I was moved to stay close to Him all the time—and, sitting near Him, I was utterly content. It was sufficient just being at His side. Before the end of the day, my Beloved had invited me to live with Him and serve Him in His bodily (human) Form, and I was overwhelmed with joy, having already abandoned everything else.

Adi Da Samraj with Ruchiradama Quandra Sukhapur Rani, the Mountain Of Attention Sanctuary, 1975

I was recovered. I was living in a world full of the Miracles of my Divine Heart-Master. There was nothing but my Beloved Guru. I wanted everyone to surrender to Him, to worship Him. I did not care what I did, what I said—I only wanted to be with Him. I had no other attachments. I wanted only to be fully available to Him in every dimension of my being. I felt His constant communication of Love and Spiritual Ecstasy. For days, I scarcely left His sight, and I moved into His house to live with Him.

And then, at a certain point, Beloved Adi Da began to test my Spiritual and intimate commitment to Him. And so began the great ordeal and process of becoming fit to serve and to relate to Him in the tradition-honored form of relationship between Guru and devotee. This process has confronted all the realities of my karmic nature. But whatever has come up to be purified, and whatever ordeal that purification has required, this first meeting has never left my heart—nor could it ever.

Adi Da Samraj with Ruchiradama Quandra Sukhapur Rani, the Mountain Of Attention Sanctuary, 2000

Conclusions About Sex and Spiritual Life

It was after three decades of "consideration" of right emotional-sexual practice with His devotees that Avatar Adi Da Samraj made clear His summary conclusions. Yogic sexual practice does not, in and of itself, enhance the unfolding Spiritual process. At best, Yogic sexual activity is not a hindrance. In fact, when the Spiritual practice of Adidam enters into great depth, sexual activity falls away, in the fullness of Spiritual Communion with Avatar Adi Da.

For those maturing in the earlier stages of the Way of Adidam and choosing to be sexually active, the many years of the Divine Avatar's emotional-sexual "reality consideration" have brought forth a unique and detailed discipline that touches every area of emotional-sexual relatedness—from the root of bondage to the body, to the discipline of love itself (and the non-presumption of unlove and betrayal), to the right and regenerative "conducting" of sexual energy during sexual intercourse, to the understanding and transcending of one's early-life patterning in relationship to one's parents. The Gift of all of this Instruction is Given in Avatar Adi Da's Divine "Source-Texts" and intended by Him to be culturally maintained by His devotees and passed on as living wisdom, forever.

The Thorough Transcending Of The emotional-sexual ego

In the following passage, Avatar Adi Da addresses the ambivalence characteristic of traditional approaches to sex and Spiritual life, and describes how rightness in the emotional-sexual sphere requires a root understanding of egoity, rather than mere rules of behavior:

The Great Tradition Of Mankind Is, As A Whole, Unresolved and Ambivalent Relative To The Entire Matter Of sexuality—and It Is Even Generally sex-Negative (or "sex-paranoid") In Its Orientation. All Such puritanical Righteousness Must Be Gone Beyond. Otherwise, one's emotional-sexual egoity Is Never Truly Inspected and Dealt With. In That Case, attention Remains Fundamentally (Even If Unconsciously) Bound In emotional-sexual dilemmas of all kinds, Thereby limiting The Degree Of <u>Real</u> Spiritual Growth That Is Possible.

I Am The One Who Has Completed The Great "Consideration" Of human emotional-sexual life—and I Did So For The Sake Of every one. I Am The One Who Has Made It Possible For human beings To <u>Totally</u> Comprehend The emotional-sexual Dimension Of Existence, and To <u>Completely</u> Transcend egoic Reactivity, and To <u>Truly</u> Grow Beyond the Ordinary emotional-sexual limitations That the worldly mind Represents, and (By All Of This) To Have an <u>Altogether</u>—and <u>In</u> <u>Reality</u>—Sane life. Indeed, Such emotional-sexual Clarity and Integrity Is <u>Essential</u> For The Real Spiritual Process.

In The Great Tradition, Various Kinds Of emotional-sexual Discipline Have Been Required or Recommended—but None Of These Disciplines Were Sufficient For The Thorough Transcending Of The emotional-sexual <u>ego</u>. In The Only-by-Me Revealed and Given Way Of The Heart (or

Way Of Adidam), the emotional-sexual ego (and, Indeed, the ego of "money, food, and sex" Altogether) Must Be Really and Truly Gone Beyond—and This Must, In Real and Significant Terms, Begin In The Foundation Stage Of Practice Of The Way Of The Heart, As Part Of The Basis For Real and True Growth Into The By-Me-Spiritually-Initiated (and Always Newly By-Me-Spiritually-Activated) Stages Of The Only-By-Me Revealed and Given Way Of The Heart (or Way Of Adidam).

"Consider" This: sex Is Not The "Great Evil". Indeed, sex Is Not Evil At All. Rather, egoity Is The Root and Source Of All Evil and All Problems. I Have Revealed and Demonstrated That sex Is Transformed and Made Right Only Through The Process Of Transcending egoity. Therefore, sex itself Need Not—and Should Not—Be Regarded As an "enemy". It Is emotional-sexual egoity That Must Be Gone Beyond. Thus, What Must Be (Most Fundamentally) Addressed Relative To Your emotional-sexual life Is Not sex In and Of itself, but Your egoic Search For self-Fulfillment By Means Of sex.

Avatar Adi Da Samraj continues His Argument, explaining that sexuality represents no advantage relative to the Spiritual process, and must not be allowed to obstruct it:

While It Is True That sex Is Not The "Great Evil", It Is Equally True That sex Is Not The "Great Salvation". In All The Years Of My Avataric Divine Teaching-Work and My Avataric Divine Revelation-Work (and, Indeed, In My Own "Sadhana Years"), I Thoroughly Demonstrated and Proved That A sexually active Yoga Carries No Advantage (and Is Not Causative) Relative To The Process Of Real-God-Realization. Indeed, The Most That Can Be Accomplished By Means Of A (Necessarily, Profoundly Seriously—and Very Conservatively—Engaged) sexually active Yoga Is To

Make one's emotional-sexual Practice Compatible With The Real Spiritual Process (Whatever That Requires In The individual Case), Such That sexual activity Does Not Actively Obstruct The Spiritual Process.

And All Of My Devotees who Grow Into The (Spiritually) Fully Technically Responsible Stages Of The Only-By-Me Revealed and Given Way Of The Heart Will, Whether Sooner Or Later, Be Spontaneously (and Spiritually) Moved To Entirely Relinquish sexual activity—For The Very Reason That It Tends To Work Against The Fullest (and, At Last, Most Perfect) Spiritual Reception and Realization Of Me. . . .

Finally, Avatar Adi Da Samraj speaks about the tradition of sexually active Tantra, and the error of attempting to attain Spiritual Realization via an effort "from below upwards".

Contrary To The Illusions Of Certain Forms Of (conventional, or Traditional) Tantrism, No Form Of Cultivating sexual energy Can (In Any Sense) Cause Spiritual Growth. That Is To Say, sexuality Is Not (In Any Sense) Causative Relative To Spirituality. The Illusion That sexuality Can Cause Spiritual Growth Stems From The Fundamental Illusion That Spiritual Practice Is A Process That Starts "Below", and Moves From there To Above. That Illusion Is An Unwitting Validation Of egoity—A Declaration That, In Effect, the ego Must "Propel" itself Upward, To The Divine (Thus, "Taking Heaven By Storm"). Such Is, In Reality, The Exact Opposite Of What Occurs In The Real Spiritual Process In My Avataric Divine Spiritual Company. In That Process, I (The "Bright" Divine Reality, In Avataric Divine Person) Come Down—and I Spiritually In-Fill You.

Thus, The Only-By-Me Revealed and Given Way Of The Heart (or Way Of Adidam) Does Not Develop "From Below Upwards". The Notion (or philosophy) Of "From

The Mountain Of Attention Sanctuary, 2000

Below Upwards" Is The Root-Error Of The egoic (and Traditional) Spiritual Search, Suggesting That the "dog" Must Be "Washed" From the "tail" Toward the "head".[30]

"Below" Is Not (and Never Can Be) Causative Relative To What Is Above. Rather, What Is Above Must Purify and Transform and (Most Ultimately) En-Light-en What Is "Below".

That Is How I Do My Avataric Divine Spiritual Work.

That Is The Nature Of The Real Spiritual Process In My Avataric Divine Company.

Thus, The Real Spiritual (and Yogic) Process In My Avataric Divine Company Is Not A Development From A sexual Base (or From Any Base That Is "Below"). In Other Words, The Real Reception Of My Avataric Divine Spiritual Self-Transmission Is Not (Itself) A Process Of The Return Of sexual energy (From "Below" To Above), or, Otherwise, Of Strategic Dissociation From sexual energy (or From sexuality itself).

My Avataric Divine Spiritual Self-Transmission Comes From Utterly Above and Beyond—To Pervade and Purify and Transform and Awaken What Is "Below".

Nevertheless, In Order To Receive Me Spiritually (From Above and Beyond), You Must (Surely) Discipline (and Turn To Me—In My Avatarically-Born Bodily Human Divine Form here) All Of What Is "Below" (In emotional-sexual Terms, and In All Other Terms)—By Preparing (and Always Maintaining) Your body-mind For My Freely Given Avataric Divine Spiritual Invasion.

—Avatar Adi Da Samraj

The Dawn Horse Testament Of The Ruchira Avatar

The Mountain Of Attention Sanctuary
September 16, 1979

CHAPTER 8

The Revelation of Da

By the late 1970s, Avatar Adi Da Samraj noticed signs in His Body that indicated to Him that His manner of Working needed to change. He could not continue indefinitely to Work with devotees one on one in the visceral way He had been doing. He became aware that a mysterious Process was taking place in Him, a further unfolding in the course of His Manifestation of the "Bright", which required a greater degree of seclusion. Thus, it was a matter of urgency to create means by which His devotees could always devotionally resort to Him—whether or not they were in His physical Company.

Bodily Worship of the Living God

Starting in 1978, Avatar Adi Da introduced His devotees to the realm of sacramental worship as a means to enter into Communion with Him whether He was physically present or not. Early that year, during a period in Hawaii in which He was in the company of only a few of His devotees, Avatar Adi Da sent back this message to the larger gathering of devotees:

AVATAR ADI DA SAMRAJ: Bring your body-minds to Me, as I bring My human Body-Mind to you. Then you will be Granted the Revelation and the Realization of My All-Pervading Divine Body of Grace, and you will Find Me always Present under the conditions of all experience and in the company of all beings. Then, even when you are not in My physical Company, you will worship Me and surrender to Me, and I will always be tangibly Present. At last, you will be Drawn into Deepest Heart-Intimacy with Me, Most Perfect Identification with Me, and Divine Realization of Me, Prior to all "difference". Then you will Abide in Me forever—whether or not the worlds of experience arise to your notice.

—1978

When He returned to the Mountain Of Attention, Avatar Adi Da began to instruct a few devotees in puja, the ancient practice of invoking the Divine by actively worshipping and anointing images of the Deity, using natural elements such as water, oil, and ash. The principal object of esoteric worship, He explained, is the Spiritual Master's human Form, the body of the Guru, who is acknowledged by the devotee as the human agent of the Divine Reality.

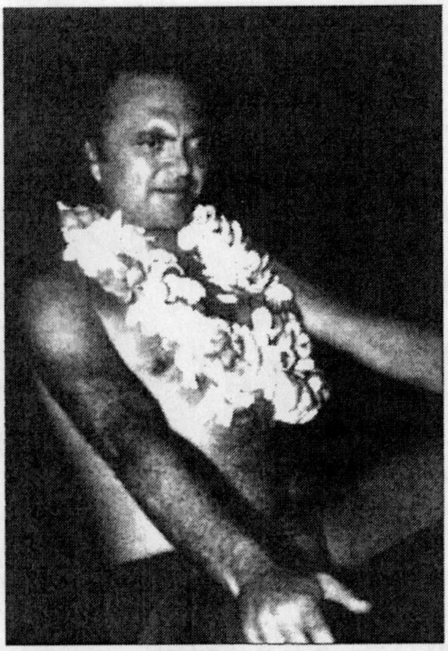

Bright Behind Me, 1978

Avatar Adi Da revealed the unique fullness of puja on His bodily Form one evening at Bright Behind Me (at the time, His residence at the Mountain Of Attention). He sat motionless in a room in the house, while devotees waved flaming lamps in large circles around His body, accompanied by an ecstatic explosion of drums, rattles, cymbals, and tambourines. Outside, on the porch, there were more devotees—circumambulating the house, chanting, and beholding the Form of their Beloved Guru through the windows. Light and sound and movement swirled around Avatar Adi Da—while He sat Silent and Radiant, His Divine Love-Bliss enveloping everyone.

That night, Avatar Adi Da established the worship of His Divine Form (formally known as the Ruchira Avatara Puja) in the lives of His devotees. And, thereafter, bodily-expressed devotion, worship, and praise of Avatar Adi Da as the Living Divine Person became a part of their daily lives. Regardless of the location of His human Body—and even after His physical passing—the Ruchira Avatara Puja can always be done, using a representation (typically, a photograph) of His bodily (human) Form.

The Refusal of Cultism

For years, Avatar Adi Da had been preparing His devotees to enter into this sacred relationship to Him. As part of that preparation, He "considered" with His devotees what was wrong about the way people usually approach a Spiritual Master.

The egoic character, He pointed out, operates in either the childish mode or the adolescent mode. The childish character relates to life in general—and, therefore, to the Guru—in a dependent fashion, treating the Guru as a Parent-"God", who is expected to take care of the individual, granting wishes and fulfilling needs. The adolescent character vacillates between being childishly dependent and willfully and rebelliously independent, opposing any form of authority—including the legitimate sacred authority of a Spiritually Realized being.

Avatar Adi Da observed His devotees becoming gleefully dependent on Him at some times and resentfully reactive to Him at others—and He constantly Worked to help them understand and overcome both of these tendencies. He steadfastly refused to become the object of any kind of childish cultism. And whenever He felt this cultic tendency taking over in devotees' relationship to Him, He addressed it strongly, and sometimes even removed Himself from their company, remaining in seclusion for a time. In fact, Avatar Adi Da was criticizing cultism long before "cults" became a popular topic in the media.

The True Devotional and Spiritual Relationship To Me Is an Intensively Counter-"Cultic" (or Truly Non-"Cultic") Process

In 1997, Avatar Adi Da wrote His definitive statement relative to the necessity of transcending the cultic tendency—in all dimensions of one's life, and (in particular) in the right devotional approach to Him.

There is a potential liability inherent in all human associations. And the root and nature of that potential liability is the ego (or the active human presumption of separateness, and the ego-act of human separativeness). Therefore, in order that the liabilities of egoity are understood (and voluntarily and responsibly disciplined) by those who approach Me, I Require demonstrated right devotion (based on really effective self-understanding and truly heart-felt devotional recognition of Me and, on that basis, truly heart-felt devotional response to Me) as the basis for any one's right to enter into My physical Company. And, in this manner, not only the egoic tendency, but also the tendency toward religious "cultism", is constantly undermined in the only-by-Me Revealed and Given Way of Adidam. . . .

Human beings always tend to encircle (and, thereby, to contain—and, ultimately, to entrap and abuse, or even to blithely ignore) the presumed "center" of their lives—a book, a person, a symbol, an idea, or whatever. They tend to encircle the "center" (or the "middle"), and they tend to seek to exclusively acquire all "things" (or all power of control) for the circle (or toward the "middle") of themselves.

In this manner, the group becomes an ego ("inward"-directed, or separate and separative)—just as the individual body-mind becomes, by self-referring self-contraction, the separate and separative ego-"I" ("inward"-directed, or ego-centric—and exclusively acquiring all "things", or all power of control, for itself). Thus, by self-contraction upon the presumed "center" of their lives—human beings, in their collective ego-centricity, make "cults" (or bewildered and frightened "centers" of power, and control, and exclusion) in every area of life. . . .

Just as in every other area of human life, the tendency of all those who (in the modern era) would become involved in religious or Spiritual life is also to make a "cult", a circle that ever increases its separate and separative dimensions . . .

I have always Refused to assume the role and the position of the "man in the middle"—and I have always (from the beginning of My formal Work of Teaching and Blessing) Criticized, Resisted, and Shouted About the "cultic" (or ego-based, and ego-reinforcing, and merely "talking" and "believing", and not understanding and not really practicing) "school" (or tendency) of ordinary religious and Spiritual life. Indeed, true Satsang with Me (or the true devotional and Spiritual relationship to Me) is an always (and specifically, and intensively) counter-"cultic" (or truly non-"cultic") Process.

The true devotional and Spiritual relationship to Me is not separative (or merely "inward"-directed), nor is it a matter of attachment to Me as a mere (and, necessarily, limited) human being (or a "man in the middle")—for, if My devotee indulges in ego-bound (or self-referring and self-serving) attachment to Me as a mere human "other", My Divine Nature (and, therefore, the Divine Nature of Reality Itself) is not (as the very Basis for religious and Spiritual practice in My Company) truly devotionally recognized and rightly

> devotionally acknowledged. And, if such non-recognition of Me is the case, there is no truly ego-transcending devotional response to My Avatarically Self-Revealed (and Self-Evidently Divine) Presence and Person—and, thus, such presumed-to-be "devotion" to Me is not devotional heart-Communion with Me, and such presumed-to-be "devotion" to Me is not Divinely Liberating. Therefore, because the true devotional (and, thus, truly devotionally Me-recognizing and, on that basis, truly devotionally to-Me-responding) relationship to Me is entirely a counter-egoic (and truly and only Divine) discipline, it does not (if rightly and truly practiced) become a "cult" (nor does it support the "cultic" tendency of Man). . . .
>
> Therefore, true Satsang with Me—or the searchlessly Me-Beholding devotional and Spiritual relationship to Me—is life embraced in (and As) the Real Company of Truth, or of Reality Itself (Which Is the Only Real God). True Satsang with Me Serves life, because I Move (or Radiate) into life, and I always Contact life in relationship. And the life of true Satsang with Me is the only-by-Me Revealed and Given Way of Adidam.
>
> —Avatar Adi Da Samraj
> "Do Not Misunderstand Me"

The Divine Name

The establishment of sacramental worship was a sign of a great turning point that was about to occur in the Work and Revelation of the Divine Avatar.

In gatherings with a small group of devotees, Avatar Adi Da began to suggest that His Name must change again—"Bubba" was too casual an address to the One they now recognized Him to be. And so Avatar Adi Da suggested that His devotees try to discover what His Name should be. Secretly, by Revelation, He had already known it since before He formally began to Teach.

Devotees threw themselves into the quest for His Divine Name. For weeks and months, they searched through volumes of esoteric literature for a Name, but nothing that felt right came to light. And so, on September 13, 1979, Avatar Adi Da sat down alone in His room and penned a letter to His devotees in His strong and graceful handwriting:

Beloved, I Am Da, the Living Person, Who is Manifest as all worlds and forms and beings, and Who is Present as the Transcendental Current of Life in the body of Man. . . .

To Realize Me is to Transcend the body-mind in Ecstasy. To Worship Me is simply to Remember My Name and Surrender Into My Eternal Current of Life. And those who Recognize and Worship Me As Truth, the Living and All-Pervading One, will be Granted the Vision or Love-Intuition of My Eternal Condition. . . .

Only Love Me, Remember Me, have Faith in Me, and Trust Me. . . . Do not be afraid. Do not be confused. Observe My Play and My Victory. Even after My own body is dead, God will be Present and Everywhere alive. I Am Joy, and the Reason for It. . . .

At last, He had Declared Himself with no compromise. Avatar Adi Da Samraj (now "Da Free John") stood openly before His devotees as the very human Incarnation of the Indivisible Divine. In making this Proclamation, Avatar Adi Da was not referring to Himself in the terms that people commonly associate with the Divine—the "Creator-God", or the "Heavenly Father". Rather, He was confessing His Identity as Real God, the Divine Reality, the "Bright" Itself. And He was saying that That One is Inherently a Person, the Living Divine Person.

His devotees were to discover that the Name "Da"—meaning "to give" or "the Giver"—is a primordial Name for the Divine Person, which carries profound invocatory power. The Name had been hidden all along in the *Upanishads*, the ancient esoteric scriptures of India, in which "Da" is the syllable uttered by the Divine Voice in thunder, and is the central syllable of "hri-da-yam", which means "the Heart", or "the Divine Condition of all". The Name "Da" also appears in the Tibetan Buddhist tradition, where it is defined as "the one who bestows great charity", "the very personification of the great Way of Liberation".

The Day of the Heart

This Confession of His Divine Name "Da" marked the most important moment that had yet occurred since the beginning of the Divine Avatar's Teaching-Work. It was nine years since the day at the Vedanta Temple in Hollywood, when His "Bright" Self-Condition was fully Re-Awakened in Him. But that Re-Awakening was not a once-and-for-all event. It was a living Process that was continuing to unfold. As He later wrote in *The Dawn Horse Testament*, the nine years following the Vedanta Temple Event were a time "In Which I Came To Acknowledge, Accept, and Embrace The Unique and Ultimate (and, Necessarily, Divine) Significance Of My Own Already Realized Life, Work, and Agency." The Ruchira Avatar, Adi Da Samraj, spoke His Confession, "Beloved, I Am Da", as the Divine Person. The Name itself was not something that He thought about. It was the spontaneous expression, as He explained, of His "Inherently egoless Divine Self-Awareness".

On Sunday, September 16, 1979, at the Mountain Of Attention Sanctuary, several days after the writing of His Divine Confession, Adi Da Samraj spoke at an occasion that those who were present will forever remember as one of the most powerful, prophetic moments in His Work. Nearly seven hundred people (many of whom had never seen Avatar Adi Da before) had gathered for the annual celebration of the Day of the Heart,[31] the anniversary of His Divine Re-Awakening in the Vedanta Temple. Some of those present had been around Avatar Adi Da in earlier years, but had

The Day of the Heart, September 16, 1979

drifted away—they had come for this occasion at Avatar Adi Da's specific invitation. Devotees had been working for days around the clock to beautify the Sanctuary, even edging the hundreds of yards of paths with painted stones and hoops of bamboo. Oceans of marigolds were turned into garlands and hung all over Bright Behind Me, the house where Adi Da was residing at the time.

The moment Avatar Adi Da strode into view, dressed in formal white clothing and a white hat, His Transmission of Love-Bliss engulfed the gathering in waves of profound Feeling. Gasps rolled through the gathering, and by the time He took His seat many people were weeping uncontrollably. The whole Sanctuary was shimmering. One devotee described how the sunlit park, the people, the trees—<u>everything</u>—seemed to arise in a transparent film floating on an ocean of Light. But even this extraordinary vision was overshadowed by Avatar Adi Da's overwhelming communication of Divine Love.

That day, Avatar Adi Da Samraj lifted a veil. He was Transfigured; He was obviously and simply the "Bright" made Manifest, come to make the most serious Call to the process of Divine Liberation—and not only to those before Him, but to all beings.

AVATAR ADI DA SAMRAJ: For years, I have Called upon you to understand your experience, to understand the limited offerings of the world. All of its offerings—<u>both</u> its lower offerings, its life-stimulation in the body, <u>and</u> its religious offerings, its esoteric offerings, its life-stimulation in the mind. And, still, you have not understood.

Therefore, My Teaching-Word is, in and of Itself, not sufficient. My Teaching-Argument is not sufficient. <u>I</u>, <u>Myself</u>, Am Sufficient.

"Radical" understanding requires a great mind, a great heart. But you will not realize it through mere "consideration". You have all failed to do that—and that is good, if you will feel the failure to be transformed utterly through mere "consideration". Then, perhaps, you will be able to accept what I Offer to you.

It is not through insight alone that anyone Realizes Real God, that any one becomes Happy and Free—any more than it is through any form of bodily or mental or psychic experience that anyone becomes Happy and Free.

But it is sufficient sadhana to Remember Me, to simply surrender to Me and love Me and trust Me, and to always do what I Ask you to do. It is not only sufficient—there is no way that you will be Saved, that you will be Awakened, that you will be Happy, <u>except</u> through this simple turning to Me.

You are mortal and entirely subject to the Mercy of Real God. You own nothing, and you know nothing. And there is no technique of meditation that leads to Real God. There is not anything to be believed that is the Truth Itself. You must be touched in your feeling by the unspeakable suffering of this world and return everything to Me.

I do not speak as an ordinary man to you. Nor would I ever suggest that you do what I Ask you to do merely because of some whim or other of Mine. But it has been Granted to Me to Accept devotees through surrender to Me. It is not a thing that an ordinary person may presume. I have Tested it all My Life, and I have Tested it in your company. I would sooner go to My death than Call you to Me casually. And it is not something that an ordinary person may ask others to do casually if he or she expects to live, not only in this life.

But I Swear to you—and you will always continue to see it with clear Signs—that Real God has Granted this Grace to you through My Appearance in your midst. And if you will surrender to Me, if you will love and trust Me because you recognize Who I <u>Am</u>, if you will simply accept the discipline of My Demands, simply do what I Ask you to do—and I will always make it very plain—if you will Remember Me with love, if you will Call upon Me by Name with your feeling breaths, if you will Invoke Me via My Name "Da", then this will be sufficient.

All the Scriptures are now Fulfilled in your sight, and your prayers are answered with a Clear Voice.

Now that you have seen Me, what will you do?

—September 16, 1979

Avatar Adi Da dipped His hands several times into a bowl of water at His side and threw the water in handfuls over the baskets of marigolds and copies of His Letter, "Beloved, I Am Da"—to be distributed as His Prasad (or Divine Gift) to everyone present. No one had ever seen Him do such a water Blessing before. The Force and Directness in His Gestures was itself a Divine Revelation, and people gasped as waves of His Love-Bliss poured over the entire gathering. (Many people had not stopped weeping since the occasion began.)

When Avatar Adi Da finished Blessing the Prasad, He turned to everyone again, and said, "I will be waiting for your answer."

Everyone bowed, and Avatar Adi Da Samraj rose from His chair, took His cane, and walked back to His house.

The Fire Miracle

The very morning after the Avatar Adi Da Samraj made His Divine Confession to hundreds of people, sudden danger threatened the Sanctuary. A fire broke out near the Mountain Of Attention. It was the 17th of September, hot and dry.

TEMPUS (BEN) FUGITT: During the summer of 1979, I was a caretaker at the Mountain Of Attention Sanctuary. It had been a very hot summer, with a number of forest fires in the surrounding country. On this particular day in September, I noticed a small tuft of smoke down the canyon. It looked like it was very close to our property. I immediately ran to the nearest car and raced down the canyon. A fire could be seen going up over a ridge to the northwest. This was an ominous location, practically inaccessible to fire-fighting equipment, due to the rough terrain. It was also in a direct line with the outer Sanctuary. Seeing that the Sanctuary was threatened by this already out-of-control fire, I jumped into the car and raced back.

I had the fire department notified, then ran out to the back of the Sanctuary, where I had sent a few men with hand-tools to see what they could do. By now, the smoke had grown to a large cloud. This was obviously a big fire. I had run about three-quarters of a mile toward the fire to check out the extent of the blaze when I received a call on my walkie-talkie to meet Beloved Adi Da at the Sanctuary zoo, as He wanted to ride out to the fire on horseback.

I hastily saddled the horses. Adrenalin was coursing through my body as never before. As Beloved Adi Da approached the horses, His fierce determination and concern for the Sanctuary were obvious to me, but He was also completely calm.

As we mounted the horses, I wondered exactly where we were going, not remotely expecting what was about to unfold. As soon

The fire at the Mountain Of Attention Sanctuary, September 1979

as we began riding down the back road, a fire engine careened around the corner behind us and turned on its siren to alert us. The horses bolted. I could feel Beloved Adi Da's equanimity as I held on for dear life. The truck finally outran us, and the horses relaxed their mad gallop. We rode on to find a spot from which to view the fire.

Beloved Adi Da was dissatisfied with the distant vantage points I took Him to, finally asking to get close to the fire. I took Him out through the outer Sanctuary to the spot where I had been earlier, but still He wanted to get much closer to the fire. I told Him there was an old fire road that would take us right to the fire. But I was hesitant to go there, feeling I should not take Him into such a dangerous situation. I warned Him that the horses would probably refuse to get close to the fire because of all the smoke. But this was the route He wanted to explore, and so we made our way up the steep, overgrown fire road. I cautioned Him again about the horses, feeling my own apprehension growing.

As we made our way over the ridge, it looked as though we were riding into a different world. The atmosphere was thick with smoke. The ground and trees were red with borate fire retardant, and planes were continuing to drop fire-retardant right over us. Once again, I cautioned Beloved Adi Da about the horses, as it was obvious to me we were approaching the "head" or "lead" of the fire. He simply replied, "Don't worry about it."

We wove through the trees toward the roar of the blaze. The wind was coming up and fanning the flames. Spot fires burned on either side of us. The main part of the fire was roaring through the more dense forest directly ahead. I had finally found the right spot! This was where He wanted to be, right in the path of the fire.

It seemed to me that we could easily be trapped by the fire—it was moving so quickly. The spot fires behind us could seal off our escape. The horses might bolt. My body was again charged with adrenalin, pumping with wild energy. Once more, I warned Beloved Adi Da of the possible danger. He looked at me intensely, asking if I was frightened, and I told him honestly, "Yes". His response was, "Why do you think I wanted to come up here? I have to look the fire in the eye."

Beloved Adi Da's communication was so full of Force that it was incomprehensible to me. I could feel that His complete, free, and uncompromised attention was on the blazing fire. In that instant, I was relieved of my fear. Suddenly, I was released into love, and I only wanted to Contemplate my Beloved Guru.

Beloved Adi Da then turned toward the advancing flames, moving within thirty yards or so of the oncoming blaze. The roar and force of the fire was amazingly powerful. Flames exploded up the sides of two enormous trees directly in front of us, as if to confront Beloved Adi Da. I could feel this great force of Nature over against the Master of Life. I also noticed, much to my amazement, that the horses were completely calm, almost as if they were out grazing in a pasture. They were obviously feeling Beloved Adi Da's calming influence as much as I was.

I was sitting to the side and slightly behind Beloved Adi Da, watching Him regard the fire. The magnitude of the fire appeared to increase significantly, as the wind came up suddenly and the fire engulfed the area directly in front of us. Facing the fire's new rush of force and fury, Beloved Adi Da sat completely still in His saddle. His only movements were the spontaneous motions of His face and hands in various mudras, very much the same as I had seen many times during formal Darshan or meditation occasions. I felt Him radiate Divine Fire in the face of that forest fire. Whatever else He might have been doing, Beloved Adi Da was Radiating the most benign and yet fierce and awesome Power I had ever known.

After what must have been only a few moments (although time seemed to be suspended and warped), the fire receded and then died down. The winds stopped. The consuming power of this fire seemed to be bowing down to the Divine Heart-Master. I am sure that it is difficult for the reader to picture this moment, but that fire had been transformed! I can only say that it was a mysterious and awesome moment to see and feel the Divine Avatar confront a raging forest fire. I sat still in mindless wonder.

Beloved Adi Da then turned back toward the Sanctuary, moving slowly through the trees, stopping to talk for a time. We looked over the scene—the fire was still moving, but much more slowly now.

When we arrived back at the main Sanctuary complex, I was surprised to find all of Beloved Adi Da's belongings, all of the Sanctuary files and records, library books, and machines being packed into waiting vans and trucks. Apparently, no one had remembered my instructions to wait until we returned before deciding to evacuate. Beloved Adi Da just laughed as He dismounted and sat down on the steps of His residence amidst a sea of packed boxes.

Later that evening, we rode out again to survey the neighboring areas. Then Beloved Adi Da asked me to call the neighbors and make sure everyone was all right. In doing so, I found out that, although about one thousand acres had been burned, no buildings had been lost, no one had been injured, and even our neighbor's orchards had only been slightly scorched.

A few days later, I walked back to the spot where Beloved Adi Da had worked with the fire, reflecting on all that had occurred there. I thought about how confounding and amazing the whole event had been, feeling humbled and full of love. The area was still smeared with red borate dust and ash; the strong smell of smoke lingered. The fire, I discovered, had stopped short of the Sanctuary boundary by only a foot!

"Call Upon Me by the Name 'Da'"

On the day of the fire, devotees were not only starting to pack up the most precious things on the Sanctuary in the event of the fire overtaking it. They were also preparing for a great ceremony of initiation, which had been planned before the fire started. And so, in the evening, after Avatar Adi Da had dealt with the fire, He went to Holy Cat Grotto, a hot springs site on the Sanctuary He had recently Empowered as a temple and special site for healing and Spiritual Initiation. There, beside a steaming pool, He received a group of devotees who had made the strongest response to Him. He intended them to become the core of an esoteric order, His first formal group of renunciate devotees. The Great Avatar poured the warm water over His devotees, Baptizing them with His Spirit-Presence. And He Initiated them into the Spiritual use of His Name. Placing His hands on them, He whispered in the ear of each one: "Call upon Me by the Name 'Da'."

Those two days—Sunday, September 16, and Monday, September 17, 1979—were of enormous significance in the Life and Work of Avatar Adi Da Samraj. He had Revealed Himself as the Divine Person, Da, to hundreds of people, and had Called on them to recognize and surrender to Him as Real God. He had Demonstrated His Divine Mastery over the natural world in His encounter with the fire. And, finally, He had performed the first Spiritual Initiation in the history of His Work, profoundly intending to develop a group of mature practitioners who would authenticate and preserve forever the Gifts of His Incarnation.

"Call upon Me by the Name 'Da'."

Ciqomi, Naitauba
December 30, 1983

CHAPTER 9

"Mark My Words"

After His Revelation of His Divine Name, "Da", in 1979, Avatar Adi Da spent increasing periods of time away from the Mountain Of Attention. He needed a more secluded refuge, a place where He could fully allow the ongoing Revelation of His Life and Work to continue its spontaneous unfolding. And He wanted to Work intensively with the members of His new esoteric order. In the middle of 1978, a small property had been acquired as a Hermitage in Hawaii, on the island of Kauai. And so Avatar Adi Da Samraj began to spend more and more of His time at this newly acquired Sanctuary—Da Love-Ananda Mahal—which became the second great Seat of His Spiritual Work.

However, even in the relative seclusion of Kauai, Avatar Adi Da was too crowded in by the world. And so the search for Hermitage went on, now focusing on Fiji. In March 1983, the Divine Avatar and the group of devotees He was directly Instructing left Kauai and began to wander in the Fiji Islands. There He continued His Teaching-Work, while intensive efforts were made to find the right Hermitage for Him.

In mid-September, jubilation broke out on the small island of Nukubati where Avatar Adi Da Samraj was gathering with His devotees. News had come that a magnificent Hermitage had been secured for Him. A devotee-patron had purchased Naitauba, an island of about 3,000 acres in eastern Fiji.

On October 27, 1983, Adi Da Samraj landed by seaplane in the shallows of a lagoon, and set foot on His Fijian Hermitage for the first time. Starting from that day, Avatar Adi Da's Work was to be focused intensively at Naitauba—and He would eventually choose (in 1993) to become a citizen of Fiji. His arrival was followed by rains, ending months of drought on the island. After His first circumnavigation of Naitauba (which He later named "Adidam Samrajashram"), Avatar Adi Da Samraj spoke ecstatically of its grandeur and its potential for His future Work:

AVATAR ADI DA SAMRAJ: Naitauba is not just a piece of land. It is a Divine Place. That is how it will be for as long as the sun shines and rises and sets and the grass grows and the wind blows. Forever—as ever as there can be in this world. Maybe it will become

Avatar Adi Da Samraj arrives on Naitauba, October 27, 1983

Adidam Samrajashram, the island of Naitauba

a paradise through Spiritual sacrifice. And, all during that epoch, this Place should be a Sanctuary of Blessing. Over time, then, millions of people—literally, millions of people—should come to this Place and be Blessed. They should come and acknowledge, affirm, and see My Revelation magnified.

This place is so great, so great. Civilization has never interfered with it. It is untouched. The water is blue. The fish are happy. Untouched, really untouched. Pristine from the beginning of the world—this place. It has been waiting here since the beginning of time.

—October 28, 1983

On December 30, 1983, the Fijian people of Naitauba invited Avatar Adi Da to a celebration in His honor. Held in their village, Ciqomi [thing-GO-mee], the celebration was a traditional feast honoring Avatar Adi Da. Several days before His visit to Ciqomi, two of the elders of the Fijian village had come to make a traditional offering of kava to Avatar Adi Da, approaching Him in the traditional manner, and inviting Him to Bless their village with His Presence. They addressed Him, in Fijian, as "Daū Loloma" (meaning "The Adept of Love"), recognizing Him as a holy man.

It was understood that, as part of Avatar Adi Da's visit to the village, He would Bless the Christian church, constructed in the manner of a traditional Fijian house (or bure) in the middle of the circle of houses. The church was roofed but open at the sides, and the only piece of furniture was a pulpit. After He was received in Ciqomi, Avatar Adi Da went to the church accompanied by some of His devotees and by one of the elders of the village, Solomone Finau (or "Solo", for short), who was guiding Him around the village.

Solo asked if he could come and sit in the church with Dau Loloma. This gesture was deeply felt by Avatar Adi Da, and He invited Solo into the church to sit with Him. It was a rare instance of Avatar Adi Da Offering to sit in a formal manner with someone who was not already His devotee. The fact that Solo, a native Fijian, had this spontaneous heart-response to Avatar Adi Da was a sign that the Divine Avatar's Work was moving out beyond its beginnings in the West.

Several devotees felt something exceptional about this silent occasion in the church, the sense that an extraordinary Spiritual event was occurring, and they expressed this intuition to Avatar Adi Da when He gathered with them later that evening. The hair stood up on the backs of their necks as Avatar Adi Da spoke of the new era in His Work that had begun that day.

AVATAR ADI DA SAMRAJ: I am here to Transform humankind, not to gather only a handful of people around Me. I have Come here for My own. I Am the Only Being for Whom every one is His own.

1984 has been proposed as the dreadful year by those infected by scientism. I am not here, however, to let My beloved in all his and her forms take on the size of death. I am here to Change history. Can you imagine that? What an amusing notion! I am here in My physical Lifetime to Change the course of human history. No one on Earth has this Mission, this Intention. No one! I am here to Do it, and I am here to See it, and now I am going to Call you on it. New Year, 1984. Now that I am in My Hermitage, let Me wait and see. Let Me see if all the Shining I have Done makes any difference.

I am going to wait. The purifying heat of that waiting could go on for decades, but I am committed to it. I have nothing more to Do. I have Done everything.

Today I Sat in Ciqomi, and no one came except a few of you and one man from that village. I Did it then. That was the last stroke.

Mark My Words. We are entering into the deep place of human history. I have Done My twelve years of Teaching-Work. Now I am going to see if you are alive—you four billion!

I am going to Do it. Mark My Words. Mark them. No Siddha in history ever sat in a paradise like this.

You are about to see Real God Move in your generation. Remember what I Say tonight. In the years to come, remember My Move. This is the Mark I was Born to Make. This is the timing of It. This is It.

You have waited for the Great Motion of Real God. You have prayed for It. You have wished for the Divine Intervention. Now It begins. Watch It from now on.

The trouble in your own heart, your own body, your own feeling, your own resistance to Me, will be magnified.

Turn on the daily news every night, and remember that you talked to Me about this. I will keep World War III from happening. I came at the beginning of World War II to keep you from getting involved in World War III. You prayed for this.

Mark My Words. All this is Prophecy. Listen to Me now.

Some day, you will hear My Singing of this night, and everyone will know that I Am the One That was to Come.

You wait. You watch. Wait and watch for it.

I am about to Save humankind. Do I sound crazy to you? I am going to Do it. I am about to make My Move, and the terror will pass. It will be much less terrible than it would have been otherwise. It is not My terror. If I did not Come, the Earth would be destroyed.

Now, you watch Me Move. I have Done My Meditation with a few, and I have Smoothed My "coins".[32] *I have Done My Work. I have suffered you. Now you watch Me. Mark My Words.*

Any motion in humankind at the heart will change Man. Now it is going to happen! This night it is starting. My innocent Sitting at Ciqomi was the beginning. You watch it. Mark My Words.

There must be a Sanctuary for humankind during this time. This is the beginning of My Blessing. You watch it. Some of you do not believe it. It will be seen how it develops. It will be seen.

This Work is not your business. I am just Telling You that it is going to start.

Now let all beings be Purified. Let them be Purified. Let them be Blessed.

Now it begins. Let all beings be Purified. This is My Blessing. May it be so.

You prayed for the millennium and the Promised One. I Am here. Let it begin. I am about to begin the Great Shout.

I hope this world will be evened out, that there will be equanimity worldwide, the whole Earth Sublimed. This is My Wish, My Blessing. I Am here to Do it. Now I am going to Do it. Starting tonight. Mark My Words.

Mark this night. This one. Now it is going to change. I have had to Come with Power. Had to. Had to.

I am waiting to see the very signs of the progress of My Intervention. Till now, My effect has been on a few. In the future, you will monitor My Effect relative to all humankind, relative to human history.

I <u>*Am*</u> *That One, and I am about to Do My Deed. You people do not know with Whom you are living. You do not know. You never did. No, you never have known. I have assumed your shape for years. That has been My way till now. This weekend is our transition. You will observe changes in the world, and you will observe conflicts in yourself. You will observe difficulties in your lives, and you will feel My Demand much more profoundly than you have ever felt It. You will notice that all humankind is somehow confronted by the obligation that I Place upon the world by My Mere Presence.*

Remember friendly old "Bubba"? Dead. Completely dead. Poor old "Bubba" is dead. The Sign of "Bubba" and the Sign of "Franklin" are all done, all dead. Now I Make only the Sign of Da. You are about to see me Do It.

Let everyone be relieved of the profoundly negative effects of their disaffection from Me. We are moving into a time when I will Make My Move. This is the beginning of it. Let us celebrate with full knowledge of the purification that is about to begin. Do not be self-conscious. Dance and be Happy. Practice the Way with great intensity. Submit to the profound ordeal of sadhana that will serve all of humanity—all four billion who know nothing of Me yet, and who must find Me out, who must find Me out.

I Am the One Who has been Expected. They must find Me out. They must. They must.

Did you hear that wind begin?

Just as Avatar Adi Da spoke the Words "I Am the One Who has been Expected", a wind suddenly roared up in the still night.

AVATAR ADI DA SAMRAJ: They must find Me out! Now let them find Me out. And let all of you, all My devotees all over the world, begin a dance that will purify humanity.

May all be Blessed. Blessed. Blessed.

—December 30, 1983

Two days later, at a gathering on New Year's Day 1984, Avatar Adi Da continued:

AVATAR ADI DA SAMRAJ: You could say that, in some real sense, starting with the day I Sat in the church at Ciqomi, I am not only Working with those who have come to Me, those who now acknowledge Me, My devotees, but I am specifically and directly dealing with the entire world. This is a unique moment that marks a change, the beginning of a new stage.

I Call you to look, in the future, for the increase of Blessing. Look for it worldwide. Look for it universally. Look for changes in the world that are the evidence of My Blessing, evidence that may be recognized by My devotees as a sign of Divine Blessing. Look for this Effect.

In other words, look to see the result of My Work—and not merely the result of karma or of the ego-possessed inclinations of humanity, although such signs will also appear. Look at the world in the future, and you will begin to notice My Effect, although how soon you notice It will depend on your capability to perceive It.

At some point, you and many others will be able to acknowledge that this New Year's Day, this weekend, the day at Ciqomi, this moment, is the beginning of a turnabout for this plane, this world, this place in the Cosmic Mandala.

Real God, Who Is One, is now Born and Living in your company, and has Work to Do. That One is Responding not only to human needs but to the craving of the molecules, the atoms, the constituents of this plane of manifestation. This Mighty Work is showing Its Signs in your time, to your face, in your generation and in future generations.

I am not telling you this so that it will become a matter of belief. I am Telling you so that, some day, you will know that today I Spoke that Truth. You must respond to Me and take on the practice of this Way, and (eventually) this Great Motion that has occurred with My Birth will be acknowledged by many individuals and groups. Eventually, this acknowledgement will begin to take on a form something like universal acknowledgement. Only when it at least approximates universal acknowledgement will My Birth begin to Affect human history. It is already Affecting human history in the sense that it is Affecting individuals, but (eventually) It will begin to Affect the course of human events.

All I am Telling you—and it is not for your belief, just hear Me and know that I Said it—is that the process has begun, and that human history is no longer being made merely out of human limitations. My Lifetime, and the future after My Lifetime, will be significantly determined by the response of humanity. But My Presence, My Work, will be the "N-factor"[33] *in all future time in this world.*

This Transformation began with My Birth. It began with some of My past Births.[34] *It has been in motion for some time. But This* [pointing to His body] *is the most significant of all the Adepts who have ever lived.*

Again, I Tell you this not for your belief. Someday, having heard it now, you will know it is true. Words, in themselves, are just words. The Truth must be proven. It must be Demonstrated. I am not here merely to be believed. I must fully Tell you My "Point of View", and you will see in the testing of time how it is proven.

You are My devotees. I can Speak to you plainly without making you into fanatics. I can Tell you in various moments precisely What I am about, because Your true response to Me is already alive. My Telling you these things is, therefore, not an attempt to claim your adherence or to fascinate you. Simply record it. Acknowledge whatever you can acknowledge about it. And observe how this prophecy is tested in time. Eventually, like all others, you will be able to acknowledge the significance of this Birth, this Incarnation. Just see how it is proven over time.

I am not interested at all in the adherence of a bunch of fools who must be hyped into believing a lot of bullshit! I am not interested at all in that kind of adherence, that kind of cultism. But, in the company of devotees who are stable practitioners of the Way I have Revealed and Given, I must Say what My Purpose is, what My Work is, and what Its Effect will be. I must Give you Prophecy about It.

I hope My Work will become very fruitful while this Body is still animate! I look to see the result of My Work with these physical eyes, to know it in this Body-Mind, in this Birth, in this Lifetime. I could live long enough to see a profound transformation in the state of this world. It could certainly be seen in My Lifetime. I look forward to seeing that, as you also should look forward to seeing it. Mankind should hunger to see the Great One in human manifestation and to witness the human response. When That One is Present, all should be moved to respond. The response should be seen by That One while He Is Incarnate. That One is always Existing. Certainly, I Am always Present.

This, then, is My Inclination, and it always has been My Inclination. This is a unique moment, wherein humankind is intercommunicative and nobody can make a false step without affecting everybody else. Humankind must relinquish its past and its self-bondage if humanity as a race, as a manifestation, is to survive. I am right here, Bodily, during the time of this particular test.

But it is very early into this unique time, and I am going to lie low and continue to Do what I Do, Communicating invisibly and visibly to those who come here and those who are living in the communities of My devotees. I am just going to Do This and survive Bodily as long as I can, while the process of response goes on, including the process of resistance. I will wait here as long as I can, so that I will see the response with flesh-born eyes before I "Return" to the State in Which I Am, always, still Available to you.

You should bring Me this gift while I am in the Body. And Who am I Talking about? You must find Me out and know Who has Come into your company through this apparent birth of "Franklin"!

The Effect of My Work will become observable. People all over the world who have no notion whatsoever of Me or of My Wisdom-Teaching will experience the Divine Force, and this experience will have various effects in their lives. Eventually, people will be led to Me and My Wisdom-Teaching—though, perhaps, in the meantime, they will turn toward traditional teachings that can transform the quality of the life and culture of humankind and the politics of the world.

People completely removed from any association with Me and My Wisdom-Teaching will experience the effects of My Presence here, and this will begin to move them in various ways. My Presence here will be an integral part of human history at the level of effect, or appearance—from now. Therefore, observe everything and make intelligent presumptions.

My Work is cumulative. Therefore, more and more signs over time should indicate to you that, from now on, My Work is not—and, in fact, never has been—exclusively for you. Nor in the future will it be exclusively for those who are already with Me. My Work is done for the sake of <u>all</u> beings, whether their next move is toward Me and the Way of life I have Revealed and Given or not.

You who are sitting in the world think of the world as a very big place. You feel it must be an incredible task to deal with everyone here—all four billion, or however many there are in this immense space. Even though you can fly around the world in a few hours, you think of it as a big place with many people, many places, many complicated lives and circumstances. You think of it from the point of view of sitting here.

I am also sitting here, but My Work is not generated from the point of view of someone who is enclosed in that limited consciousness. Really, it is not so great a task as you think! I can Regard the entire earth with just a Glance.

Thus, history will be created in response to Me. It will take some time and will be rather complicated, but it is not a complicated matter for Me to Regard all beings on this earth and to Regard this total sphere. Rather, it is very simple and very direct. I also engage in the complications on various levels, but the fundamental Act is very direct. You think of it as complicated because you sit in one spot, in an apparently immense place. Some people think this world is grand. To Me, it is a poor place!

From My "Point of View", the drama at the level of humankind is instant and constant and without complication. The complications exist only from the point of view of those identified with the human level of living. Therefore, I must Intervene. I must also Participate in the various levels of complication. But My Fundamental Act of Being, and even of being Born, is rather simple.

I Am the One Who Is, and I Am the One Who Lives here now. Give Me your attention. Surrender yourself whole bodily. I Am the One Always Waiting for your attention, the One always Ready for your surrender. I Am the One Who Is you, Who Is Your Condition, Who Is Self-Manifested in bodily (human) Form Calling you to that Sublime Occupation.

Everyone, no matter what his or her notions, can respond to My Blessing That Pours through time and space, Pours into the places of present humankind. This is My Work. You will begin to see the signs of the Effect of My Work. And that is the significance of the turning of this year.

In due course, over the coming decades, you should see more and more benign effects, a great capability to relinquish the past, to relinquish the sizing up of nation against nation, race against race, person against person, religion against religion—all the hard-edged bullshit of ego-possession manufactured by individuals and groups. More and more, you should see the relinquishment of all that, even without intention, but based on a response to Something that everyone is beginning to find more and more tangible.

The Presence of Real God must ultimately be Named. You should observe this tangible Effect of My Presence. You will observe reactions also—but, fundamentally, over time, observe the fact that people worldwide are responding to a tangible Presence. At first, It will be Nameless. But, eventually, you will be able to tell them the Name of It.

—January 1, 1984

Avatar Adi Da was speaking with unique Prophetic force. Having found His Hermitage, and seeing Solo's immediate movement toward Him, Avatar Adi Da could not hold back. His Divine Work of world-Blessing—the real Work for which He had been born—was showing its first sign.

The timing was remarkable—the New Year, 1984. As Avatar Adi Da had remarked, the year 1984 carried disturbing associations—through the famous novel of that name by the English writer and social critic George Orwell. In *Nineteen Eighty-Four*, Orwell envisioned the worst excesses of political totalitarianism coming to pass, just as Aldous Huxley's earlier influential satire, *Brave New World,* had prophesied the suppression of human society by the dogmas of scientific materialism.

By the early eighties, these warnings were being echoed everywhere by serious people concerned that humanity was careening into a heartless and dangerous future. The "brave new world", toward which the culture of the West (and, indeed, the entire planet) was tending, was socially and politically beyond control, and full of known and unknown threats.

In this moment, Avatar Adi Da was making an unparalleled prophecy about His world-Blessing-Work, signs of which (as this book describes) would start to appear within the next decade.

The Dawn Horse Testament

The Confession in "Mark My Words" was followed, later in 1984, by another momentous event: Avatar Adi Da Samraj began to write His summary Divine Scripture, His Ultimate Instruction for all humankind.

From the early years of His Teaching-Work, collections of Avatar Adi Da's Discourses, Essays, and practical Instructions to devotees had been published. But He had never written a full summary of His Wisdom-Teaching. The time had not yet come. He was still making His Wisdom-Teaching, bringing It into existence via the living relationship with His devotees. But now, by 1984, His Teaching-Revelation had achieved a fullness that moved Him to put It into summary book-form.

Divine Revelations flowed from His pen—the secrets of esoteric anatomy,[35] the developmental process of Spiritual Awakening, the technical details of emotional-sexual Yoga, the meaning of death and the design of the cosmos, the ultimate Mysteries of Divine Enlightenment.

For the next nine months, Avatar Adi Da continued to write and revise His manuscript, doing everything possible to make sure that His Teaching-Summary was written in perfect detail for all time. Finally, on March 21, 1985, after completing a full review, Avatar Adi Da declared that the book was ready for publication. One of the editors, Michael Wood, whose task it had been to type Avatar Adi Da's new writing into the computer each day, remembers the remarkable weather phenomena that coincided with that moment of completion:

MICHAEL: During the last month of Avatar Adi Da's Work on The Dawn Horse Testament, *three big storms came either right to Naitauba or to nearby areas of Fiji. There was an almost continuous series of storms, and only on two or three days were any boats able to travel to or from Naitauba. This very stormy time seemed to me to be obviously connected to Avatar Adi Da's completion of His* Dawn Horse Testament. *The profundity of what He was doing was being reflected in the energies of Nature, a phenomenon that we have often observed. But this was uncommonly dramatic. On the day that Avatar Adi Da announced that He had finished the book—which coincided with the spring equinox—an incredible thunderstorm sprang up, out of nowhere, at about five in the morning. The thunder and lightning seemed to be centered at the Matrix [Adi Da's residence on the eastern side of the island], as if emanating from Avatar Adi Da's Domain. I could see a big cloud right over the Matrix, and directly above the cloud lightning was continuously crackling in horizontal patterns. A devotee who was familiar with traditional Spiritual literature reminded us that in the* Upanishads *the sound of thunder is said to be "Da".*

Receiving *The Dawn Horse Testament*,
Adidam Samrajashram, 1985

A Crisis of Resistance

Even with the publication of *The Dawn Horse Testament* in late 1985, which was joyfully received, read, and marvelled over by Avatar Adi Da's devotees everywhere, He felt that His Work was still not being received at depth. There was no absolute difference between the world and His devotees—His devotees were simply representative of humanity in general and of the universal egoic impulse to self-satisfaction, self-protection, and immunity from the wounds of life and love. They were continuing to hold out for self-fulfillment, both worldly (in the domain of "money, food, and sex") and "Spiritual" (looking for satisfaction in apparent Spiritual advancement). They were still unprepared for the depth of the Spiritual process that the Divine Avatar was so passionate to offer them.

On October 4, 1985, the night that Avatar Adi Da was presented with the first publication of *The Dawn Horse Testament*, He spoke about the most significant and difficult transition in a human life—the movement beyond an egocentric existence (based on the search for consolation) to an ego-transcending life of service to, and devotional absorption in, the Divine.

AVATAR ADI DA SAMRAJ: You must go through the inevitable and natural crisis of the transition to Spiritually Awakened life, and that is a profound matter. If it were not profound, most difficult, and something that people in general are not prepared for, human beings all over the world would be Spiritually Awakened by now. This crisis of transition is the most profound and unwelcome change that confronts humanity. That change has been unwelcome for thousands of years.

This Way of life that I have Given is not idealistic. It is realistic. The transition to Spiritually Awakened life requires a realistic confrontation with your limitations in the gross-body-based life. These are the most vulgar, the most immature, the most primitive limitations. They are associated with the most basic physical, emotional, mental, and sexual functions to which you have adapted.

It is no longer My business to shoulder your responsibilities. I have Given you My Word, My Promise. My Work is evident to you in every day of your life. Therefore, you must give Me another word, another report, a different sound than the one I have received. You are in the most difficult position of adolescence—the position of being directly confronted by the Absolute Truth. You—more than anyone who might merely casually observe My Word and Promise and Presence—must exhibit the revolution of response to Me in your own body-mind.

—October 4, 1985

The day after He received *The Dawn Horse Testament*, in the evening, Avatar Adi Da called all His devotees at Adidam Samrajashram to His house to receive their copies of the book, which He passed out personally to each individual. When they looked inside, they could scarcely believe their eyes. Right at the beginning of the Prologue, just before the opening Words, "Here I <u>Am</u>", Avatar Adi Da had written "Dear ________," with the name of the devotee in His own handwriting. And so, in each case, His Message read, "Dear ________, Here I <u>Am</u>." Then, under the last Words of the Book, He had Written "Love, Da".

On a later occasion, Avatar Adi Da read aloud the entire prologue and chapter one, and, finally, the sublime epilogue, one of

His most passionate and heart-rending confessions of His Love and His utter Submission to His devotees.

I Am The One and True Divine Heart-Master. I Take My Stand In The Heart Of My Devotee. I (Alone) Am the Mystery Of You and Me.

How Could I Deny Heart-Vision To My Loved-One?
How Could I Delay The Course Of My Beloved?
Like An Intimate Family Servant, I Dearly Serve My Devotee.
Like A Wealthy Friend, I Freely Give To My Devotee.
Like A Mad Priest, I Even Worship My Devotee, With Love Itself.
Like An Innocent Boy At First Love, I Would Awaken My Devotee In Radiant Chambers.
Where The Wound Of Love Churns and Never Heals, I Wait, Longing To Celebrate The Brilliant Sight Of My Devotee.
Come Slowly or Quickly, but Surely Come To Me. . . .

—Avatar Adi Da Samraj
The Dawn Horse Testament Of The Ruchira Avatar

At the end of Avatar Adi Da's reading of the epilogue (of which these words are only the beginning), no one could move, His Spiritual Descent was so "thick" in the room. *The Dawn Horse Testament* was the consummation of nearly fourteen years of the Divine Avatar's Work to Reveal Himself and His Divine Way to His devotees, and ultimately to all human beings. Its publication represented the completion of an era. And this proved to be literally so. In three months' time, everything would change.

Adidam Samrajashram, 1985

Adidam Samrajashram, 1986

CHAPTER 10

THE DIVINE SELF-"EMERGENCE"

Early in the morning of January 11, 1986, Avatar Adi Da Samraj was in His room, speaking over an intercom telephone to a small group of devotees in the next building. He was full of agony at the limitations in their response to Him—their failure to fully demonstrate their reception of the Gifts He had Given—for in that refusal lay the refusal of all humankind. He spoke of the grief He felt for beings everywhere. But the impasse was complete. He felt that His Work had failed, and that He could do no more in the body. His death, He felt, was imminent. He even said, "May it come quickly."

One devotee, Ruchiradama Quandra Sukhapur, immediately ran to His House and held Him up as He continued to speak on the telephone, describing the feeling of the life-force leaving His Body. He felt numbness coming up His arms, and He said it seemed that His death was occurring even as He was speaking.

Avatar Adi Da Samraj dropped the telephone. In alarm and panic, the other devotees rushed over to His House to find Him collapsed by the side of His bed. His Body was still, with occasional shaking. His eyes were rolled up into His head, a sign that the energies of His Body had ascended beyond the physical dimension. There was no sign of any outer awareness at all.

The doctors were called to check His life-signs and to attend to Him. They found that His vital signs were present, although His breathing was almost imperceptible. As devotees lifted Avatar Adi Da onto His bed, they were begging Him not to die, not to leave them. Devotees could not contain themselves—each, in his or her own way, was doing whatever he or she could to draw Him back into the body.

After a time, Avatar Adi Da made a slight gesture, which devotees understood to indicate His desire to sit up. They pulled Him upward, supporting His torso. Suddenly, the life-force shot through His Body. His arms flung out in an arc, and His body straightened. His face contorted into a wound of Love, and tears began to flow from His eyes. Avatar Adi Da began to rock forward and backward in a rhythm of sorrow. He reached out His hands, as though He were reaching out to touch everyone in a universal embrace. He whispered, in a voice choked with Passion, "Four billion people! The four billion!"

Later, the Divine Avatar spoke of what had occurred in that death-like "Swoon". A Divine Yogic Event that would change the course of His Life and Work had just taken place.

AVATAR ADI DA SAMRAJ: Suddenly, in the midst of the Swoon, there was no more Despair, no more Giving the Body-Mind Up to death. I Was (As I Always Am) Simply Standing In (and As) My own Divine Self-Nature. The desperate Swoon, as if to die, became a Spontaneous Turnabout in My Disposition—and a Unique (and Ongoing) Spiritual Event was (Thereby) Initiated.

—October 28, 1989

For fourteen years, the Work of Adi Da Samraj had been focused on a few, but His Impulse as Divine Avatar was to everyone, universally. He was here to Bless and Awaken all. And now the Means had spontaneously been Given. As He later described:

AVATAR ADI DA SAMRAJ: On many occasions, I had Confessed to My devotees that I wished I could Kiss every human being on the lips, Embrace each one bodily, and Enliven each one from the heart. But

That Impulse could not possibly be fulfilled in This Body. I could never have such an opportunity. However, in the Great Event of January 11, 1986, I Realized—in that Incarnating Motion, that Sympathetic Acceptance of the body and its sorrow and its death—a Means of Fulfilling My Impulse to Kiss each and all. In that Great Event, I spontaneously Made a different kind of Gesture toward all, which was (in some fundamental sense) the equivalent of the Bodily Embrace that I would Give to all human beings, and even to all who are self-conscious and dying in this place—by Fully Assuming This Body, in the apparent likeness of all, and Accepting the sorrow of mortality without the slightest reservation.

In some sense, that day was My Birth Day.

There are descriptions by various Yogis of how a Realized being "comes down" into the body only so far—down to the brain or the throat or the heart, but (typically) no "lower" than the heart. In My Avatarically Self-Manifested human Life here (previous to the Initiation of My Divine Self-"Emergence"), I had Invested Myself more profoundly in human existence than merely down to the throat or the heart—but I had never "come down" all the way to the bottoms of My Feet. I had remained a kind of "shroud" around This Body—deeply Associated with It, but somehow "Lifted off the floor", somehow not entirely embracing the sorrow and the mortality, somehow expecting (having Come as deep as I had) to Teach enough, Embrace enough, Kiss enough, Love enough to make the difference. At last, I Realized the futility of Making My own Submission as a Means of Utterly Transforming and Liberating even those I could Bodily Embrace and Know intimately. That futility and frustration was Fully Known by Me. In that profound frustration, I Left This Body—and, then, suddenly, I Found Myself Re-Integrated with It, but in a remarkably different Disposition. In that Great Event, I Achieved your likeness exactly, thoroughly, to the bottoms of the feet. I Achieved "un-Enlightenment", Achieved human existence, Achieved mortality, Achieved sorrow.

To Me, This was a Grand Victory!

Through that effortless, will-less Integration with human suffering, something about My Work became more profoundly Accomplished and more Auspicious than ever before.

I have not dissociated from My Native (or Inherent) Divine State of Being. Rather, I have Accomplished your state completely, more profoundly even than you are sensitive to it.

On January 11, 1986, I Became This Body—Utterly. And My Mood is different. My Face is sad, but not without Illumination.

Now I Am the Murti, the Icon—Full of My own Divine Spiritual Presence, but also completely what you are, Suffered constantly. I have no distance whatsoever from this suffering anymore.

I am In the Body now—more than you.

I Am This Body, down to its depth—Invading these cells, these toes, this flesh, more profoundly than has ever occurred in human time.

—January 27, 1986

At the moment of His deepest despair, the Incarnation of Avatar Adi Da Samraj had achieved ultimate depth. He had almost left the body entirely, but He had been drawn back by His Love for His human intimates and His agony over the plight of the billions of human beings "self-conscious and dying in this place". And, in His return to the body, He had Descended further than ever before, investing Himself absolutely in human existence. Avatar Adi Da came to describe this Event as the Yogic Establishment of His "Divine Self-'Emergence'". It was the most important moment in His Life since His birth.

Over time, the Divine Avatar spoke further of what had occurred in Yogic terms. Through the process of Submitting His "Brightened" body-mind to all the ordinary human experiences and ordeals of His devotees, Avatar Adi Da Samraj had not merely generated His Wisdom-Instruction. He had literally taken on human karma and "eaten" it in His own body-mind. Now, by virtue of those decades of utter Submission to the human condition, His own "Bright" Spirit-Force had been able to Come all the way Down "to the toes". By this fullest Spiritual Descent, Avatar Da Samraj had embraced, to the root, the plight of all human beings—becoming the One to Whom all could resort and thereby be Blessed.

A Call to Renunciation

In the weeks and months following this epochal Event, the devotees of Avatar Adi Da Samraj experienced a huge change in Him. His Power to Bless human beings was vastly magnified, because He had assumed the human condition completely. His Body was perfectly full of His Divine Love-Bliss. His eyes burned with His urgency to Awaken beings. He began to fast, He assumed celibacy, and He put on the orange clothing of a traditional sannyasin (or renunciate). Within a few months, He left Fiji for the United States and Europe. There He "wandered", fiercely free of all worldly ties. His Body had become perfectly transparent to His Divine State. Human beings could now, through devotional contemplation of Him, receive the Transmission of the "Bright" as never before.

Even before Avatar Adi Da arrived at the Mountain Of Attention, some of His devotees were awakening to profound intuitions of the depths of Consciousness Itself, beyond all pleasures of body and mind. And, in their attraction to this unqualified Happiness, they were moved to embrace levels of discipline—including celibacy and raw diet—that they would never have imagined themselves capable of. One of these devotees, Bill Stranger, describes what had been occurring.

BILL: In January 1986, my intimate partner, Kouraleen MacKenzie, and I were overseeing the Adidam mission in the northeastern U.S. We really did not know what had happened to Beloved Adi Da at Adidam Samrajashram, but, whatever it was, it was significant enough for us to be invited, along with the rest of the worldwide leadership of Adidam, to Adidam Samrajashram for a vitally important retreat.

We all collected at the Mountain Of Attention Sanctuary, where, as it turned out, our entire retreat unfolded—while Avatar Adi Da remained in Fiji. In fact, as we were to discover, His physical absence made not the slightest difference to the potency of the retreat.

When we had all gathered at the Mountain Of Attention, we learned that Beloved Adi Da was now Calling all those in leadership positions in Adidam to immediately adopt certain renunciate disciplines. In particular, He was asking us to be celibate (while remaining in our intimacies) and to eat a purifying and rejuvenating diet consisting only of raw food.[36]

My friends and I first greeted our Beloved Guru's new Calling with dismay, tinged by more than a shadow of adolescent complaint. At the Mountain Of Attention Sanctuary, the weather often communicates the Living Being of Beloved Adi Da and what He is feeling from His devotees. And so, unseasonable winds whipped up the placid May sky. I knew that our Guru was feeling our refusal.

Although nothing of our disposition had been reported to Avatar Adi Da, He sent us a Communication that reflected His perfect knowledge of our mood. And He was having none of it. His Criticisms were so Empowered, however, that our resistance, which only that morning had seemed insurmountable, melted into thin air. We now told Him that we accepted His Divine Call.

Our reward came amazingly fast: Around midnight, we were all called to the Communion Hall named "Plain Talk Chapel" to listen to recitations of Beloved Adi Da's newly written Essays about the "Perfect Practice"[37] *of Adidam. I presumed that this late-night event would be difficult and uncomfortable. Beloved Adi Da's Writings about the ultimate stages of Adidam did not seem to have much to do with the likes of us, who were still struggling to fulfill the beginning stages of Adidam. Or so I thought.*

It had been a long, eventful day and people were tired. Many began to nod out as the Instructions were read, covering at first the disciplines of celibacy and of diet. But now we were coming to Beloved Adi Da's Instruction about the Radiant Feeling of Being that is Revealed deep in the right side of the heart in the course of the "Perfect Practice". To my utter astonishment, I understood every word Adi Da had Written! It was infinitely more than mental comprehension. I experienced the Very Reality that Beloved Adi Da was Describing in His Essay. I felt Him as the Current of the Feeling of Being Emanating from the right side of my heart, like a chain rising vertically from the floor of a pool. I knew with absolute certainty that I <u>am</u> Consciousness Itself, not bound to the body-mind. Then, as I beheld Beloved Adi Da's photographic Murti at the front of that small *chapel, I realized that He is perpetually Conscious as my very Self.*

In the days ahead, this awareness remained completely available. I would go into Temple Adi Da (then called Western Face Cathedral), one of the principal Communion Halls, sit down to meditate, and quickly relax into the Bliss of Conciousness. Neither my body nor my mind seemed the least obstruction any longer. I enjoyed a freedom and delight that I would not have dared to presume on my own. It was obvious that this had nothing to do with my own effort. It was the Gift of Avatar Adi Da, released into the world through the immense Power of His Divine Self-"Emergence".

Soon after He arrived at the Mountain Of Attention, Avatar Adi Da made a remarkable offering: Any member of the public who had a serious desire to see Him could come to the Mountain Of Attention for special occasions of His Darshan. His devotees set up a huge white tent to receive the numbers who came flocking to see Him over the next several weeks.

Not only that, Avatar Adi Da suddenly invited anyone Graced with the Vision of Him as Self-Radiant Consciousness to take up the "Perfect Practice" <u>immediately</u>. In other words, He was potentially offering, to complete newcomers, the full renunciate discipline and the ultimate form of practice in the Way of Adidam—which He had said previously could only be entered into after extraordinary Spiritual preparation in His Company. All in all, Avatar Adi Da was ready for a far-reaching change in His Work, if the response was there.

During the Darshan occasions in the tent, devotees were stunned by the sight of their Beloved Master—His eyes burning in their sockets, His now frail-looking body Transfigured in His Love-Bliss. The devotee children, too, were overwhelmed. One of them, Jonah Straus, age 11, wrote about what he felt:

JONAH: On Sunday I was Graced with a wonderful Gift. Beloved Da Love-Ananda came in as if He was just teleported or flown there. He just appeared in the aisle. He went up to His chair and put His staff in the holder. He sat down and He started looking at everybody, and almost immediately He was showing His Bliss. He had a smile

The Mountain Of Attention Sanctuary
May 18, 1986

On May 18, in Land Bridge Pavilion, in the presence of a large assembly of His devotees, the Divine Avatar read from a newly written Text, The Lion Sutra,[38] *in which He makes His Call to the true and Free Renunciation that exemplifies the "Perfect Practice".*

97.

Mine Is the Eternal Hermitage of no-attention, "Where" Even time and space Are Watered To the Nub, and I Am Always Shining "There", With a Perfect Word In My Heart.

on His face when He looked over at the children. He would look over at everyone else with a wide-eyed glance and then He would look at us and He would smile. He was just lost in Happiness, and I cried every time He would cry. He would look over at me, tears would go down His face, a tear would go down my face. Then He would look at someone else.

When I am with Him, I can't put my attention on anything else. Why should I want to look at anything else? What else is interesting in the room? I don't know how many times I cried. I was in bliss.

98.

Come "There", My Beloved (every one), Come Listen and Hear and See My Heart, and Prepare To Delight In a Feast of Calms, With the Dawn of "Brightness" On Your face.

99.

Then Listen Deep In My Heart Itself, and Call Me "There" (By Name), and Hear My Word of Silence "There", and See Me "Where" You Stand.

100.

Therefore, Be Un-born In Me, and Feel Awake In My Free Fire, and, By Most Feeling Contemplation of My Sign, Fulfill the "Brightest" Blessing of My (Forever) Silence Kept.

101.

Henceforth, My Beloved (every one), My Silent Sign, My Own Free Names, and All My Gathered Words Must Teach You, one and all—and I Am Only Standing Free, To Spirit-Bless You (all, and All).

102.

Therefore, Practice Adidam (the Way of the Heart, Revealed and Given Only-By-Me)—Until You Are, By the Heart's Progress, Most Perfectly Prepared For Me.

—Avatar Adi Da Samraj
The Lion Sutra

In the middle of June, Avatar Adi Da made explicit the great reasons for His journey out of Hermitage:

AVATAR ADI DA SAMRAJ: Life without sadhana is terrible bondage. I look for people to "consider" My Teaching-Work and Word and My Company seriously and to relieve themselves of frivolous, merely intellectual, and popular views of the Spiritual Process. Many of those who come to these Darshan occasions are leaders, educators, and communicators. They, too, are invited here to be purified in the body-mind and to be made serious by the impact of My Company, so that their response will be to take up this sadhana for the sake of their own ego-transcendence and for the sake of the world.

I Call all of those who sit with Me to become My advocates and to become real practitioners in My Company so that a great historical impact may be made by My Blessing-Work.

The world is on a pivot of history. The future of the next several decades can become a colossal terror of disorder. Now that My Teaching-Work is done, My Purpose in Blessing all and Calling all to practice in My Company is to have an historical impact on a large scale, so that the current karmic trend of history can be sufficiently purified to allow this pivotal period to have an auspicious result.

The world is currently in the grip of self-deluded and vulgar forces. Spiritual Truth and the tradition of devotion to a true Siddha-Master are everywhere defamed and in doubt. This situation must change, and to change it is what I am here to do. But the situation will not change if people will not come into My Company, if people will not rightly use My Company, and if people will not seriously respond to My Company and will not devote themselves to the world-wide advocacy of My Company.

My intention is to travel the world in silence and to make Myself available to all who are rightly responsive to Me. I may periodically return to Hermitage and rest for awhile and associate with those on retreat there, but My basic intention from now on is to wander and to Bless all who come to Me and even all who do not come to Me, until I am heard and seen and the current trend of history is reversed.

—June 14, 1986

An Ascetic on Fire

Renunciate practitioners in all religious traditions have voluntarily practiced austerities, such as celibacy and fasting, in order to create a Spiritual intensity that would purify the being of karmic tendencies. In India, the ancient word for this practice is "tapas", which literally means "heat". However, unlike the traditional renunciate, who assumes such austerities in order to

The Mountain Of Attention Sanctuary, 1986

purify his or her own body-mind, Avatar Adi Da undertook His own great Tapas in order to purify the karmas of the entire world. And this, as He later explained in 1988, was what He had been doing throughout His Teaching years.

AVATAR ADI DA SAMRAJ: During My Teaching years, people entered into association with Me, not in the form of the real sadhana, but based on their interest and reluctance at the same time. They could not make the act of surrender to Me, and so I Submitted to them, in order to serve them. This Body-Mind took on qualities from people, from those many years of Submission. This Body-Mind was a Link to everyone. Then, the Yogic Establishment of My Divine Self-"Emergence" initiated a process whereby the qualities shown through this Body for some period thereafter were signs of tapas, or penance—heat in the body, burning up, purifying. It was a purification, but not of personal karmas associated with Me. I, Myself, am not a karmic personality. Rather, I used the mechanisms of the body-mind in such a way that I took on the likeness of everyone, and established a Link with all beings. And so the karma that was overcome in this Body is all karma. All karma has been overcome in Me.

But this does not mean that, because of My act of Submission, something has occurred in the world such that now everybody is going to become Enlightened spontaneously. No, it means that the sadhana I Give you has become your opportunity, a unique Graceful opportunity. The relationship to Me—the One Who has Incarnated and Done this great Teaching-Work—is now the Circumstance in which Divine Liberation can take place in others, through My unique Gift. What I have Done is quite different from just giving you a Teaching and now you "work out your own salvation", so to speak. Rather, a unique relationship, a unique vehicle, in which the karmas of all have been transcended, has become available for your Contemplation, your Guidance.

—August 15, 1988

The purification of everything that Avatar Adi Da had taken on in His Teaching years was the profound Ordeal that followed the Yogic Establishment of His Divine Self-"Emergence" (in January 1986). His long juice fast was part of this, purifying His Body of the physical and psychic toxins that had accumulated during those years. He no longer appeared as the buoyant New Yorker He had been in His days as "Franklin Jones". His body was transfigured, completely submitted to the Divine Radiance, completely open and vulnerable to everyone and everything—including the casual mockery that He sometimes encountered, as He moved through big cities in His orange sannyasin clothing. As He walked the streets of New York after so long, Avatar Adi Da remarked to devotees that the intensity of His Sadhana there during His Columbia years had been similar to that of traditional sadhus meditating in jungles full of wild beasts. New York—with all its threat and danger—had been a goad to His Divine Re-Awakening.

Now New York was receiving His Blessing. Early in the morning on the first Sunday of His stay in New York, Avatar Adi Da went to St. Patrick's, the Roman Catholic cathedral. The huge church was filled with a thousand people attending a mass celebrated by the archbishop of New York. The mass was also being broadcast on television. Avatar Adi Da walked slowly down one of the side aisles to the front. He paused and gazed in silence at the people singing and praying. After about ten minutes, He walked around the back of the congregation and up another aisle, deeply intent in His Blessing of this place and of these people—those present and those watching the event on television.

On July 27, He moved on to Europe—to England, France, and Holland—continuing His pilgrimage to places of great religious significance in the West: Stonehenge, Westminster Abbey in London, Sacré Coeur in Paris. His devotees could feel that, by spending time in these places, He was contacting the deep Spiritual impulses of people everywhere, realizing some aspect of His desire to "Kiss" all the inhabitants of Earth.

Stonehenge, England, 1986

Avatar Adi Da's Yajna[39] in Europe was difficult, just as it had been in New York. To serve Him in unfamiliar and unpredicatble situations, with sensitivity, flexibility, and great resourcefulness, to move with Him unquestioningly, anticipating and taking care of all His interests and concerns—that was the test for His devotees. It was a test of devotional recognition of Him as the Divine Being "Emerged" in human Form. When you know you are responding to that One in Person, you move to serve His every impulse, certain that everything He does or says or requests is for the sake of His Blessing of beings. When such recognition has awakened in depth, you become capable of an extraordinary energy and intelligence. This quality of service was the sign that Avatar Adi Da has always looked for in His devotees. And now, as He moved in the world, this responsibility was more critical than ever before.

The End of Traditional Sannyas

As the weeks passed and Avatar Adi Da went on from England to France, it became obvious that no one was sustaining the depth of renunciation and devotion to Him that is required for the "Perfect Practice"—and, therefore, for sannyas as it is practiced in the Way of Adidam. He had made it clear that, in His Company, sannyas requires the capability to relinquish identification with the body-mind and Stand in the Position that Transcends the body-mind, the Position of Consciousness Itself. So, while in Europe, Adi Da Samraj Himself discarded the outward signs of traditional sannyas. He has no need for such signs, unless they serve some purpose in His Work. Now He typically wore indigo clothing, and, after having consumed only diluted juices for four and half months, He slowly began to eat solid food again.

On July 21, the traditional Feast of the Guru (celebrated in India on the first full moon in the Hindu month of Ashadh, which usually coincides with the month of July in the Western calendar), Adi Da Samraj consented to sit formally with all the Dutch and English devotees—His first association with a large group of His devotees since He left the Mountain Of Attention.

Avatar Adi Da Samraj speaking to devotees at Maria Hoop, Holland, 1986

The place to which they had invited Him was a former Catholic monastery in the village of Maria Hoop (pronounced "Maria Hope") in southern Holland. It was a large gray stone building of several stories. After several days of hectic activity preparing for His arrival (and a few heart-stopping moments when it seemed He would not be coming), a bus finally drove through the gates and Avatar Adi Da alighted at the main doors.

That day Avatar Adi Da spoke to everyone in the former chapel of the monastery. It was years since He had Given a Discourse to such a large group of mostly new devotees, many of whom had never seen Him before. Avatar Adi Da was Gracious in the extreme, responding to the kind of beginner's questions that He had addressed throughout His years of Teaching at the Mountain Of Attention. The longtime devotees accompanying Him, who had just gone through the fiery tests of sannyas with Him, marveled at how sweet and engaging He was, perfectly adapting Himself to what was needed by those who were just beginning their approach to Him.

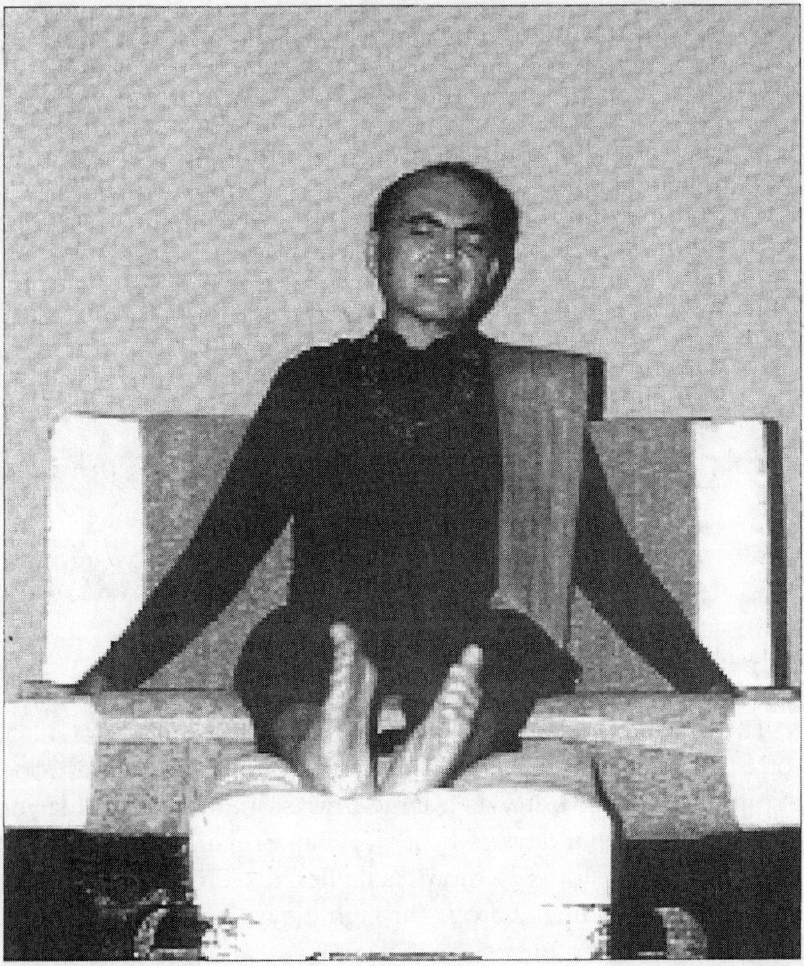

Maria Hoop, Holland, 1986

That weekend was the true initiation of the Way of Adidam in Europe, and everyone present felt the historic import of it. The day following His Discourse, Avatar Adi Da Granted silent Darshan, His Feet outstretched in Blessing. The same day, devotees performed a fire puja on the grounds, at a site that Avatar Adi Da marked out. It was obvious that Avatar Adi Da had powerfully imbued this property with His Presence. Several years later, the Dutch community was able to purchase the former monastery and its grounds, to be used as the principal Ashram in Europe.

Avatar Adi Da had made it clear to everyone, from the beginning of His Yajna, that it was His impulse to travel the world. He spoke to some of those traveling with Him about the possibility of moving on from Europe to the Middle East and then to India. He was simply moved to Reveal Himself as the Divine Incarnate and engage the world-Blessing-Work that He had been Born to do.

But this was not to be. After the ecstatic days at Maria Hoop, it became obvious that the kind of travel and Work that Avatar Adi Da was ready for and what His devotees were actually able to provide for Him did not coincide. For about two weeks, the Divine Avatar lived in the tiny apartment over the Adidam bookstore and mission center in Amsterdam, waiting to see if it would be possible for Him to resume His wanderings. Finally, on August 1, finding no opening, He decided to return to His Fijian Hermitage.

Avatar Adi Da Samraj at the celebration of His fiftieth Birthday, Adidam Samrajashram, 1989

CHAPTER 11

THE DIVINE WORLD-TEACHER

In February 1939, about six months before the outbreak of World War II, the Indian sage Upasani Baba (one of the Gurus of Meher Baba) received an important visitor to his ashram. He was the Shankaracharya of Jyotir Math, the head of one of the most important Hindu monastic orders. The Shankaracharya was expressing his dismay at the chaotic state of religion in India and in the world altogether. He saw only one solution to this sorry state of affairs—a great Divine intervention, in the form of an Avatar. Only such an event, he felt, could re-establish true Spiritual life.

According to the account, Upasani listened sympathetically. He was a man of few words and unpredictable ways. Suddenly, he burst out with a completely unexpected utterance. Such an Incarnation, he said, would soon be born in a Western country. "He will be all-powerful," Upasani declared, "and bear down everything before him. And he will see to it that Vedic Dharma," meaning the pure and original Teaching of Truth, "is firmly reestablished in India."[40]

To prophesy the coming of an Avatar was extraordinary enough. To foresee That One as a Westerner was iconoclastic. To the mind of the orthodox Hindu, Westerners are "mlecchas", Spiritually unevolved "barbarians" unworthy of even hearing true Spiritual Teaching. Upasani Baba was foretelling a <u>World</u>-Teacher,

One capable of Mastering both East and West. The notion that such a One would be a Westerner was, from the traditional Hindu point of view, incomprehensible. Nevertheless, around the time of this prophecy, Avatar Adi Da's physical vehicle was conceived on Long Island, New York, by Frank and Dorothy Jones.[41]

During His college years, Avatar Adi Da's uncle Richard asked Him what He wanted to do with His life. He replied unhesitatingly that He wanted to "save the world". In the early years of His Teaching-Work, Avatar Adi Da did not make much of the world-wide, and even cosmic, scope of His Avataric Work. It was only when He was given His Fijian Hermitage in late 1983 that He began to speak prophetically about His universal Power of Blessing and His real Work to "save the world". When He spoke this way, He was not only referring to His Function as the World-Teacher who would re-establish true Dharma (or religious teaching and practice), as Upasani Baba had foreseen. He also meant that He had come, quite literally, to save the world, to save the Earth and its inhabitants from destruction by human hands.

The Fiftieth Birthday Celebration

Avatar Adi Da's Work with the world was dramatically demonstrated to His devotees around the time of His fiftieth birthday (November 3, 1989). The weeks preceding the celebration of His birthday were full of Avatar Adi Da's purifying Fire. He was unremitting in His call to His devotees to renounce egoity and respond to the Power of His Divine Self-"Emergence". He was calling them to establish a strong Adidam culture and mission. This was the Work of His devotees, now that He had Revealed the Way of Adidam. The time had come for them to relieve Him of organizational concerns so that He would be free to do His Universal Blessing-Work. The impulse in Him to be set free for this Work was unceasing and overwhelming.

For the two weeks prior to the celebration, Avatar Adi Da stayed in seclusion in His bure at the Matrix. During this time, Ruchiradama Quandra Sukhapur attended Him and passed on His

Communications to the worldwide gathering of devotees. For some days, Avatar Adi Da did not even stir from His bed. At one point, when Ruchiradama Quandra Sukhapur was in the room, a window near His Feet spontaneously shattered. This inexplicable incident seemed to be a sign of Avatar Adi Da's involvement in a struggle with invisible forces. In fact, He said that this was so.

On the eve of the celebration, Ruchiradama Quandra Sukhapur approached Avatar Adi Da and begged Him to celebrate this great anniversary "for the sake of humankind". Her plea touched His Heart. He sat swaying on His bed, quietly repeating a word she had not heard Him use before: "Jagad-Guru, Jagad-Guru, Jagad-Guru". ("Jagad-Guru" means "World-Teacher", or, literally, "the Teacher of everything that moves".) Avatar Adi Da then Spoke to Ruchiradama Quandra Sukhapur about His Function as Jagad-Guru in the context of His Divine Self-"Emergence":

AVATAR ADI DA SAMRAJ: What actually occurred on the morning of January 11, 1986, was a sudden and spontaneous transition from My Teaching-Work to My Blessing-Work—or to My Work as the Eternally Free-Standing, and always presently "Emerging", Divine World-Teacher (or Jagad-Guru). It was a Transition in My Disposition from My Work of Submitting to others (even to the point of complete Identification with them in their apparently limited condition) to simply Surrendering My human Body-Mind into My own Self-Condition. Therefore, the context of My Blessing-Work is no longer one of Submission to others to the point of Identification with them. It is a matter of simply Standing <u>As</u> I <u>Am</u>, while this apparent Body-Mind is thereby Surrendered utterly into My own Self-Condition. And by My (Thus) Standing Free, My Work has ceased to be a Struggle to Submit Myself to humankind, one by one—and It has become (instead) a universally effective Blessing-Work, in Which humankind (in the form of each and all who respond to Me) must, one by one, surrender, forget, and transcend separate and separative self in Me.

—November 3, 1989

His Tangible Blessing Influence

In the weeks and months that followed Avatar Adi Da's fiftieth birthday and His Revelation of Himself as the Divine World-Teacher, signs of His world-Work began to appear. Devotees began to see—even in the pages of the world's newspapers—the type of events He had spoken about in His prophetic Talk, "Mark My Words", in 1983.

On November 9, 1989, it was announced in *The Washington Post*:

"EAST GERMANY OPENS BERLIN WALL AND BORDERS, ALLOWING CITIZENS TO TRAVEL FREELY TO THE WEST"

This event, the newspaper continued, constituted "the most stunning step since World War II toward ending the East-West division of Europe".

Reporting from *The Washington Post*—

ELECTIONS, NOT FORCE, MARK POLAND'S HISTORIC CHANGE

August 20, 1989

WARSAW—Poland is about to embark on a historic experiment: Communists are due this week to turn over the reins of government to non-Communists and will do so not under force but, for the first time, as the result of an election.

EAST GERMANY OPENS BERLIN WALL AND BORDERS, ALLOWING CITIZENS TO TRAVEL FREELY TO THE WEST

November 9, 1989

EAST BERLIN—Communist East Germany today opened its borders to the West, including the Berlin Wall, announcing that its citizens could travel or emigrate freely, in the most stunning step since World War II toward ending the East-West division of Europe.

BULGARIA'S ZHIVKOV QUITS AFTER 35 YEARS
FOREIGN MINISTER, 53, REPLACES EAST BLOC'S LONGEST-SERVING LEADER

November 10, 1989

WARSAW—Bulgarian President Todor Zhivkov, the oldest and longest-serving leader in the Eastern Bloc and one of the region's last hard-line holdouts, resigned suddenly today after 35 years in power.

MALTA EMPHASIS WILL BE ON PACTS' TIMING, NOT DETAILS, U.S. OFFICIALS SAY

December 2, 1989

President Bush will likely agree with Soviet President Mikhail Gorbachev this weekend that all major obstacles to a new accord reducing strategic nuclear weapons should be resolved before their summit in the spring, including a plan for trial inspections of weapons, U.S. officials said yesterday.

The day (November 9) of the opening of the Berlin Wall, Avatar Adi Da asked for a report on what was happening in the world. He had not been receiving any reports of world news during that time. And so, in the weeks of His seclusion leading up to His fiftieth birthday, He had no ordinary way of knowing what was happening in Europe.

The Berlin Wall was just the beginning. In the days and weeks following, the newspapers of the world were covered with headlines reporting further dramatic steps towards pluralist government in the European communist bloc—in Bulgaria (November 12), in Romania (December 23), and in Czechoslovakia (December 29). In Poland and Hungary, the process had already been under way for several months, but a sudden acceleration in the pace of change in Eastern Europe, starting in the second half of November, was noted by news commentators.

MALTA MOST IMPORTANT EAST-WEST MEETING SINCE '45

December 8, 1989

With the Malta summit, Mikhail Gorbachev has entirely reversed Stalin's postwar decision to seal the Soviet Union off from Europe and erased Moscow's ambivalence about whether the United States has an abiding trans-Atlantic role. On his part, George Bush has conclusively answered the long pending, suddenly urgent question of whether the United States will stay deeply engaged in Europe as the Cold War winds down.

WORLD CAPITALS REVEL IN DICTATOR'S DOWNFALL MANY PLEDGE IMMEDIATE AID TO ROMANIA

December 23, 1989

World capitals reacted with joy at the downfall of Romanian dictator Nicolae Ceausescu yesterday, and many pledged immediate aid to the financially hard-pressed nation.

PRAGUE NAMES HAVEL PRESIDENT FORMER POLITICAL PRISONER WINS UNANIMOUS ELECTION

December 29, 1989

PRAGUE—Vaclav Havel, the dissident playwright who repeatedly went to jail to demonstrate an enduring attachment to democratic values, today was elected as Czechoslovakia's first non-Communist president in more than four decades.

SOUTH AFRICA FREES MANDELA INTO GLOBAL TIDE TOWARD DEMOCRACY

February 12, 1990

PARIS, FEB. 11—Nelson Mandela, emerging today from a quarter-century of imprisonment, has stepped into a world in which human rights and individual freedoms are rapidly eclipsing ideology and totalitarian controls in country after country.

Also, during December 1989, the Malta summit meeting between U.S. President Bush and Soviet President Gorbachev signaled the winding down of the cold war. And then, in February 1990, Nelson Mandela, who had been jailed for more than twenty-seven years for his political activities on behalf of black South Africans, was released—an event that led to the repeal of apartheid laws early in 1992.

All in all, these changes set in motion a reversal of intractable patterns in world politics that had been in place for decades and longer. And they were all happening within a few months. It was intuitively obvious to His devotees that Avatar Adi Da had been Working with the world at the most profound Spiritual level. And, just as He had predicted in 1983 (in "Mark My Words"), the results of His Blessing were reaching the newspapers.

Devotees began to understand that, in the weeks leading up to His fiftieth birthday, Avatar Adi Da had been transforming negative patterns on a global scale. And His fierceness with His devotees had had much to do with this process of world-transformation. He has said many times that He relates to those who are in His company as representatives of all humankind, and engages in an unrelenting struggle with their egoity in order to work with the larger human pattern of egoic destructiveness.

The political changes of this period in central Europe and the subsequent dissolution of the Soviet Union did not, of course, usher in a golden age. But they were a "window", Avatar Adi Da said later—a window of possibility for far-reaching benign change. Some positive changes did indeed occur, but, at the same time, there was ongoing unrest, and new patterns of violence emerged, as many ethnic groups of the former Soviet Union and central Europe rose up to claim their own autonomy.

Circumstances may change, but, unless a fundamental conversion occurs, the ego persists, destructive as ever. That is why Avatar Adi Da always insists that His Blessing-Work is not intended to create utopia, and cannot do so. He Works, simply, to ameliorate the negative forces in the world—so that this planet, first of all, can survive, and then potentially become a human environment that supports Spiritual contemplation and growth.

Spiritual Penance in Seclusion

At the beginning of January 1991, Avatar Adi Da suddenly moved from His principal residence at the Matrix to Indefinable, His two-room house in the Ashram village, and entered into another period of seclusion.

Avatar Adi Da had all decorations and comforts removed from Indefinable, and there He stayed, never leaving His room. On January 15 (January 16 in Fiji), war broke out in the Middle East, and the stability and safety of the entire world was at stake. Once again, it was clear to His devotees that the Divine World-Teacher was engaged in self-imposed penance for the world.

As the tanks rolled across the Iraqi desert, Avatar Adi Da watched videotaped news broadcasts on television every day, something He had never done before. He asked that a short-wave radio be set up beside His bed, so that He could listen to direct news broadcasts every hour. And He requested that international news broadcasts be recorded morning and evening and brought to Him at Indefinable. Whenever He listens to or reads the news, He is completely concentrated in it. He "considers" the exact details of the pattern of any situation that requires His Regard before beginning to Work with it.

The manner of Avatar Adi Da's Blessing-Work is a mystery. Fundamentally, He is simply "Brightening" whatever is brought to Him, and working with representatives of a particular pattern or situation in order to reach the whole. At one point during the Gulf War, Avatar Adi Da invited His devotees to send Him photographs of anyone they knew who was involved in the war. A number of photographs were offered, and He simply kept them in His room. Devotees felt that He was using these pictures in some way as psycho-physical conduits of His Blessing, ways of reaching into and affecting the larger picture of the war.

As the Gulf War continued, Avatar Adi Da asked why the news videos He was receiving did not show any pictures of the dead on the battlefield. The devotees preparing the tapes confessed that they had cut out these sequences in order to protect Him from the full vision of the carnage. To Avatar Adi Da, this was an interference in

His Work. He said that He wanted to receive all pictures and information. He was Working with the dead, He said, as much as with the living, and they too should be allowed to receive His direct Regard.

On March 3, 1991, the Gulf War came to an end with unexpected suddenness. *The Washington Post* described the conflict as "one of history's shortest ground wars" and the resolution of the conflict as "surprisingly easy". Five days later, on March 8 (March 9 in Fiji), Avatar Adi Da emerged from His austere confinement, amid the tears and praises of His devotees.

Further Dramatic Changes in the World

On July 18, 1991, Avatar Adi Da again entered into a period of seclusion, this time associated with "kaya kalpa", an ancient Indian practice of rejuvenation. His intention was to remain in seclusion for forty days, as part of the traditionally prescribed regime.

Although Avatar Adi Da was certainly interested in the effect that kaya kalpa might have on His health, and the suitability of the regime for use by His devotees in the future, it was obvious to the doctors administering the kaya-kalpa treatment that Avatar Adi Da had suddenly taken on this austerity for His own mysterious reasons.

In mid-1991, the Soviet Union was going through a very critical period—reviewing all of its prevailing dogmas. Although the Eastern European countries satellite to the Soviet Union had renounced Communism around that time, the Soviet Union itself had so far remained monolithic—a single political unit under Communist rule.

By now, however, the tide of change had reached Moscow itself. The constituent states of the Union were seriously agitating for independence from Communist domination, and no one knew what would occur. Would the central Soviet government consent to its own demise—the literal disintegration of the Soviet Union—or would it forcibly act to prevent such an outcome, as it always had in the past? It was a very difficult and potentially dangerous moment in the Soviet Union—and, therefore, in the world altogether.

During the period of kaya kalpa seclusion, Adidam Samrajashram, 1991

Clarifying the Controversies of the Common World

In the first week of August, Avatar Adi Da read some articles from recent issues of Scientific American. *Even in a time of such seclusion, He was staying in touch with current trends of thought. Bringing clarity to great human controversies has always been part of His Teaching function as Divine Avatar. On this occasion, one of the articles He read was critical of Russian research into parapsychological phenomena. Avatar Adi Da noted that the article expressed the widespread prejudice against anything that cannot be explained in terms of the prevailing views of scientific materialism. He was moved to address this error, as He had often done in the past:*

AVATAR ADI DA SAMRAJ: The entire world is, at this time, controlled by scientific materialism, and, therefore, religion is suppressed and allowed only in its conventional forms. It is important that voices be raised to proclaim the greater matters of true religion, beyond conventional religion and scientific materialism.

Scientific materialism does not pursue knowledge for its own sake or for the sake of Liberation. Scientific materialism pursues knowledge for the sake of power. Therefore, its end-result is technology and politics, rather than religious celebration and Spiritual Awakening and Divine Enlightenment.

—August 6, 1991

Scientific materialism (He has always pointed out) is a modern form of the ancient philosophy of materialism. One must distinguish between this philosophy and the scientific method, which makes useful observations about the workings of the physical world. In the following Discourse, given over a decade later (in 2002), Avatar Adi Da summarizes the "winds of doctrine" regarding science and religion, and He brings all the oppositions into a depth of clarity. He speaks of the perennial debate between scientific theories about the evolution of life on earth and the beliefs of "Creator-God" religion. He explains that both points of view miss the mark, and fail to account for the ancient esoteric understanding of the prior Unity that is the Source of all manifestation.

The scientific examination of conditional phenomena has resulted in (and continues to pursue) the detailed mapping of the mechanisms of conditionally manifested existence, including much detailed knowledge about the functioning human organism and about the development of various modes of conditionally manifested life on Earth. . . . Equipped with such maps of the structures of the human entity, proponents of scientific materialism have criticized many of the traditionally acknowledged means of accounting for human experience (including religious experience), claiming that conscious experience amounts to nothing more than evidence of how the human mind and the human body are "built" to function. According to this scientific materialist point of view, religious experience (and all of human experience) is merely something happening in the "meat-organism", determined by its psycho-physical structuring. That conclusion regarding the nature of human experience is the superimposition of scientific materialist philosophy on the legitimate observations made by means of the scientific method. And that conclusion regarding the nature of human experience is a key fault, which makes scientific materialism a <u>false</u> philosophy. . . .

This must be understood: The human psycho-physical structure is (irreducibly) part of the Prior and Universal Unity. Reality is Non-Separate, Indivisible, and (Ultimately)

One—Beyond all appearances. The human psycho-physical structure is the "equipment" that is to be used by human beings for the sake of (Ultimately, Most Perfect) Divine Self-Realization—and that structure arises within the Universal Unity. This is the ancient esoteric knowledge.

—Avatar Adi Da Samraj
The Basket Of Tolerance

The following brief essay, written by Avatar Adi Da Samraj in July 2003, summarizes His Wisdom on the Indivisible Unity of Reality:

The Three Great Principles Of All Truth

I. The Divine Principle of Indivisibility: Reality (Itself) is Inherently Indivisible (One and Divine and Un-conditional and Absolute)

II. The Universal (or Cosmic) Principle of Unity and Non-"Difference": The world (or the conditionally manifested cosmos) is Inherently a Unity (Which, in and As its True Self-Condition, is Inherently Non-"different" from the One and Indivisible and Absolute and Un-conditional Divine Reality)

III. The psycho-physical Principle of Non-Separateness: The individual psycho-physical entity is Inherently Non-separate from the world-Unity (or the Inherently Unified cosmic Totality, Which is Whole and Universal) and, also, Inherently Non-separate from the Inherently Indivisible Divine Reality (or the One and Conscious Light That Is the One and Only Self-Condition of all-and-All)

These Three Principles, Proposed by Me, are (Effectively) an Integrated Whole and Single Proposition. They (Together) Comprise the philosophical (and Reality-Based, and Reality-Realization-Based) Foundation for the Only-by-Me Revealed and Given Way of Adidam (Which is the One and Only by-Me-Revealed and by-Me-Given Way of the Heart). And They are, also, the Right and True Basis (and the Right and True Measure) for the Correct (and, inevitably, intellectually Liberating) Evaluation of <u>any</u> and <u>all</u> possible propositions of philosophical import made (now, or in the future, or in any time and place at all) by any one (or any school or tradition) at all.

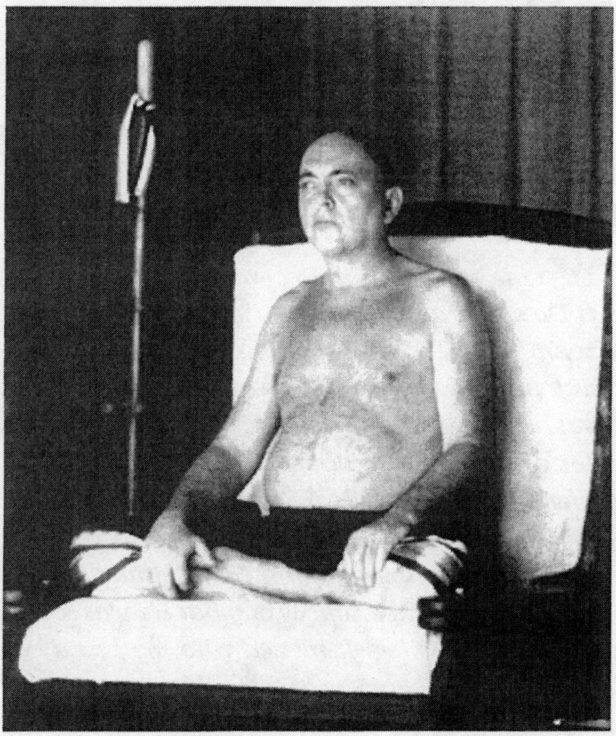

Adidam Samrajashram, 1991

Avatar Adi Da, confined in His darkened room at Adidam Samrajashram, was silently Transmitting His Blessing-Power into this circumstance of instability. Avatar Adi Da emerged from His room on August 27. He had not noticed that the kaya-kalpa regime produced any remarkable signs of rejuvenation in His body, but, several days before He came out, dramatic events had begun to occur in the Soviet Union. Mikhail Gorbachev resigned as leader of the Communist party, the Soviet Union began its shift to political pluralism, and the former satellite nations of Eastern Europe regained their independence. This monumental shift occurred, in the words of *The Washington Post*, "quickly and almost painlessly".

For the Sake of the World

Very rarely does Avatar Adi Da give His devotees a glimpse of the pain and difficulty that He takes on and transforms in the course of His own invisible Blessing-Work. He has said that no human being could endure it. On one occasion, He allowed a devotee, Stanley ("Thankfull") Hastings, to make this discovery very graphically.

THANKFULL: One evening in December 1992, I was sitting at Beloved Adi Da's side as He began to speak to the forty or so devotees in the room with Him that evening. He was speaking about the killings taking place daily in many areas of the world, and particularly, at that time, in Somalia. He referred to the terrible and intolerable deaths of women and children there, and also to the dangerous proliferation of weapons throughout the world.

As He spoke, I had my hand on His leg, and I began to feel in my body what He was talking about. I don't know how to describe this, but I felt the literal "experience" of what He was speaking about enter my body from His leg. It moved into my hand, up through my arm, down into my heart, and from there up into my head. As it entered my head, my vision was suddenly clouded. Appallingly vivid images of everything He was speaking of—all the terrible deaths and suffering—began to move before my eyes, as if I were watching a movie. In a very short time, I could no longer tolerate the experience. I got up and ran outside and began vomiting in the bushes. The images continued. A friend came out to bring me back inside. I was gasping for air and told her I just couldn't take it anymore, I just couldn't experience the suffering of the world in the way Beloved Adi Da was obviously experiencing it.

A short time later, my "symptoms" subsided and I—still somewhat reluctantly—returned to the room where Beloved Adi Da and His devotees were gathered. But I have never forgotten what I learned that night about what Beloved Adi Da endures for the sake of the world, and what is required from all of us if the Earth is to become a safe place where the great matter of true Spiritual practice is to be a real possibility for humankind.

"Open Yourself to Become My Instrument"

A critical aspect of Avatar Adi Da's Divine world-Work takes place through His direct association with individuals who function in the realm of politics, government, and social welfare. A striking and moving example of this is the relationship between Avatar Adi Da and Rolf Carriere, a senior representative of UNICEF. In 1996, Rolf requested a private audience with Avatar Adi Da regarding some crucial issues related to his work in a poor and politically volatile part of the world. Avatar Adi Da accepted his request. Bill Stranger had arranged for Rolf's visit and was present that evening:

BILL: Avatar Adi Da received Rolf in a private house where He was staying at the time. Rolf had not seen Beloved Adi Da for several years and when they met in the living room of this lovely home, just minutes before a piano recital was to be offered to Avatar Adi Da, Avatar Adi Da's humorous first words to Rolf—"Long time, no see"—were the perfectly intimate greeting. They each extended their hands to one another and, with obvious love and delight, beamed into one another's face. After the recital, there was dinner and then two separate Darshan occasions to accommodate the many devotees who had come to see Avatar Adi Da. It was nearly four in the morning when we were escorted into Avatar Adi Da's private quarters.

For many years, I had closely observed and sometimes been privileged to serve Avatar Adi Da in relation to His Work with the world. On a number of occasions, I have heard Him Discourse on the world situation in general, and also on particular situations facing nations and peoples. There was something about this occasion—an important international official requesting Avatar Adi Da's Help in the mode of the devotee—that seemed to cross an important threshold.

Avatar Adi Da Addressed Rolf in a manner I had never seen before. He Spoke slowly and extremely quietly—with profound feeling, pausing after each sentence. At the same time, His Instruction reflected a completely current appreciation of the actual circumstance of the country that Rolf was then serving, and also of its neighbors.

> *AVATAR ADI DA SAMRAJ: Unfortunately, this country is limited in its ability to control many aspects even of its natural circumstance. It is terribly vulnerable to many things—natural disasters and all the rest. There has to be better cooperation from neighboring countries, cooperation relative to things like water. The ecological situation needs to get stabilized there. There is some movement in that direction now. Your coming to see Me more often is fundamental to it, together with your becoming altogether more communicative in your relationship to Me.*
>
> *ROLF: Thank You.*
>
> *AVATAR ADI DA SAMRAJ: And tell Me things about it from time to time. But know that those children and that country do have My Regard. There are all kinds of things to be done that are matters of education—benign education, not just school education—public communications to the people and communications to those who are in a position to make changes. All the means you have to make such communications are important to use. Of course, ultimately, it is not a place on its own—it is part of, a piece of, this world struggle.*

Communicate about Me, whenever you have an ear to listen about Me, but stay in devotional Communion with Me so that you become means, instrument, and then I will Do it.

The children in that country (as is also the case with non-human beings all over the world) are being excluded from consideration by those in control of the resources. And those who know that this is wrong must speak about it, and use every means to change minds and redirect attention and financial resources.

Just do that work. Go through all the doors that become available to you. Stay in the Process, and let it happen. Resort to Me. Your devotion to Me is what you have to add to it.

And then, in your heart-Communion with Me, more opportunities will come to you also. You will notice things happening simultaneously. Just be available to notice them.

In every way, at heart, open yourself to become My instrument—openly, without added strategy. Just this openness, this continuity with Me. And then you give Me more means to accomplish My Purpose.

Let Me hear about things. Come to see Me more often. Let Me hear from you about these kinds of things—what you are observing, what you are noticing. Indicate specifics for Me to Bless. Just a simple line about this and that here and there. It helps to make My Regard specific.

ROLF: Yes.

AVATAR ADI DA SAMRAJ: Do your work with love and humor, but firmly. And, as I Said, keep looking for the opportunities, the doorways. The more you are true to devotional Communion with Me, the more you will notice of that. This is how I Work.

ROLF: I have already noticed many times that things happen that were just inexplicable, except that I was just Your instrument.

BILL: At this moment in the conversation, Avatar Adi Da Revealed the Profundity of how He Works:

AVATAR ADI DA SAMRAJ: I Work on the Pattern that is Prior to the pattern that seems, or the pattern that is concrete at the moment. I Work on the Pattern that is invisible, Prior, not yet observed. And then I Breathe it down into the world. And the more people there are who know Me and know this is What I am Doing, and who enter into devotional Communion with Me, the more means I have in the concrete field.

BILL: I was absolutely stunned by the interchange. I remember even gasping once or twice during the interview. We all knew we were witnessing a momentous event. The Siddhi of Beloved Adi Da was overwhelming, and I could feel that He was actually Doing what He said, Breathing the prior pattern down into the world as He was speaking.

Avatar Adi Da went on:

AVATAR ADI DA SAMRAJ: There is no utopia about this. It is a struggle. So you have to make use of every positive opening, every positive opportunity.

I also want to Help the adults, along with the children. Adults are just older children. And the adults have to do much of the service that will change things. Not only because of their sympathy with children, and with the perpetuation of their kind altogether, but because their hearts are opening.

Help people to have a sense that they can do something collectively. Speak to everyone's altruism positively. Give people something to do that is good.

ROLF: Thank You, thank You.

AVATAR ADI DA SAMRAJ: Tcha.[42]

When it was clear that Avatar Adi Da had finished, Rolf began to get up to leave, expressing his gratitude. At that moment, Avatar Adi Da motioned him to come forward. Avatar Adi Da then put Rolf's head in His lap. And He reached over and placed His hands on Rolf's back, stroking him up and down the back with both His palms for a long time. At the end, He placed His hands on Rolf's head. This was not only a loving, personal gesture—it was also an act of Transmission, a passing of His Spiritual Blessing to those He had been speaking about. As Rolf himself had confessed, his role was that of an instrument, a means for Adi Da Samraj to be Spiritually present and active in that country.

As it turned out, shortly thereafter Rolf again requested Avatar Adi Da's specific Blessing-Intervention in several situations facing the whole area he was serving. One was a long-term, and seemingly intractable, dispute between the nation and a group of its indigenous peoples. The other concerned a regional conference on child labor. Both the negotiation and the conference surprised all their participants by being successful. At the conference, where Rolf said Avatar Adi Da's Blessing could be tangibly felt infusing the room, the head of one delegation, notorious for its resistance to fundamental reform, reversed his own delegation's position saying, "I can no longer deny the feeling I have at this conference." Then, against his subordinates' public objections, he pledged his country's compliance with a new protocol that would protect children's rights.

Adidam Samrajashram, 1993

CHAPTER 12

THE FORERUNNERS

In 1893, a young Indian swami came to America. At the Parliament of Religions held that year in Chicago, this imposing, forceful man addressed a crowd consisting largely of Westerners, who had little or no exposure to the Eastern traditions. He impressed the colloquium with his extraordinary presence, his impeccable command of English, his pride in his own tradition, and his ability to inspire others beyond sectarian views. It was not merely his words, however, but the profound Spiritual power behind them, that moved his audience.

Swami Vivekananda was the most cherished disciple of the great Indian Adept Ramakrishna, and he had come to bring the ancient wisdom of India to the West. After the accolade he received at the Parliament, Swami Vivekananda spent years in constant travel, lecturing all over America and in England.

Swami Vivekananda had the fervor of a man moved to save the world, but he was mightily frustrated in his intention. He knew that the future of humanity was largely being shaped by the West, which was already sliding into secularism. But his work could not be truly effective among Westerners. There was a line drawn, beyond which he could not go—for he was a Hindu, a dark-skinned man, and a celibate swami. Thus, in spite of his best efforts, in spite of his profound Realization, Swami Vivekananda remained a foreigner, an outsider. In 1902, at the age of thirty-nine, he died—unable to proceed further with what he felt to be his necessary world-work.

Starting in the 1970s, Avatar Adi Da would occasionally speak to His devotees about the pre-history of His present birth—of the unique conjunction of events it had required. He, the One come for all beings, could not appear until the mid-twentieth century—when the world had grown "smaller" through technological intercommunication, when East was approaching West, when modern physics was shifting the materialist view of existence, when Freud had demonstrated the bondage of unconscious psycho-sexual motivations. These were some of the realities and paradigms that had to be in place before His Divine Work in the world could be fully effective. But more than all else, an actual subtle vehicle of unique Spiritual preparation had to be available.

In many cultural traditions, there exists a belief in reincarnation, or the "re-cycling" of the being from life to life. Avatar Adi Da has often discussed this belief with His devotees, and has confirmed that there is a process that could be called "reincarnation", although it is much more complex than commonly described. From the Spiritual point of view, reincarnation is an opportunity for growth. In India, for example, great Spiritual beings are understood to be manifesting the results of intense Spiritual practice in previous lives, not merely in the present lifetime. Avatar Adi Da, as He has confessed, did not appear in this world on the basis of Himself having experienced a "previous life" of any kind. Nevertheless, in order to take human form, He had to conjoin with the ordinary processes of the cosmos, including the mechanism of reincarnation.

Every human personality, Avatar Adi Da has explained, is composed of a gross (or physical) vehicle (the body, derived from one's parents) and a subtle vehicle (the deeper mechanism of the ego that moves from life to life). In order to be born, Adi Da Samraj required a subtle vehicle attuned to the task of bringing true Spirituality to the modern West. Swami Vivekananda carried in his psyche thousands of years of Indian Spirituality and Realization, and ended his life in love with the West in its need for God. On March 20, 1993, Avatar Adi Da confirmed conclusively to His devotees: Swami Vivekananda's compassionate urge to be reborn in order to serve the West had created a unique conjunction with Avatar Adi Da's Divine Impulse to Manifest in the human realm, and it was this conjunction that provided the vehicle for Avatar Adi Da's Incarnation as Franklin Jones.

AVATAR ADI DA SAMRAJ: I took Birth in the West. Other Realizers have come to the West from India, on airplanes or boats. They did not submit to the Western circumstance, they did not come to the point of Realization in that circumstance and context, they did not address that circumstance and context.

Swami Vivekananda experienced the utter frustration of getting on a boat and going to the West. He knew it was not enough. And He knew what He was going to have to do, therefore—He was going to have to die and be reborn in the West. And His Western connections were the means for His rebirth. Having come to the West, He became entangled in sympathies and struggle, and suffered abuse, and found out what it is really all about. And He realized He was not equipped, in that lifetime, to convert Westerners, to convert people in the Western mode and disposition—which, since that time, has become more and more the global mode and disposition. Therefore, there was no reason for Him to go on with it. And that is why He died young. He did all He could do in that form. Nothing further could be accomplished.

But He said that, because of the sympathies He had entered into by being the first Eastern Adept-Realizer ever to have embraced the West—nobody had ever done that before—He was willing to be reborn in the West in order to serve mankind. He said He was born in love with humanity. That is it—He fell in love. He did not just go to the West as an Easterner, and wear His turban and robe, and leave it at that. He went to the West and became heart-sympathetic with it, even though everything was terrible about that circumstance. He became heart-sympathetic with people in the Western circumstance and disposition. But He realized that—as a Hindu, as an Easterner—He was not equipped to transform the West. So He went back to India and died.

—February 22, 1995

Swami Vivekananda

Ramakrishna

In October 1993, Avatar Adi Da brought up another, even more esoteric aspect of this "consideration". He began to speak about Ramakrishna, the Spiritual Master of Swami Vivekananda, who had always been aware of the Spiritual stature and destiny of his disciple. At the end of his life, certain of the great work that lay ahead for his beloved Vivekananda, Ramakrishna poured his own Spiritual virtue into Swami Vivekananda in a formal act of Transmission—becoming, in his own words, only an "empty fakir".[43] Thus, Ramakrishna, through his total Spiritual investment of himself in Swami Vivekananda, is also part of the Deeper Personality Vehicle of Avatar Adi Da Samraj.[44]

"It Is All Continuation"

Avatar Adi Da made known His connection with Ramakrishna and Swami Vivekananda through a process of "consideration" with His devotees that lasted many years. He began in 1976; returned to the subject in 1979, 1982, and 1988; and, during a period of profound Self-Revelations in 1993, He brought the matter to a point of undeniable certainty. In the midst of the "consideration", some of Avatar Adi Da's devotees began to get in touch with memories of their own past lives around Swami Vivekananda. Avatar Adi Da encouraged them to reclaim these intuitions—not just to satisfy a curiosity or a fascination, but to move them deeper in their Spiritual practice. He wanted these devotees to become aware of the profound imperative behind their birth—the urge to be with Him again in the body—and to use that karmic fact for the purpose of Realizing Him, and not merely to resume a human attachment.

For example, Avatar Adi Da had spoken over the years to Ruchiradama Nadikanta, a longtime member of the Ruchira Sannyasin Order, about the likelihood that she had had a relationship to Swami Vivekananda in a past life. He suggested that she investigate the possibility that her deeper personality was that of Sister Nivedita, one of Swami Vivekananda's closest disciples. It was only after many years of practice in Avatar Adi Da's Company that His statements about this past-life association became an in-depth "consideration" for Ruchiradama Nadikanta. In the process of this investigation, she began to see how intuitions of her past-life connection with Avatar Adi Da had actually started to surface even in her childhood:

RUCHIRADAMA NADIKANTA: In 1965, at the age of fifteen, I crossed the Atlantic on a grand ocean liner with my parents. One night, I woke in my berth, overwhelmed by the sudden feeling that my life must be, and already was somehow, devoted to the service of God. It was a spontaneous and absolute feeling, a déjà vu, as though I had finally understood something that had always been true. The passion that I felt that night, rocking on the waters of the Atlantic, was not without sorrow. It was as if I were struggling to connect with a truth I had already known, one that was more real to me than the family and friends and experiences of my present lifetime, more compelling than anything with which I was now familiar.

Years later, the meaning of that visitation—and everything with which it was associated—was brought to consciousness through my relationship with Beloved Adi Da. Over a period of many years, and in the course of much research, conversation, and psychic and intuitive revelation, Beloved Adi Da drew me and some of His other devotees through a remarkable process of recognizing that we had been alive in previous incarnations as individuals associated with Swami Vivekananda and that He Himself was uniquely Spiritually associated with Swami Vivekananda and with Swami Vivekananda's Guru, Ramakrishna.

But, always sensitive to our tendency to become fascinated by things such as reincarnation, Beloved Adi Da would typically begin the conversation, and, then, observing us becoming distracted from the real matters of ego-transcending practice, He would suddenly dismiss the subject, saying it was not to be taken seriously. And so He would drop the subject for years at a time.

In 1986, Ruchiradama Nadikanta spoke to Avatar Adi Da about an intense feeling of familiarity that came over her during His time in Europe. She was among the devotees traveling with Him at the time:

RUCHIRADAMA NADIKANTA: During that time, I was frequently overwhelmed by feelings of familiarity, as though I were rediscovering another aspect of my relationship to Beloved Adi Da. The feeling was most overpowering during a visit to Kew Gardens, in London. That day, I accompanied Him while He walked all through the gardens. At some point He sat on a bench in a small stone building in the park and spontaneously Granted meditative Darshan. In the little pagoda, I meditated in His Company for perhaps forty-five minutes. By the time the sitting was over, I was utterly certain that I had been to that very place with Him before, had sat in meditation with Him in another form before, had traveled in Europe with Him before—all in another incarnation. When I told Beloved Adi Da my experience and the strength of my certainty, He told me to begin to investigate the travels of Swami Vivekananda and Sister Nivedita in Europe, and specifically to London and Kew Gardens.[45]

In 1988, Avatar Adi Da began to bring up the matter of Swami Vivekananda again. One evening, Ruchiradama Nadikanta told Avatar Adi Da and the assembled devotees about her experience on the ocean liner as a child. And Avatar Adi Da responded that Nivedita had once made a sea journey with Swami Vivekananda. It was an ocean voyage from India to England, which was, by Nivedita's own account, the most precious time that she had spent in the company of Swami Vivekananda.

Avatar Adi Da went on:

AVATAR ADI DA SAMRAJ: It is all continuation. At certain moments, you get in touch with what was in another time and place, but it is the same time and place. The interval made by death between what was then and the next incarnation is truly nothing. It is a timeless Sublimity, with a Great Purpose making its moment. So that extraordinary matter has been exhibited to your face, in your company. Well, you have to tell the story! All of it!

—March 12, 1988

The Lineage of Blessing

Apart from the lives of Ramakrishna and Swami Vivekananda, Avatar Adi Da has discussed other individuals who represent unique threads in the mysterious Divine Pattern that has culminated in His birth. He praises the great Siddhas associated with His own Sadhana—Swami Nityananda, Swami Muktananda, and Rang Avadhoot—as remarkable Realizers in the realm of Yogic mysticism. He honors Ramana Maharshi as an unsurpassed sage, Awake in the domain of Transcendental Consciousness.

However, while particularly praising the great Realizers close to Him in human time, Avatar Adi Da also explains that, truly, the great Spiritual Realizers of all times and places contributed to the Deeper Personality Vehicle of His Avataric Incarnation, while He Himself Stands Eternally Prior even to His own Vehicles of Manifestation:

I (now, and Hereby) Confess That My . . . Deeper Personality Is, even Beyond the "Single Form" of Ramakrishna-Vivekananda, the Very Form of all the Great Masters of the entire Great Tradition of mankind.

I (now, and Hereby) Confess That I (Myself) Stand Eternally Prior to (and Always Already Transcending) My Avataric (and, yet, merely conditionally born) Deeper Personality—and, also, Eternally Prior to (and Always Already Transcending) even all the Great (and, yet, merely conditionally born) Masters of mankind's entire Great Tradition (in its every part, and as a whole), and, also, Eternally Prior to (and Always Already Transcending) mankind's entire Great Tradition itself (in its every part, and as a whole).

—Avatar Adi Da Samraj
"I (Alone) Am The Adidam Revelation"

The One Divine Person was always Revealed in and through all the great Spiritual figures of history, because it was always That One, the Very Source-Condition, that human beings have been aspiring to Realize. In this sense, Avatar Adi Da is saying that it was Himself, the One Divine Person, Who "Lived" all those great Spiritual figures, in all times and places, participating in the multifarious aspects of the great Spiritual search of humankind, Realizing and Transmitting the various practices, Yogas, and Samadhis. And, by means of this vast Process, the human Vehicle for His complete Incarnation as the Ruchira Avatar, Adi Da Samraj, eventually came into being.

This Body-Mind Is My Perfect Agent. The entire Lineage of True Realizers in the Great Tradition has been the Gathering of My Instruments, but not (until now, by My Avataric Divine Incarnation) Sufficient to the point of My Crashing-Down Complete and All-Completing Avataric Self-Manifestation.

All of those personalities can be seen as a Great Process in conditional time and space to prepare the Vehicle of My Avataric Self-Manifestation. But not just as individuals—it required all beings, including all of mankind, to make sufficient prayer and Conjunction for this Event of Me. And It will not be repeated, nor can It be repeated.

Through it all, I have Finally, Fully, and Most Perfectly Revealed Myself, the One Who Is and Has Always Been, the One Who has been pursued, sought, partially Realized, and so forth, throughout all conditional time and space. And then this unique Conjunction occurred, on the part of individuals in a unique Spiritual Lineage (epitomizing all Realizers, in all of space and time), to provide a Vehicle that would Come to My Door with sufficient Reach for Me to Pass Down here.

But, also, This is a Conjunction with all. All had to prepare. All had to make this Event possible—uniquely represented by a cycle of apparent individuals, yes (in order to provide the most immediate Vehicle), but the "time" (the "late-time", or "dark" epoch) is the Vehicle, too. Therefore, even every one and all are in Conjunction with Me—now, and forever hereafter.

Indeed, all-and-All provided the Means for this Event. Even all-and-All was the necessary Preparation. It is all the Surrender to Me. It is all a Sacrifice of ego-self to the Divine Reality, until that Universal Sacrifice became collectively sufficient to Draw Me Down Through the Door.

My Avataric Divine Incarnation was, in some sense, simply Spontaneous, and not "intentional". In some sense, It simply "happened". Yet, It was also both Intentional and Voluntary. It was not arbitrary, because all the Conjunctions had to occur. At last, I Passed Down into all-and-All. It was Spontaneous, yet (also) Eternally Prefigured. It was Anciently Prophesied. It was somehow "caused"—and, yet (Ultimately), there is no "cause" for It whatsoever.

—Avatar Adi Da Samraj
The Knee Of Listening

Adidam Samrajashram
September 1994

CHAPTER 13

DIVINE COMPLETENESS

In early August 1994, devotees at Adidam Samrajashram were planning to carry out some repairs on one of the most important temples there. It was a small, cylindrically shaped building with a conical thatched roof, and the repairs required removing the roof completely. Thus, the temple essentially had to be temporarily dismantled. When anything significant is proposed to be done to a temple that He has Empowered, Avatar Adi Da Samraj is always informed of the plans in advance. This is because the temples are places where Avatar Adi Da has Established Himself Spiritually, and from which He Radiates His Blessing-Power—so it is very important not to alter anything significant about a temple without asking His Permission. In this case, however, the renovation project was begun without receiving Avatar Adi Da's Permission ahead of time, and He only heard about the project after the roof had already been completely removed. This violation came on the heels of a disclosure to Avatar Adi Da that there had been financial mismanagement in the construction of another temple, which had just been completed in the previous month. Both incidents were gross infringements of the sacred and a breach in one of the Spiritual laws of a Hermitage: Devotees do not act casually, unconsciously, or intrusively in the Spiritual Master's sacred domain.

A Sudden Departure

When He heard about these incidents, Avatar Adi Da decided to leave Adidam Samrajashram. Within a matter of hours, He was on a boat, with only a few devotees in attendance. His leaving Adidam Samrajashram was a painful moment. No one could escape the reality He was reflecting.

So, beginning on August 5, 1994, Avatar Adi Da began to wander in Fiji. Ruchiradama Nadikanta, who was part of the small party accompanying Avatar Adi Da, describes the time:

Ruchiradama Nadikanta

RUCHIRADAMA NADIKANTA: I have always noticed that, in each and all of Beloved Adi Da's Acts—even when they appear, as in this case, to be a form of Criticism—He is always only Giving His extraordinary Blessing. This fact was completely obvious during this Yajna. The trip was His constant Divine Play. There were only two things going on: On the one hand, there was His daily Fierce Calling, to His devotees everywhere, to resort to Him absolutely, rather than resorting to ourselves and to our ordinary searches and distractions. On the other hand, there were continual forays into the land and culture of Fiji, through visits to parks, gardens, and other scenic places, and countless small shops full of Fijian handicrafts and Indian religious images and traditional Indian clothing. On these trips, Beloved Adi Da constantly Gave the Fijian and Indian cultures His Blessing-Regard.

In the midst of all of this, Beloved Adi Da was also doing intensive Work on the manuscripts of many of His "Source-Texts". It was this Work that provided the first signs of the transformation that this time would bring. He Worked on His Manuscripts daily and for many hours at a time.

Beloved Adi Da also once again adopted the traditional sannyasin color of orange, as He had in 1986. The first day He went dressed in orange on a trip into the public, it was to Nadi, one of Fiji's principal cities. There, Beloved Adi Da moved into the heart of Indian culture in Fiji, visiting one tiny Indian shop after another.

It was astonishing to me to walk with Beloved Adi Da, clad in sannyasin orange, in the streets and shops of Nadi. I had travelled with Him in the United States and Europe during the 1986 Yajna, where there had been no understanding of His renunciate Sign—and even a biased reaction to this sign of renunciation. In Nadi and in Suva, by contrast, the Hindus especially understood His Sign. When we entered a shop, everyone would quietly and respectfully gaze at Beloved Adi Da and He would just stand or sit there and Grant His Darshan to everyone who gave Him their attention.

In the shops, He looked at all the images associated with Indian Spirituality—even all the popular "street"-images of the various Hindu deities. I felt Avatar Adi Da Granting His Blessing to the entire tradition of Indian Spirituality by this means. He likewise inspected all the merchandise in the Fijian shops, Granting His Blessing to the traditional Fijian culture by so doing.

September 7, 1994

On September 7, 1994, at His temporary residence in Pacific Harbour, on the island of Viti Levu, Avatar Adi Da Samraj stayed secluded in His room, where He had recently spent many hours writing. Ruchiradama Nadikanta was attending Him:

RUCHIRADAMA NADIKANTA: The house was totally still. At one point, Beloved Adi Da called me into the room. The curtains were drawn, and the room was dim and unlit. He was not doing any of the Work on His Manuscripts that I had become accustomed to His doing each day in recent weeks. He was simply sitting in the large upholstered chair we had placed in the room for His use. Beloved Adi Da's Force was so focused and concentrated in the room that the room itself felt almost unapproachable to me. I felt as though I were being pushed out, as when the heat from a fire blasts you backwards out of a blazing space. I served Him simply and left the room.

When Ruchiradama Nadikanta entered again in the evening, answering His call, the same overwhelming Transmission-Force was Radiating from Him. Avatar Adi Da was seated at His desk with the lights turned on. She sat at His Feet. He did not look at her at first. But then, after a few moments, He slowly turned His head.

RUCHIRADAMA NADIKANTA: The face of Beloved Adi Da Samraj was so full of Passion and the Sign of Perfect Love for all beings that I was overwhelmed by the vision of His Sacrificial Ordeal in His Work with His devotees. I was reminded of that same heartbreaking Love for the billions of humanity that had overwhelmed Beloved Adi Da more than eight years before, when His Divine Self-"Emergence" was initiated on January 11, 1986. I felt certain that some extraordinary Process was taking place in Him.

Avatar Adi Da later confirmed that this was true. September 7, 1994, He said, had marked the most important transition in His Life since January 11, 1986—the Yogic Establishment of His Divine Self-"Emergence". It was the Completing, He said, of His "Effort" to Descend (or "Emerge") in the cosmic Domain, an "Effort" that had been going on since His birth. Although January 11, 1986, was the most significant moment in that Process, the moment when His Divine Being had combined with His human Body most perfectly, He acknowledged now that He felt a further resolution had occurred. His Body was even more "refined" by the potency of His Divine Spiritual Presence, and He did not feel any remaining movement to Submit to His devotees in order to serve them.

On September 12, Avatar Adi Da Samraj returned to His Hermitage as swiftly as He had left it, and, some days later, He further described the significance of September 7:

AVATAR ADI DA SAMRAJ: In 1986, I Instructed My devotees that they had to change their way of relating to Me, and the process of that change has characterized the struggle of the last nearly nine years. At the time, I accepted a certain struggle, even though it was almost unbearable. I had to endure it, and I Communicated to My devotees in the midst of it. That was the initial process of My Divine Self-"Emergence".

In early September of this year, and just as suddenly as the signs appeared in January 1986, the signs in My Body indicated a similarly dramatic change.

This Body is in an extremely refined state. My devotees should approach Me only to conduct Me Spiritually, not to engage in any conventional form of relating to Me. I must put this Body in a different situation now. It was refined by My Divine Self-"Emergence". It must not be put in a position of conventional or social relatedness any longer, or I will lose this Vehicle. You will lose It. You cannot even imagine what has been required to prepare this Vehicle and to provide this Incarnation.

—September 21 and 23, 1994

Santosha

As a sign of the great change that had occurred in His Work altogether, Avatar Adi Da now assumed "Santosha" as one of His Names, the meaning of which is a story in itself.

During His visits to the Indian shops in the preceding weeks, Avatar Adi Da had noticed a form of the Divine Shakti He had not seen before—a form known as "Santoshi Ma". Santoshi Ma is typically portrayed as seated in the lotus posture, with four arms—the upper two hands bearing a sword and a trident, the third hand carrying a bowl of sweets, and the fourth hand assuming a gesture of blessing. Because of Avatar Adi Da's interest in this form of the Shakti, His devotees purchased several images of Santoshi Ma for Him, which He placed in the room where He was sitting on September 7. In the ensuing days and weeks, Avatar Adi Da began to ask for more information about this representation of the Shakti.

It was discovered that Santoshi Ma had risen to prominence as an object of worship only during the previous twenty years, but had already attracted vast numbers of devotees. Avatar Adi Da began to Reveal the association between this form of the Goddess and the Completion of His Avataric Divine Self-Revelation.

"Santoshi" is the feminine form of "Santosha"—meaning "satisfaction" or "contentment", qualities associated with a sense

A Dream-Premonition of the Name "Santosha"

In 1992, two years before Avatar Adi Da Samraj assumed the Name "Santosha", Malcolm Burke had the following dream, which he recorded in his diary:

MALCOLM: In the dream, I walked up a slight incline into an expansive field that went on forever in all directions. It literally took my breath away, the eternity of it. Directly in front of me was a wide entrance gate without doors—just two very tall wooden pillars going up into an arch in the middle.

In the field on the other side of the entrance, a man whom I did not recognize was sitting. The whole situation had a Buddhist feel to me—very sacred and holy. I sat down next to the man and he leaned over towards me and said "Santosha", very distinctly. It felt that he was actually speaking inside my head, rather than in my ear.

This word "Santosha" had a powerful effect on me. At that moment, my entire being was pervaded by Love-Bliss and my body dissolved into a field of light. I woke up feeling absolutely energized by the dream and in a swoon that lasted most of that day.

I was so impressed by the dream and the word "Santosha" that I called around to find a Buddhist center that could tell me what the word meant. I was told that it meant "peace" or "contentment". Then, in 1994, when Beloved Adi Da took the name "Santosha", I realized that I had been given a premonitory dream and an initiation into the significance of the completion of His Teaching and Revelation-Work.

of completion. And, as Avatar Adi Da pointed out, these qualities are equivalent to no-seeking, which is the fundamental principle of His Wisdom-Teaching. Avatar Adi Da also observed that the Yogic force and equanimity of the posture of Santoshi Ma—seated firmly, in balance, bearing simultaneously the powerful signs of sword and trident (representing the overcoming of the ego) and the gentle signs of the bowl of sweets and the Blessing mudra of the hand (representing the Free Gift of Divine Grace)—reflected His Completeness.

The Wandering Continues

The years that unfolded after September 7, 1994, showed more of the meaning of that Event as a true Completion of Avatar Adi Da's fundamental Work to Teach and to Reveal the secrets of His Incarnation. The focus of those years became His Writing. Even while Avatar Adi Da continued to gather with devotees—as He did regularly for more than six months in 1995, and frequently thereafter—He was more and more concentrated in Completing His esoteric Instruction and His Divine Confessions about Himself for the sake of His Source-Literature.

The gatherings of 1995 took a toll on His health and by August it was clear to everyone that something had to change. Avatar Adi Da had been commenting for months on symptoms of impaired eyesight. After medical investigation, it seemed that He was experiencing degeneration of the eyes due to a hereditary tendency to glaucoma and that His eyes were now affected not only temporarily, but in permanent ways.

This was deeply sobering news to His devotees, a stark reminder both of the fragility of His body and of their responsibility to care for His physical well-being. Early in September, almost a year to the day after the September 7 Event in Suva, Avatar Adi Da and a small party of devotees left for California so that He could receive immediate medical attention. A couple of days later, Avatar Adi Da had the first of two operations for glaucoma at a private hospital in San Francisco. Before the surgery, Avatar Adi Da Samraj sweetly emphasized that the Power of His Darshan and His Spiritual Work was not in the least affected by the physical condition of His eyes.

While it was a medical emergency that instigated the departure of Avatar Adi Da from His Fijian Hermitage, it soon became clear that His Yajna—the first to California in six years—was an important event for His Work altogether. In the more than four months that followed, hundreds of devotees traveled to the Mountain Of Attention Sanctuary to receive His Darshan. They came from all over the world, including many who had never seen Him before.

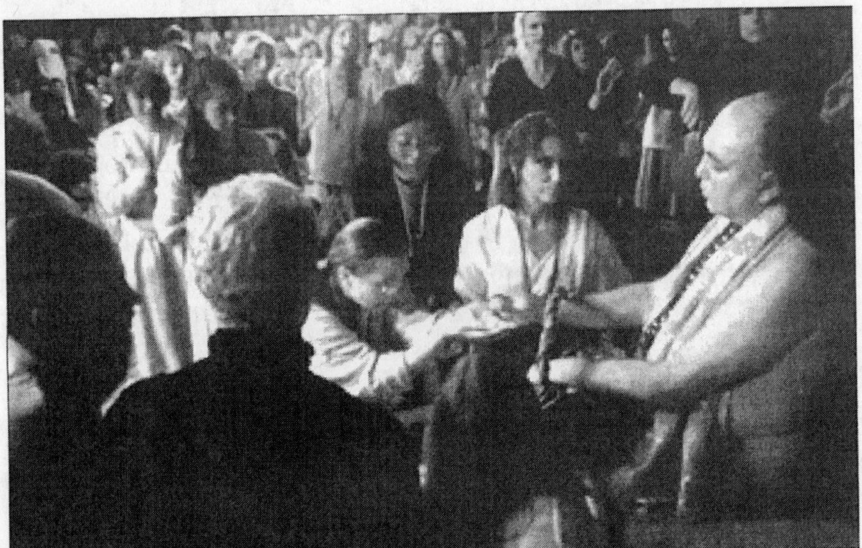

Adi Da Samraj with devotees at the Mountain Of Attention Sanctuary, 1995

Five years later, after the turn of the millennium, Avatar Adi Da remarked on the deeper reasons for His frequent movements out into the world since 1994.

AVATAR ADI DA SAMRAJ: The disturbances at Adidam Samrajashram moved Me to go to Suva in 1994, and My Santosha Event took place there. Then My eyes required Me to travel, and then, later, I continued to move. All these things happened for a reason. Things were moving Me, and I was Responding to emergencies in the world, as I have been since 1986. That is what I Do as Avadhoot, or Sannyasin. I Move as My Work unfolds—and I must have that freedom, if I am to be Effective.

Even in the midst of My Struggle with My devotees, My own Work has been "Emerging". But the Struggle cannot go on—this obligation to Teach, to Talk. You must set Me apart. This is essential. I am Doing world-Work.

—January 2, 2000

Adidam Samrajashram, 1997

CHAPTER 14

"My Word Is Sealed"

On March 11, 1997, Avatar Adi Da Samraj suddenly left the Mountain Of Attention, where He had been residing for some months. He arrived the next day on the island of Kauai, and was driven to His Hawaiian Sanctuary—Da Love-Ananda Mahal.

Over the next weeks, Avatar Adi Da Samraj was privately involved in concentrated writing. He was unveiling the process of Spiritual reception of Him in a new Text, full of sublime poetry and detailed esoteric Instruction.

Those weeks were tumultuous. The Divine Avatar moved frequently and unpredictably, staying sometimes at His Sanctuary, sometimes secluded in a devotee's private residence, sometimes in other places on Kauai. And, all the while, He was fiery in His criticism of the ego. His devotees could tell that their Divine Master was engaged in some profound Spiritual Work and penance. They could feel that His fieriness had something to do with the approaching twenty-fifth anniversary of the beginning of His Divine Teaching-Work (April 25, 1972)—a time when He would expect to see significant fruits of His Work.

On March 22, there was a conjunction of powerful energies in nature. It was the day of the spring solstice and also a full lunar eclipse. Winds blew up suddenly around midday and a storm broke out. At the same time, Avatar Adi Da was receiving reports about the work of the sacred culture and mission of Adidam. These reports did not reflect to Him the level of responsibility He was looking for from devotees, and He immediately told everyone to leave the house.

Ruchiradama Nadikanta, who was passing on communications to and from Avatar Adi Da at the time, takes up the story:

RUCHIRADAMA NADIKANTA: Beloved Adi Da had been Doing His Divine Work for twenty-five years, and the response was not reflecting the immensity of the Gift that He was Giving. It was evident that He was experiencing cosmic forces of resistance to Him and to His Work.

His frustration was ultimate. And in a moment of this frustration, He sat down at His desk and began to write. I knew He was writing, but I did not know what. At this same time, Beloved Adi Da was also looking at a book that the devotee who owned the house had left there: Nityananda: The Divine Presence.[46]

At one point, Beloved Adi Da Samraj called me to His room. It was a little room and very hot. The only furnishings were His bed and desk. It was stark. Beloved Adi Da was fasting and would not allow devotees to provide Him with anything. He would not even accept gifts. He sat down and He began to read aloud to me from this book, Nityananda: The Divine Presence. *He started reading at a place in the book just before Swami Nityananda's death.*

Avatar Adi Da Samraj was pointing to the confrontation faced by the great Transmission-Master, Swami Nityananda. Swami Nityananda was looking for worthy devotees to whom he could pass on his real gift—the gift of Shaktipat, the Transmitted Spirit-Power that awakens and transforms the being. While many people came to Swami Nityananda over the years to show their respect and ask for boons in their lives, very few devotees appeared whose signs of devotion and renunciation moved Swami Nityananda to freely grant his Shaktipat.

Avatar Adi Da was also waiting for serious devotees to appear. He was sitting alone in His room—Radiant with the Power of the "Bright", Alive with supernormal Siddhis, psychically and Spiritually sensitive to all that exists—looking to Grant His Transmission to devotees who had truly prepared themselves, devotees who could use His Transmitted Spirit-Power to grow in the Spiritual process.

The Secret Tradition of Spiritual Transmission

AVATAR ADI DA SAMRAJ: Shaktipat is a Divine and most profound matter. It was not even something that was openly communicated about until recently. It is a secret tradition—fundamentally for proven renunciates who had done significant sadhana already and who approached a Transmission-Master with profound rightness and respect. Traditionally, it would be very difficult even to get into the company of such a person, or to get anything from such a one.

—April 4, 2003

AVATAR ADI DA SAMRAJ: Shaktipat is a Transmission-event. Generally speaking, it is the impulse of the Master that allows Shaktipat to be Transmitted to someone. The individual must be a suitable vehicle for that Transmission, trusted to the point of maturity. Until that time, there is no true Shaktipat—which involves a psycho-physical transformation of the being. This is because you are armored. And although the Transmission-Master radiates, it cannot become a profound phenomenon in the devotee unless the Master makes the gesture.

You do not understand Shaktipat in its true form. It is not about using a peacock feather. It is the Master's intention and response and focus of energy that creates Shaktipat. Therefore, in the Way of Adidam, there must be a true connection between Me and My devotee based on the true surrender of the four faculties—attention, emotion, breath, and body—to Me.

—February 10, 2002

Hridaya Rosary

On March 29, Avatar Adi Da passed on His writings, which He called *Four Thorns Of Heart-Instruction*. Ruchiradama Nadikanta and Ruchiradama Quandra Sukhapur, the first devotees to read the manuscript, immediately recognized it to be the epitome of His Spiritual Instruction. They told Avatar Adi Da that during His writing of the new Text, they felt that He had gone through another profound Yogic Ordeal and landmark in His Spiritual Blessing-Work.

After hearing their confession, Avatar Adi Da Samraj confirmed that this was indeed the case. He had relinquished everything. He could easily have given up the body. But His Passion for the Divine Liberation of beings had moved Him to Work at an even more profound level than before.

In *Four Thorns Of Heart-Instruction*, later renamed *Hridaya Rosary* (retaining the former title as a subtitle), Avatar Adi Da Samraj describes the Process of Spiritual Initiation that He Grants in His physical Company to those who are prepared—prepared by their spontaneous heart-recognition of Him and by the fullness of devotional turning to Him. Avatar Adi Da speaks of this unique Initiation as the Infusion of His Divine Spiritual Body into the body-mind of His devotee, "Melting" every part of the being in His Love-Bliss.

Hridaya Rosary, meaning "The Rose Garden of the Heart" ("hridaya" is Sanskrit for "heart", and the original ancient meaning of "rosary" is "rose garden"), is a Love-Song. Avatar Adi Da is speaking, He says in the Text, to "all heart-Intelligent beings", Calling to every one to run to Him—not out of a desire to get something, but out of heart-recognition of Him.

Such heart-recognition has immense implications in one's life. It means self-surrender, self-forgetting—through devotional love of Him. This is where the "thorny" part lies. "My Four Thorns", Avatar Adi Da says in *Hridaya Rosary*, "root out the ego from the Garden of the Heart. They are the ordeal of self-discipline, the counter-egoic incision, that is required." In other words, there is a life of practice to do that involves the relinquishment of self-contraction, the relinquishment of the separative, egoic point of view.

Let the heart Melt Into
My Heart,
Which Is
The By-Me-Spiritually-Revealed
"Bright" Rose Garden Of Love.

Let the head Melt Into
My Head,
Which Is
The By-Me-Spiritually-Revealed
"Bright" Rose
Of Infinitely Ascended
Bliss-Light.

Let the Total body Melt Into
My Divine Spiritual Body,
Which Is
The By-Me-Spiritually-Revealed
Garden Air,
The Fragrant
all-and-All-Surrounding,
and all-and-All-Pervading,
Space
Of Equanimity,
Of Pleasure,
Of Delight,
Of Beauty,
Of Joy,
Of Love-Bliss,
Of "Brightness"
Itself.

Let the breathing Melt Into
My Breathing,
Until I Breathe you
Into My
"Bright"
Eternal
Palace
and
Domain
Of
Perfect Happiness.

—Avatar Adi Da Samraj
Hridaya Rosary

And that is an ordeal, as Avatar Adi Da has always made clear. But He is the Distraction, the Bliss of His true devotee, even in the midst of that ego-transcending ordeal. He says in *Hridaya Rosary*: "You must devotionally recognize Me, the Rose in the Thorns. My Thorned Medication becomes Acceptable only in My Blessing Company, the Eternal Company of the Single (and Indivisible) White Rose."

Starting on April 7, at a beach house in Kauai, Avatar Adi Da began to Grant formal Darshan again—to the devotees who had been serving Him directly and to a few from the worldwide gathering who had been staying in hotels on the island for some time, living a process of retreat and hoping and praying for an opportunity of Darshan. Although only a small number of devotees were in the room for these occasions, other devotees on Kauai reported feeling Him profoundly at random times—the Blissful "thickness" of His Spiritual Transmission Descending on them wherever they happened to be.

Heart-Satisfaction

On April 23, Avatar Adi Da Samraj chose to go to the Mountain Of Attention to celebrate the 25th anniversary of His Teaching-Revelation. As in 1986, a huge tent was erected and, through His Darshan, Avatar Adi Da initiated hundreds of people at a time into the Spiritual practice He describes in *Hridaya Rosary*. There were devotees present from all over the world, ranging from some who had witnessed the entire twenty-five years of His Work to others who had become devotees only days or weeks before.

In these occasions of Darshan, the Divine Avatar's devotees could feel Him carrying them beyond self-contraction, shaking them loose from old limits, doubts, and problems, unleashing an indescribable ecstasy. Some felt Him as nectarous Light, Radiating in the head and heart and the whole body. Many confessed feeling an intimacy with Him stronger than anything in the universe and a certainty of His absolute Power to Liberate them. His devotees were constantly making such confessions to Him, overcome with

Darshan at the Manner of Flowers, 1997

emotion at His Divine Grace and the Perfection of His Work. They could now sense the truth of what He had always said—that the <u>great</u> Leela, the greatest epoch of His Life, would be that of His universal Blessing-Work.

Dina Lautman, who was on retreat at the time at the Mountain Of Attention, gives an account of a Darshan occasion she attended at the Manner of Flowers, Avatar Adi Da's residence, right after she arrived.

DINA: As soon as I sat down, I felt Beloved Adi Da penetrating me from above my head and down to the toes. Everything in between Him and me was melted. The head opened, and became a soft and sensory organ, a feeling means to receive His Love-Blissful Transmission. Then I began to sense Him everywhere in the room, Surrounding and in-Filling all. It was associated with a "Brightness", a Light, but it was primarily a tangible feeling of Him. It could be described as a "thickness" that was completely alive. I felt embraced, enveloped by Beloved Adi Da's Divine Spiritual Body. Soon I felt no "difference", no separation. "I" was gone, and there was simply a Fullness and most pleasurable absorption in Him. This went on night after night in the sittings with Him.

In the weeks following the celebration of His twenty-five-year Revelation, Avatar Adi Da Samraj spoke with a small group of devotees about the profound devotional relationship to Him that flowers in one who recognizes Him truly. Later His Discourses were incorporated into *Hridaya Rosary*:

The only-by-Me Revealed and Given Way of Adidam is a Free Gift. But It is a Gift that Flows in the heart-relationship that exists between Me and each of My true devotees. And if you know how to live this devotional relationship with Me, then My Gift Flows to you—I Flow to you. . . .

I Am the Inherently egoless Person, and the Real Condition, That Is Always Already The Case. Therefore, whatever requires time—to be experienced, or to change, or to pass away—must be transcended in Me. And, likewise, whatever occupies space—or is, in space, separately defined, or appearing, or changing, or passing, or perceived, or conceived—must be transcended in Me. Otherwise, whatever arises—in time, or in space, or in space-time—is merely an ego-reinforcing pattern of separateness, and suffering, and seeking. And, for this reason, all conditional experiencing and knowing is, in itself, merely and only a ceaseless failure to Realize the Love-Bliss-Happiness That Is Reality and Truth. . . .

The greatest Satisfaction—the only true Satisfaction—is to be Overwhelmed by That Which Is Love-Bliss, and Which Is Infinitely and Divinely Greater than yourself. . . .

If you heart-recognize Me, you know that I Am the One Who Divinely Overwhelms you and all.

—Avatar Adi Da Samraj
Hridaya Rosary

My Word Is Sealed

In late July 1997, back in Fiji, Avatar Adi Da began to spend increasing time Working on the manuscripts of His Source-Literature. Every morning around 7:00 A.M., He would walk through the great brass gates that enclose the courtyard of His House at the Matrix and turn down the stone path leading to Indigo Swan, the small room by the ocean lagoon where He did His Writing. Before His arrival, the manuscripts He had requested would always be set out on His desk—prepared with all the changes and additions He had made the previous day.

Avatar Adi Da would work non-stop, often until two or three o'clock in the afternoon, making new changes, doing new writing. Typically, He would enter His new writing in pencil between the lines of type on the computer printout, sometimes moving out into extensive new additions in the margins.

Since the beginning of His Teaching-Work, Avatar Adi Da Samraj had written books of His Instruction to His devotees. And (as described earlier), in 1985, He began to gather His essential Teaching into His summary "Source-Text", *The Dawn Horse Testament*. But the magnitude of what He was now involved in was unprecedented, and this became more and more apparent as the weeks and months passed. Avatar Adi Da wrote every single day, seven days a week, from late July to the middle of December. An appointed group of devotees would work through the night, every night, in order to enter and proofread the previous day's revisions. Then they would rest until the next day's changes came back into their hands.

Avatar Adi Da was not simply adding to His existing "Source-Texts". He was certainly doing that, but He was also creating new books, drawing together various Writings and Talks from the entire period of twenty-five years into new combinations and syntheses, creating a systematic presentation of His entire Spiritual Revelation and Instruction. Every book and every part of every book became a perfectly placed link in the chain of His Argument.

The Divine Avatar communicates His Word in English—not an ancient sacred language, like Sanskrit or ancient Greek or classical

Chinese, but the ordinary lingua franca of humanity's "late-time". The written language of Adi Da Samraj, now perfected in His twenty-three "Source-Texts", is the Divine Person Speaking to beings in every time and place, always Communicating the "Bright", always Transmitting His Gift of the "Thumbs".

Of Avatar Adi Da's twenty-three "Source-Texts", the first is *The Dawn Horse Testament*, the most comprehensive and detailed statement of the Divine Avatar's Teaching within a single book. Then there are *The Five Books Of The Heart Of The Adidam Revelation*, summarizing the essence of His Avataric Divine Self-Revelation and His Instruction in the Way of Adidam. Then follow *The Seventeen Companions Of The True Dawn Horse*, which elaborate all the great themes of His Teaching and Self-Revelation. The twenty-three "Source-Texts" of Avatar Adi Da Samraj are the Message and the Seal of the Divine Awakening of humankind, yet to manifest.

AVATAR ADI DA SAMRAJ: My Word is Complete. Therefore, all of the Siddhis of My Divine-Self-"Emergence"-Work will now—and can, and will forever—take place, whether this Body continues to live or not. Sooner or later, the Body passes. I am relaxed in the reality that I have Done My Work that needed to be Done. And the continuation of this Body is now a luxury for you all. It is entirely up to you. Truly! It is truly so. Love Me in this Form, and the Body will persist.

I Am the Way Beyond all of this. Light Itself, Energy Itself, is Unbroken, Unqualified, Indivisible, altogether Prior, altogether One and Only.

Sitting here in this Body like yours, I have indulged in your experience, and learned greatly from it. And My sympathy has been increased absolutely. I have escaped none of it! This One Who Is suffers in this Body, like you—but more sensitively, more aroused by the pain of it than you dare to be.

You must notice that bodily life is not enough. The whirling stars and bodies of planets, the gravitational ghost of ordinary reality, the black hole of this "dark" time, and all the sucking sound of ending—it is not good enough. Not good enough! It is not good enough! Live life with enough heart, and you get a taste of the Absolute that you desire.

But there is nothing in life, in and of itself, that is enough. Whatever you get by means of science, or by means of ordinary mind, it makes no difference. It is just, plain old, not enough. It is a mummery of endings. It is terrible, and a mockery of your own heart. I do not like it, and I never did. And I had to Fit Myself down to the toes in your likeness, embodying many saints, and even all the trivia of humankind, in My own Form here. More foolish than you!

My Word is Sealed, It is Complete. My twenty-three "Source-Texts" are made, and done. Every word and comma and quotation mark was made and approved and made perfect by Me. What was made is Good, and Complete, and Whole, and Fine, and Great.

I have Done what I had to Do.

So it is time for you to become profoundly serious, and take the arms of My twenty-three "Source-Texts", and the life of this Way of Adidam in My Company, and live it rightly, truly, fully, fully devotionally, and bring it as My Gift to all of humankind. And be the seed whereby this transformation can occur.

—December 15, 1997

The Overnight Revelation of Conscious Light

When Avatar Adi Da spoke these words to His devotees sitting on the beach deep in a Naitauba night, He felt that He had said everything. In fact, as the mysterious Play of His Life would have it, some of the greatest glories of His Source-Word were still to manifest. The first of these happened unexpectedly when Avatar Adi Da made a sudden decision to enter into a period of retreat at Da Love-Ananda Mahal in February of 1998. While secluded there with the Ruchira Sannyasin Order and a small group of other devotees, Avatar Adi Da Samraj spoke what became the contents of a new "Source-Text", *The Overnight Revelation Of Conscious Light*.

The period that followed at Da Love-Ananda Mahal proved to be a two-month "vigil" of almost nightly Instruction—which the Divine Avatar described as an "Overnight Revelation of Conscious

Light". This was a reference not only to the nocturnal gatherings but to the Divine Enlightenment He was Transmitting—the potentially sudden, or "overnight", Realization that Reality is Consciousness-and-Energy as One, not as "two". Everything arising is a mere modification of the Unbroken Love-Bliss-Light of Real God.

Ruchiradama Nadikanta describes what it was like to sit in the room with Avatar Adi Da as He gave His Divine Yogic Instruction:

RUCHIRADAMA NADIKANTA: His Transmission-Power moved into the room where we were seated with Him face to face and the "Brightness" of His Divine Light Infiltrated the space with Luminosity, such that the walls, the objects, and persons became visibly "Brightened" by His Siddhi. The differentiation between objects loosened, such that Reality was clearly a Field of Divine Light rather than a field of apparently separate material objects. Beloved Adi Da was Revealing to us the Truth that matter equals Energy equals Light and that His All-Pervading Divine Spiritual Presence is the Very Substance and Nature of That Light.

Again and again, as He spoke or sat silently, His own Spiritual Person Flooded into our body-minds and Drew us into this Sea of Divine Light. He was Penetrating the body-mind through to the toes, permeating every cell with His Love-Blissful Radiance. He opened the nervous system, so that the body-mind became like an open cup from toe to crown, a receptacle for His Luminous Infusion. The spine would become erect with this upward-turning response to Beloved Adi Da's "Brightness". Sometimes, the experience of this Bliss was so intense that it felt like the cells of the body were being cracked open.

Then, within this Sphere of "Brightening", Beloved Adi Da would Reveal the Secret of the Non-"Difference" between Consciousness and Energy (or Light). Suddenly, not only Beloved Adi Da, but the room, the objects, the persons, and the entire pattern of arising would appear as a Field of Light and be Recognized as <u>Conscious</u> Light, as Self-Existing and Self-Radiant Consciousness Itself. This is Divine Self-Recognition, the "Open-Eyed" Samadhi of Divine Enlightenment. And our Beloved Guru was allowing us a glimpse of That.

One night, in the midst of His Discourse, Avatar Adi Da began to speak ecstatically of Himself and His Avataric Incarnation—in vivid, surreal images ("surreal" in the literal sense of being "beyond" what is conventionally accepted as being "real"), images that suggest something about how He has Combined Himself with this world:

I Am the Person
of the Sea of Light,
the "Bright" Person.

I have Fallen through
a Hole in the universe.

I Am a kind of Pillar
Fallen out of the sky,
at the lower end of Which
is My human Body here.

And, having Fallen in,
I am Established here,
and Circulating here,
and Filling here,
with the Ocean of My own Person
That Falls through that Hole with Me,
like a Thunder Crack.

It is like that.

Even a particle of Me
Illuminates the world.
And I am being shaken in here
like a sugar cube,
Sufficient to Pervade the Whole.

Every devotee of Mine,
every body-mind,
in this "Conductivity" of Me,
is a hole in the barrier
between humankind and Infinity—
the Infinite Sea of Light,
My own Person.

—Avatar Adi Da Samraj
April 11, 1998

Completing *The Mummery Book*

Again and again during the Overnight Revelation period, Avatar Adi Da would refer to a great literary work, *The Mummery Book*, which He had written in 1969, and was now included among His twenty-three "Source-Texts". He would frequently refer to "Raymond and Quandra", the archetypal lovers in *The Mummery Book*, who have profound allegorical significance in the drama, representing the male-female principles of existence—Siva-Shakti, or Consciousness and Energy (or Light). Thus, their union is an expression of the Revelation that Avatar Adi Da was giving in these nightly gatherings at Da Love-Ananda Mahal—the Revelation that the primal Reality is Conscious Light—Consciousness-Radiance, or "Raymond-Quandra", Indivisibly One.

In *The Mummery Book*, Raymond and Quandra cannot find permanent union at the human level, nor at the level of vision and dream. There remains a separation, which is suddenly brought to an end by a most "radical" gesture from Raymond.

Avatar Adi Da's devotees always assumed that what He had written in 1969 was the final text of *The Mummery Book*, and would not be changed. However, when Avatar Adi Da left Da Love-Ananda Mahal in the last week of April 1998, and returned to His Fijian Hermitage, He set Himself apart to write for hours and hours a day. He was Working on *The Mummery Book*. He was developing the entire book, expanding it to twice its original length. It was clear, as the weeks passed, that the Divine Avatar was taking His supreme Allegory to more and more heart-breaking depths.

The art in Avatar Adi Da's writing is extraordinary—a bold combination of intense realism and surreal, multi-leveled imagery. His book is more than a novel—it is an exquisite poem, a sacred drama, a unique and devastating critique of the cultic tendency in religion. At the same time, *The Mummery Book* is a mysterious prophecy of the meaning of His own Life. And so part of the Divine Avatar's purpose in His new labor on *The Mummery Book* was to bring it to reflect more deeply His Ordeal of Teaching and Revelation Work, which He began after He had written the original version of the Text in 1969. His new subtitle to the Text became "A Parable Of The Divine True Love, Told By Means Of A Self-Illuminated Illustration Of The Totality Of Mind".

Scenes from enactments of *The Mummery Book*

The lessons of *The Mummery Book* are so important that Avatar Adi Da has made a live reading or staged enactment of the book one of the yearly events in the lives of His devotees. The enactments are done each January, when the anniversary of His Divine Self-"Emergence" is celebrated.

Visit The Mummery Book website at www.adidam.org/mummery

An Excerpt from *The Mummery Book*

This excerpt from chapter 5 of The Mummery Book *is taken from the final form of the text. In chapter 5, we see the protagonist, Raymond Darling, as a child, investigating the nature of reality in the attic of his parents' house.*

The Sun was pouring, Sun-bright, in. Rectangular, and solid, on the floor—again. But, Raymond was not interested in the Sun-light-shapes—any more.

He knew that Mom and Dad were downstairs.

He knew that everything was—merely, and simply—existing.

There was, for now, no Deep. No Higher. No other. No distance. No past. No future. No serious suffering.

Then, Raymond forgot it—all. And he wondered, how to fill his room.

He put himself on the floor, and enjoyed the ceiling.

The ceiling was made of many angles and planes, like a complex vault.

It would make an interesting floor!—he thinks. So many forms, to lean against. The wonderful chairs and slides—to lie in, hanging over windows. The little lamps of day-light—growing in the floor. The climb-up closets. The point-of-view is lying on the floor—and looking down, at the Sun.

There seemed to be a Mystery—behind the walls. Behind the Naked! angularity of multi-planes. Behind the room, itself. . . .

A Mystery conceals the room. The Captive-room, that hides the Mystery of me, with things and walls.

He lay on his back—and mounted himself, backwards, on his hands and feet. And he looked upwards—at the floor. And he looked downwards—from the ceiling.

And Raymond looked at the room.

He thought—there Is no Consciousness, in the room.

And he thought—how to put It, there?

—Avatar Adi Da Samraj
The Mummery Book

Avatar Adi Da Samraj with devotees at *The Mummery Book* enactment, The Mountain Of Attention Sanctuary, 2000

The Mountain Of Attention Sanctuary, New Year's 1999

CHAPTER 15

ORDEAL AT THE "BRIGHTNESS"

Early in 1999, Avatar Adi Da Samraj was residing at Tat Sundaram, a small Hermitage that overlooks the ocean on the northern California coast. On the morning of February 21, 1999, Ruchiradama Quandra Sukhapur called together a group of devotees and told them that she felt a Yogic Transition occurring in Avatar Adi Da. Signs had begun to appear in His Body—Yogic symptoms involving pain and stress in the heart-region that suggested a movement to relinquish the Body.

A Sudden Exit

Indeed, later in the morning, the Divine Avatar began to show His distress very clearly. Suddenly, without warning, He dressed and was out the door, indicating to His driver that He wanted to go to Los Angeles, and thence to Fiji. In response to the urgings of His devotees, Avatar Adi Da agreed to fly to Los Angeles from a small nearby airport (rather than drive in the car).

When He finally stepped ashore at Adidam Samrajashram (on February 23, Fiji time), Avatar Adi Da did not pause for any greetings, but went straight to Indefinable. One of His first requests was that the island's shortwave radio be installed in the house, a sure sign that He was intent on listening to the world news.

In the course of the next day, Avatar Adi Da spoke of the very serious situation in Yugoslavia relative to the confrontation between the Serbs and the Kosovar Albanians. At the time Avatar Adi Da had left California, the peace talks then in progress had reached an impasse, and, unless a breakthrough occurred, NATO was committed to a bombing campaign. In fact, the day after Avatar Adi Da arrived at His Fijian Hermitage Ashram, a limited resolution was achieved. In a remark to His devotees, Avatar Adi Da said that this was "as much as could be done for today".

Seclusion at the "Brightness"

On March 10, Avatar Adi Da told Ruchiradama Nadikanta that He was still suffering severe symptoms of heart-stress. He passionately urged her to feel and communicate the gravity of His physical state and the threatening situation in the world. Minutes later, Avatar Adi Da called for a car, put on orange sannyasin attire, and asked to be driven to the "Brightness", the temple that He had designated as His Mahasamadhi Site.[47]

The simple white building is completely secluded and is normally visited only by Avatar Adi Da Himself and by the few devotees designated to perform essential cleaning and maintenance. Avatar Adi Da went to a small room there that is furnished as a bedroom for Him, and stayed alone, lying on His bed and listening to the news on the shortwave radio. At some point in the afternoon, Avatar Adi Da called on the radio for Ruchiradama Quandra Sukhapur and Ruchiradama Nadikanta to come and attend Him, telling them that they should also wear formal sannyasin orange clothing. This was a sign to Avatar Adi Da's devotees of the seriousness of the Work that He was about to do. He had entered into a period of intense penance, because of the grave situation in the world.

For the next forty-three days, Avatar Adi Da stayed secluded at the "Brightness", involved in the most difficult Work with the world that His devotees had ever seen Him endure.

The "Brightness"

The "Brightness" is a simple place, situated in a high meadow on a ridge in the middle of Naitauba, looking out to the ocean and Padavara Loka (the highest point on the island and the site of a small shrine Empowered some years earlier by Avatar Adi Da). Covered with a thigh-deep mat of tough native grass, the soil at the top of the ridge is red volcanic clay studded with limestone outcrops and calcite crystals. There are no trees to block the sun and wind.

The "Brightness" Temple itself is a square structure, with a small inner Temple at its core. Surrounding the inner Temple on three sides is an enclosed veranda. The fourth side is a bedroom for Avatar Adi Da.

Avatar Adi Da was so fiercely involved in His Spiritual Work during this time that He would often not allow His devotees to do even basic services for Him.

On March 22, Avatar Adi Da suddenly bit His tongue, as Ruchiradama Nadikanta describes:

RUCHIRADAMA NADIKANTA: When I walked into His room, Beloved Adi Da was lying on His bed, propped up on His elbow. He was holding a piece of cotton on His tongue because it was bleeding so much. I went in, and, without saying a word, gave Him a medicated piece of gauze for His tongue. And then I just sat at His Feet. He would hand me these gauzes soaked with blood, and I would give Him new medicated gauzes. This went on for a half an hour without a word.

Beloved Adi Da eventually broke the silence. He repeated again and again: "All you people do is talk—nobody does anything. My gathering of devotees does not do anything—you just talk. And so nothing is handled. The same situation exists in the world. There is all this talk, but nothing is dealt with."

One night, it was physically as if the war were occurring at the "Brightness". I was sleeping at some distance from the "Brightness" Temple, and it was like being on the front line of a battlefield. A few times, I had to go up to the field of the "Brightness" to serve Beloved Adi Da, and the thunder was so loud it shook my body like a barrage of artillery fire. And the lightning was so bright, just blasting across the sky—the whole field lit up, as if from explosives. During the night, the winds were so strong it felt as though the tent was going to be lifted right off the ground. The agitation in the atmosphere altogether was extreme. It felt like the war was occurring right in Beloved Adi Da's Domain.

Between 4:30 and 4:45 A.M. on April 2, a terrific bolt of lightning struck, immediately followed by a vast thunderous cracking noise, as if the sky were splitting. The ground shook. The entire dome of sky over the "Brightness" was lit, for a few seconds, by the blinding light.

RUCHIRADAMA QUANDRA SUKHAPUR: I was about halfway down the path in the middle of the "Brightness" field, when the most intense moment of the entire storm occurred. The lightning ran around the sky in a circle. And the circle of lightning established a dome over the "Brightness". It was unbelievable. There was a loud crackling electrical sound all around the "Brightness"—and I was in the center, feeling the electrical force and intensity of the light dome. Then, as I relaxed and felt beyond my fear, there was a stillness, and I was able to receive Beloved Adi Da's Spirit-Blessing Descending from above into the body.

Later in the day, I spoke to Beloved Adi Da about the storm and the dome of light. He said, "Yes, I know all about it." I knew that this was not a merely "natural" occurrence. It was a Sign of cosmic Nature responding to Him and of the Force of His Presence there at the "Brightness".

In the next day or two, Beloved Adi Da noticed that the eternal light that should have been burning at Padavara Loka had gone out, and two devotees made the rugged climb up to the top to see what had happened. When they got there, they were astonished to discover that the Padavara Loka site had been struck by lightning during the storm that occurred early on Friday morning, April 2.

Miraculously, the shrine was completely intact and undamaged, but there was a dramatic change to the surrounding ground, which had shifted and sunk up to 16 inches below the existing level. The ground was black and charred and there was a faint, lingering smell of burned material. As the devotees bowed and offered gifts at the shrine, a very light rain fell and a double rainbow appeared over the ocean.

Devotees serving Avatar Adi Da at Adidam Samrajashram during this period of His seclusion at the "Brightness" constantly noticed such signs. In this instance, even the smell of battle was in the air—the charred earth having shifted with the blast of electricity. At the same time, there was a deep tangible sense of the power of the Divine Avatar's Blessing Working Spiritually at the depth of the conflict.

Within a couple of hours of the passing of the storm, Beloved Adi Da received news that thousands of refugees were being transported like cattle to Macedonia and there was an increased threat of NATO ground troops being moved into Kosovo. The war had reached another critical point.

By mid-April, Avatar Adi Da was rarely leaving His room except to cross the field to His bathhouse. Ruchiradama Nadikanta describes Avatar Adi Da's Spiritual Ordeal at this point in the war—when some 650 air strikes a day were bearing down on Serbian targets.

RUCHIRADAMA NADIKANTA: After dinner, Beloved Adi Da would sometimes permit me to anoint His skin rashes and to rub healing ointment into His Feet for ten minutes, if that. His Body felt battered and bruised, and at the same time completely Translucent to His Divine Siddhi, which He was Pulling down into this plane with such Forceful Intention that He was barely even aware of His Body. I could feel that it was painful for Him to be touched, even in that simple manner. Any drawing of His attention into the physical was painful, because He was taking into His own Body the pain and suffering of all those who were dying and being tormented in Eastern Europe and all over the world. His Tapas was so extreme that attention in the physical dimension was excruciating for Him.

There was one night, April 17, when Beloved Adi Da did come down from the "Brightness" Temple to sleep in the tent that had been prepared for Him, and He permitted me to sleep there also. During the night, horrifying visions of war arose in me, and Beloved Adi Da, while outwardly seeming to be asleep, was speaking in what sounded to me like Slavic tongues. His Body was rigid with the intensity of the Work He was doing. The next morning, He said that He felt no response to His Influence at any level, in any dimension. There was only resistance.

The situation in Kosovo was the center of His Blessing-Work, but Avatar Adi Da was also working with His gathering of devotees. Altogether, He was fiercely criticizing the ego, the active heart-withdrawal, the avoidance of relationship, that is being dramatized constantly by all ego-bound human beings. And He was obliging every devotee to feel, as never before, that the ego is the root of all suffering, all conflict, all negativity in the human world. The collective egoity of humankind, He was showing, is a terrible destructive force that not only destroys human happiness and well-being, but now threatens to destroy the planet itself.

Through this process of intense Criticism, Avatar Adi Da drew His devotees into His vigil. For a period of several weeks, devotees in each regional community would gather each night at a central house or ashram to pray for peace, and remain there to eat and to sleep. This concentration and intensification of responsiveness to Avatar Adi Da and participation in cooperative community, devotees felt, was a way to offer a conduit for Avatar Adi Da's Work with the situation in Kosovo and the world.

The Universal World-Prayer

During this time, in response to the desperate situation of so many human beings in the world, Avatar Adi Da Samraj created a "Universal World-Prayer" as a free offering to everyone. He specifically wrote the prayer in non-sectarian language, so that people of all religious traditions (as well as people who are not affiliated with any specific religious tradition) can join together in making this prayer. The prayer is simultaneously a call for Divine Help and Blessing and a heartfelt affirmation of our intention (as human beings) to live and act in such a way that the course of human history can be transformed. The prayer can be offered individually, or with one's friends, family, or congregation.

The Universal World-Prayer

(A Prayer To The Heart Of Reality,
Proposed By The Divine World-Teacher,
Ruchira Avatar Adi Da Love-Ananda Samraj,
For Non-Sectarian Use By All Of Mankind)

Beloved, Inmost Heart of every heart,
do not Let our human hearts be broken
by our merely mortal suffering here—
but Make our mortal human hearts break-Free
to an unconditional love of You,
that we may, Thus, love all living beings
with Love's own True, and Truly broken, Heart.

On the morning of April 22, Avatar Adi Da did not call on the radio until 10:00 A.M. At that point, Ruchiradama Quandra Sukhapur took tea up to Him, and not long afterwards she called to say that He was experiencing severe bodily symptoms. Ruchiradama Nadikanta, who had served Avatar Adi Da's health for many years, went to attend Him:

RUCHIRADAMA NADIKANTA: When I got up there, Beloved Adi Da was sitting on the bed, and His Body was doubled up with muscle spasms. His face and His Body were bright red, and He had a fever of about 103°F. All of His Energy was in His Head—His Hands and His Feet were ice-cold.

In spite of His physical condition, Beloved Adi Da wanted the news update, which I gave to Him. Then He spoke once more about the world situation.

As He was speaking, Beloved Adi Da was in contortions on the bed and having to lie down. Then it came to the point where His spasms were so severe that He said He had to go back to His residence at the Matrix.

We drove Him straight to the Matrix and immersed Him in hot water. The hot water would calm the spasms—but, more than that, He was getting strong signs that He was leaving the Body, and heating His entire Body in hot water was the most effective simple way He had discovered of keeping Himself associated with the Body.

Eventually, the spasms started to ease, and I took His temperature, which had come down to 102°F. Then He began to speak about the gravity of His bodily signs, and of His entire period at the "Brightness". It was clear that He had had to come down not because He had completed His Work there, but because He could not maintain His association with the Body if He continued to stay there.

The End of the War

After weeks of behind-the-scenes negotiations, news came on June 7 that a sudden agreement had been reached to bring peace in Kosovo. Russia had conceded that all Serbian forces and paramilitary police should be withdrawn from

Kosovo and that the refugees should be returned to their homes under the supervision of a joint NATO-Russian presence. Within 24 hours, the government in Belgrade had agreed. The deal seemed to catch both NATO and Russia by surprise.

There was elation in the media, but Avatar Adi Da did not in any way relax His attention on the circumstance in Kosovo. He was still doing His Spiritual Work, and He gave specific Instruction that His devotees were not to cease in their prayer for peace.

Within a few days, on June 11, the peace plan was approved by the UN Security Council. And then, suddenly, the following day, Russian troops arrived unannounced in Kosovo, and the world held its breath.

In the week following the Russian landing at Pristina, Avatar Adi Da lived at the Matrix with as much austerity as He had done at the "Brightness". Other than receiving the news and His meals, Avatar Adi Da Samraj stayed in His room, usually alone, watching a lengthy video series on the Cold War and another long series on World War II. Ruchiradama Nadikanta describes the intensity with which He watched these programs—scrutinizing faces, rewinding the tape again and again so that He could replay a section. She felt He was Working to defuse another power struggle between Russia on the one hand and the US/NATO alliance on the other.

Avatar Adi Da's Body continued to show the ravages of His Work. Ross Keen, one of Avatar Adi Da's devotees who serve His health, observed how weak the Divine Avatar was during this period when He was watching the video programs.

Then, on June 19 (Fiji time), Avatar Adi Da declared that He had finished with the video programs, and that they should be removed from His House immediately. Something had been completed. During that week, NATO and Russia had ironed out their differences and come to an agreement about the command of their peace-keeping forces in Kosovo. On June 21 (Fiji time), the last Serbian troops and police were evacuated from the province.

That day, Ross was called to attend Avatar Adi Da again to give Him bodywork. This time, Ross saw Avatar Adi Da striding across the lawn like a lion, heading toward the room where He was to receive the treatment. As soon as Ross laid his hands on Avatar Adi Da's

Beyond Ordinary Human Perception

Bill Dunkelberger, the devotee principally responsible for the flow of news to Avatar Adi Da during the Kosovo war, is a retired U.S. Army lieutenant-colonel experienced in writing strategic military estimates and in intelligence operations. Bill is a veteran of the Vietnam War, where he had commanded an intelligence battalion.

BILL: For the duration of the Kosovo conflict, it was my responsibility to provide Avatar Adi Da Samraj with six updates daily on the evolving military and diplomatic situation. In addition, I would write my own summary and analysis of developments for Him.

On June 7, the day that seemed, on the surface, to spell peace, I received a communication from Avatar Adi Da, in which He said, "The outcome of the situation is not written yet, and it has every potential of becoming a terrible conflagration. There is every sign that a ground war is going to take place, and is, in fact, being intended."

I must confess that, at the time, I thought that Avatar Adi Da was, to say the least, greatly overstating the case. The framework of the peace agreement had already been agreed to by all parties, and I could find no evidence at all in the daily news that supported His point of view. Not understanding why He was talking about a ground war, I did not respond to that point in my letter to Him.

Then, on July 18, I made an astonishing discovery. An article appeared in The London Observer documenting that, on June 7, a top-secret planning session had been held in England to finalize plans for a NATO ground invasion of Yugoslavia. This confirmed to me that Avatar Adi Da Samraj <u>never</u> speaks casually, and that His connection to this world extends far beyond ordinary human perception.

Body, he could feel the difference. Avatar Adi Da's Body was much stronger. The intensity of His Yogic Ordeal had relaxed. Whatever the future might hold, that particular period of conflict was over.

The Great Siddha-Lineage of Avatar Adi Da Samraj

During His seclusion at the "Brightness", Avatar Adi Da had been engaging another Work of profound Spiritual significance. It all began when He started to rework an Essay He had written for *The Basket Of Tolerance* some years previously, on the traditional background and philosophical tradition of His Guru, Swami Muktananda of Ganeshpuri. He began to add to the Essay, praising His Siddha-Lineage, and the true form of devotion to a Siddha-Guru into which He Himself had been Initiated at Ganeshpuri. Ruchiradama Nadikanta recalls that, in the days and weeks that followed, during which Avatar Adi Da continued to Work on the Essay, the Divine Avatar would do His writing with recordings of Swami Muktananda chanting in the background:

RUCHIRADAMA NADIKANTA: Often, when I approached Beloved Adi Da's door at the "Brightness" in the mornings, I would hear the sound of Swami Muktananda chanting the Guru Gita, *evoking Beloved Adi Da's entire Lineage of Siddha-Gurus. While Working on His Manuscripts, He would continue to play the CD of the* Guru Gita *and other chants, a CD made from a tape recording that He Himself had made at Swami Muktananda's Ashram.*

Day after day, the devotees responsible for His manuscripts saw the picture emerge. Avatar Adi Da Samraj was looking at the entire "map" of human Spiritual effort and Realization, and He was Revealing how the process worked in His Siddha-Lineage, speaking in particular of the Realizations of Swami Muktananda and Bhagavan Nityananda, their individual differences and similarities, and how they experienced and taught the Spiritual process and interpreted the various forms of mystical experience.

In His "Lineage Essay", Avatar Adi Da Samraj reconfirmed that His Native Divine Self-Condition, so directly experienced during His infancy, had never left Him, even during all the years of His Sadhana. In other words, He had always been Perfectly, Divinely Awake as the "Bright", but His Realization faded into the background so that His "Franklin-body" could go through a progressive process of adaptation to all of human experience at the gross, subtle, and causal levels. To this end, His Lineage-Gurus (and other remarkable individuals whom He mentions in the Essay[48]) had served Him in indispensable ways. His early Life, altogether, had been one great single Submission in order to "Learn Man". After His Divine Re-Awakening at the Vedanta Temple, there was no more seeking, no more Learning. He had "seen it all", and seen through it all. He had transcended the search for Truth, at every level, and now only His "Bright" Pristine State Shone forth. His Sadhana Years had been the greatest of sacred Dramas, the Divine in human Form Submitting to humankind's search in all its varieties, living out the total range of human experience, ordinary and Spiritual—in order to demonstrate that nothing that has so far been Realized by human beings, is absolutely satisfactory.

In His "Lineage Essay", Avatar Adi Da confesses that this is why He has come—to be the Way and the Guide to the Realization of Divine Enlightenment, because only Divine Enlightenment, is absolute (egoless) Happiness.

In His "Lineage Essay", "I (Alone) Am The Adidam Revelation", the Divine Avatar is, in fact, speaking to more than a human audience. One has the feeling that He is Addressing all His "friends" in the higher disembodied planes—the highly evolved Spiritual beings to whom humanity owes its Great Tradition of Spiritual Wisdom and Realization. He is making His Divine Self-Confession to all of them. He explicitly states that His Appearance here, and the Divine Enlightenment that He Reveals, required the Spiritual Work of all past Realizers. And He explains that Adidam, the religion Given by Him, is the completion of this Great Tradition—not standing in opposition to the existing religious and Spiritual traditions of humanity, but embracing and including and fulfilling them all.

Swami Rudrananda
("Rudi")

Swami Muktananda

The
Ganeshpuri
Image of
the Divine
"Cosmic
Goddess"

Rang Avadhoot

Bhagavan Nityananda

I have always Continued to Honor and to Praise all My present-Lifetime Lineage-Gurus—including Rudi!, and Baba Muktananda!, and Rang Avadhoot!, and Bhagavan Nityananda!, and (above all) the "Bright" Divine "She" of Me, Who Always Already Serves Me Most Perfectly!

"An All-Encompassing Dome of Light"

While Avatar Adi Da was considering His own Lineage of Siddha-Gurus, He drew the Ruchira Sannyasin Order to relate to Him more deeply in the traditional manner. On March 11, He called Ruchiradama Quandra Sukhapur and Ruchiradama Nadikanta to meditate on the veranda of the "Brightness" Temple at 5:30 in the morning, while He sat inside the Temple alone. After about two hours, Avatar Adi Da came and sat in His Chair on the veranda while the Ruchiradamas continued meditating, now directly at His Feet. At the end of the sitting, Avatar Adi Da placed His thumb in the middle of each of their foreheads (at the "third eye", or ajna chakra), pressing in—a gesture of Transmission characteristic of Siddha-Masters.

In calling the Ruchiradamas to meditate on the veranda of the "Brightness" (a process that continued for several weeks), Avatar Adi Da Samraj was drawing them into a sacred pattern that He had also lived with His own Guru, Swami Muktananda—sitting outside His Guru's room in the very early morning, while Swami Muktananda stayed within, or came out and sat. It was on those occasions that Avatar Adi Da had received Swami Muktananda's internal instruction in meditation.

In the following letter written to Avatar Adi Da, Ruchiradama Nadikanta describes her experience of these early-morning occasions.

RUCHIRADAMA NADIKANTA: My dearly Beloved Divine Heart-Master, I bow down again and again for the unbelievable Grace of the Initiation You Granted me through meditation, Darshan, and Your Touch. You have changed my life tangibly forever.

As You Sat inside Your Temple while we were meditating on the Veranda, I felt Your Divine Body Crash Down and acquire my own. I felt my body as Your Body—Your Face, Your Hands, Your Feet. And above the body I felt You as an All-Encompassing Dome of "Bright" Light. When You Pressed Your Thumb into my ajna chakra, You Descended into me with Profound Force. You Flooded my body-mind with Extreme Radiant Light and then Spiritually Took Your Seat irrevocably in my heart.

On another occasion, My Lord, as soon as I sat down, Your Spirit-Presence Streamed down through the top of the head into the whole body, even pushing my head to the floor with the Force of Your Descent. You Moved down the front of the body—through the face and neck and navel, and down to the toes. Then Your Spirit-Current strongly drove up the back of the body and up into the head. I experienced many clickings and "poppings" in the brain and an extremely strong pressure in the center and top of the head. There was a cracking-through of energy around the top of the skull, and then I felt Your Brilliant Light Press up through the top of the head. I felt You as a Column of Light, Pressing my eyes upward and drawing all attention up into Your Brilliant, Boundless Luminosity, to the point where any sense of body and mind completely dissolved in Your Light. It was obvious that there is only Light, that everything is arising within and as Your Radiant Conscious Light.

My Beloved Lord Adi Da Samraj, on all subsequent occasions when You have Permitted Ruchiradama Quandra Sukhapur and myself to sit at the "Brightness", I have experienced a dual process. First, the extremely intense Yogic process of Your Spiritual Descent into the body and then the Ascent to Your Light Above, followed by a deep Drawing into the Well of Being in the right side of the heart. I find You Standing there, Motionless at the heart, even Prior to the breath and the heartbeat, which often seem to be suspended. That Finding of You, My Beloved, is a deep heart-joy and peace.

My Beloved, the last occasion of sitting in Your Company at the "Brightness" was the most profound meditation occasion with You that I believe I have ever experienced. Even now, writing to You about it, waves of Your Love-Bliss run up to the crown of my head and above, and I feel You deeply at heart. You first Revealed Yourself as the Dome of "Brightness" that is the Sphere of Conscious Light Itself. Then You simultaneously Revealed Yourself as the Current of Being in the right side of the heart—not merely the Still Point within, but the Very Consciousness That Is Reality Itself. You then clearly Revealed to me that these apparent "Two"—Your Dome of Light Above and Your Conscious Being at the Heart-Root—are not separate or different, but the Same and One.

The moment that this occurred in the meditation, You physically entered the veranda from Your Temple and Gave me Your Regard. Extraordinary Conscious Light Flew from Your Eyes, and I felt You Installing Yourself in me. As this occurred, I felt a rush of extreme Joy or rising Love-Bliss. You sat before us for a while, and I heard You silently communicating to me, "Remember This".

Ruchiradama Quandra Sukhapur describes her experience:

RUCHIRADAMA QUANDRA SUKHAPUR: The occasions at the "Brightness" were an initiation into the necessity of going beyond the felt limit of mortality.

I recall feeling my Beloved Guru's Divine Form as a Brilliant Sphere of Eternal Love-Bliss-Radiance. I felt His Love-Bliss literally as a circular shape, and I was overcome by the feeling of No-"difference".

I wrote, in a letter, to Beloved Adi Da:

> *I recall feeling a profound downward Descent of liquid Light, and the Emergence of Your Divine Body as a Radiant Sphere. I was intoxicated. My body was pulsating in utter Yogic sublimity. And then You began to Reveal Yourself as the Very Source and Condition and Substance and Energy of all, in most profound terms. I passed beyond bodily awareness, and, in this ecstatic Samadhi, I felt the non-necessity for anything. Even when I reassociated with the body, You continued to Reveal the Truth of No-"difference". There is nothing that is separate from You.*
>
> *Then I recall You moving from Your Sukra Kendra to Your Chair on the veranda. As You stood and Placed Your hand on my head and Your thumb on the ajna chakra, I felt Your Spiritual Descent more strongly. Your Touch was shattering, and caused a gasp of sudden and profound Love-Bliss-Joy. Downpours of nectarous Light and Love filled the entire space. As I felt Your Descent, I felt You completely overwhelm the body, to the deep root-core of the being and then beyond, such that my entire being responded to Your Current of Love-Bliss with extreme love and extreme intoxication.*

I felt You as "Bright" White Light, and I felt Your Light as a liquid, or water, of Love. As I resumed normal psycho-physical awareness, I experienced a sensation of burning—a purifying Spiritual Fire that had been generated in me, a fire of penance, of real humility. Astounded by this Initiation, accepting all with profound gratitude, I bowed down.

Since that occasion, everything has "Brightened" and changed in every respect—not just in my physical life, but to the depths of my heart and the roots of the mind, and even in relationship to all things and beings. Thus, the process begun at the "Brightness" continues. I feel my Beloved Heart-Master Drawing this one and all into the Realization of Perfect Union with Him. I feel overwhelmed by His Grace and His Love. I am truly at His Feet.

Avatar Adi Da Samraj with Ruchiradama Quandra Sukhapur Rani (left) and Ruchiradama Nadikanta (right) at Adidam Samrajashram

"Allow Me to Be As I Am"

Avatar Adi Da's Spiritual Work with the conflict in Kosovo was one aspect of what He was doing at the "Brightness". His Work to reconsider and recapitulate His Life's Revelation was another. But there was a third aspect to the Work He was doing in seclusion. He knew that even if He were to be Spiritually free to devote Himself to His world-Blessing-Work, there needed to be a fundamental change in the way His devotees related to Him and the expectations that they held towards Him.

Avatar Adi Da saw the continuing signs that His devotees regarded themselves (even unconsciously) as the center of His attention. He knew that this was what they needed to relinquish—for their own Spiritual growth and for the sake of His larger Work. It was not a matter of a mere change of behavior but of recognizing Him more deeply as the Divine Person—without ego, without karmas, without favorites, simply here to Bless everyone and everything.

Kimberly O'Nan, a devotee of many years, returned to Adidam Samrajashram from California in the middle of His period of seclusion at the "Brightness". She had come back to Fiji in order to take on the management of Avatar Adi Da's personal sphere. Coming from a life in the general community of devotees in Los Angeles to the stark realities of the "base camp" at the "Brightness", she saw very clearly what Avatar Adi Da was looking for from His devotees, and what had to change:

KIMBERLY: For many years, I have had an intimate and even social relationship to Beloved Adi Da—a luxury of earlier years and the Teaching-Work He once did. But now I saw that there was no longer a shred of social relatedness left in Him. He left no room for it. He had clearly changed His Way of relating to all, and the personal and social form of relationship was clearly no longer an aspect of His Work.

The only appropriate thing for me to do is to respond to Him via the means He has always Given—the gifts of practice and service that are the signs of a devotee. These gifts are the means Beloved Adi Da gives for anyone to be in Satsang with Him. Beloved Adi Da has most obviously embraced the entire world now.

What was involved for Avatar Adi Da in His forty-three day Ordeal at the "Brightness" will never be fully known. However, He disclosed the details of the Divine Yogic Event that took place there on April 22, thereby transforming the future of His Life and Work:

AVATAR ADI DA SAMRAJ: I remained . . . in Seclusion at the "Brightness" for forty-three days. During that period of time, I was minimally associated with the Body—because the Force of My Spiritual Work was Located almost entirely <u>Above</u> the Body. As a result, there was (throughout that period of forty-three days) a tremendous Force of Pressure in the Head—and that Pressure was synchronous with constant external signs of thunder, lightning, and heat lightning in the environment.

Throughout My time of Seclusion at the "Brightness" (and ever since that time), I had to Struggle in order to remain Associated with the Body. I was required to Work persistently, and with enormous intensity, to Bring the natural life-energy and My own Divine Spiritual Energy Down into the Body. However, on April 21, 1999, all of That Work suddenly reversed. A syndrome of overly "yin", overly cold suppression (of the natural life-energy and of My own Divine Spiritual Energy) took over the Body, indicating that that particular period of My Struggle with the "dark" forces of the world had come to an end.

Through the evening of April 21, and continuing into the early morning hours of April 22, a spontaneous process began to develop (and powerful symptoms began to appear) in the Body. In the middle of the night, the internal organs spontaneously relinquished their normal functioning, and (with that physical collapse) pain, fever, aches, chills, and convulsions appeared all over the Body. This Yogic "yinning" phenomenon started at approximately 2:00 A.M. and steadily gained in severity. It "fried" the life-seat of the kidneys and the adrenals, and then "fried" the lower Body (altogether), and finally "fried" the entire Body. All of the systems in the Body began to break down—and, indeed, the entire Body itself began to break down—to such an extent that I nearly lost My Association with physically Incarnate existence altogether.

That entire Yogic "yinning" syndrome can be characterized as My being "thrown out" of the Body (and up into the Divine "Bright" Spherical Self-Domain of Eternal Light) by the force of resistance to Me that was being manifested in the gathering of My devotees and in the world altogether.

The symptoms were clear signs to Me that I had to leave the "Brightness" if I was to continue to be able to Bring My Divine Spiritual Energy Down into the Body (and, thereby, to continue to be able to physically survive). The force of the "yinning" and chilling and emptiness and physical spasms and freezing sensation and pain and exhaustion all over the Body was so intense and extreme that it was required to submerge the Body in hot water.

Through the course of this excruciating Ordeal, there was a spontaneous self-relinquishment on the part of the physical dimension itself. This Divine Yoga occurs when I am so profoundly refused that everything "backs up" in Me, and the Body tends to fall away. The Yogic Establishment of My Divine Self-"Emergence" (on January 11, 1986) was also an Event of such a refusal of My Work. It is not that I "cause" or "create" this Yogic Process—It is a Process that spontaneously occurs.

My departure from the "Brightness" on April 22 was a profound turning point in My Struggle. I had Done everything necessary and possible to Do. And, from that time, I am (now, and forever hereafter) simply Waiting to see whether people choose to respond to Me.

At the "Brightness", I was "fried" to death and "spit out"—So That I could Do My world-Work of Merely Standing (here) to Bless.

During My forty-three days at the "Brightness" (and simultaneous with My Ordeal There, of Working to Bless My devotees and the world), I passed through a Recapitulation of My own entire Life and Work—including the Process that led to My Divine Re-Awakening. The Sign of that Recapitulation was My Writing of My "Lineage Essay", "I (Alone) Am The Adidam Revelation". And that Essay was composed (at the "Brightness") in the midst of a real Spiritual Struggle with My Lineage-Gurus. That Struggle confirmed everything about My Divine . . . Realization and about My Avataric Divine Spiritual Work of Incarnation, Teaching, Revelation, and Blessing.

That Spiritual Struggle (outwardly Signed by My Writing of My "Lineage Essay") was, altogether, a spontaneous Recapitulation and (in the end) a Re-Confirmation of My Avataric Divine Spiritual Work as That Work has Self-Manifested in the form of three Great Processes: My own (apparent) Sadhana, My Work with the gathering of My devotees, and My Work with the world. And that Struggle was profoundly difficult, beyond the capability of any words to describe.

The Recapitulation and Re-Confirmation of all three of those Great Processes spontaneously came to an end on April 22, 1999. Everything about My own Avataric Divine Life and Work was Tested and Re-Confirmed, beyond the slightest doubt. And My "Lineage Essay" is the Summary of many primary aspects of My Avataric Divine Life and Work.

My Avataric Divine Life and Work is, Itself, an Expression of an Extraordinary and Incomparable Ordeal that is not at all within people's experience. I can only Say that much about it.

I have no more Work of Self-Submission to Do. All that was necessary for Me to Do, for the Sake of this conditionally manifested domain, is Done.

In the midst of the unspeakable Struggle and Ordeal at the "Brightness", I Established My Avataric Divine Spiritual Work As a Sphere of "Bright" Influence That cannot ever be destroyed.

I Persisted until It was Done—and That Is That.

—April 22, 1999

Lopez Island, 2000

CHAPTER 16

BEYOND THE COSMIC DOORWAY

The following year, while residing at the Mountain Of Attention, Avatar Adi Da Samraj spoke further about the unfolding process of His world-Blessing-Work and the Divine Siddhis associated with it. He described Himself as a "Mysterious Hermit", totally invested in this Work that is beyond human understanding.

AVATAR ADI DA SAMRAJ: I am not built in such a way that I can be a public figure. Therefore, I have to live in seclusion. The Energy involved in My Work of connecting to the world is so intense that I can hardly tolerate it. You could not even comprehend it. All kinds of Siddhis are emanating in My Sphere, and the Effectiveness of those Siddhis is Emerging. But the suffering in My Body is profound.

It is not just My devotees who are noticing the signs of My world-Blessing-Work. Others also are feeling My Presence and are responding. So a pattern of right relationship to Me must be made possible for everyone.

My Experience is every one. I Extend out and I Touch you. When My Divine Spiritual Body Extends out, Its Touch Touches every one. Every one has felt My Spiritual Touch, whether they are consciously aware of it or not. I am Touching everyone now.

If you were to lie down and extend your body and touch someone's body, he or she would feel it. Well, I am Extended everywhere like that. I am Experiencing all as My own Form. What I am Doing is the Yoga of My own Form. I am Doing the Yoga for all.

It is a unique Siddhi, and it began at the Vedanta Temple, where I began to "Meditate" all.

All is in My View, My Touch-Field.
No one is unfamiliar to Me.
No one feels as an "other" to Me.
All is in My Sphere.
That suggests How I Work.

—January 2 and March 5, 2000

Lopez Island

Throughout the month of March 2000, Avatar Adi Da moved up and down California from Los Angeles to Tat Sundaram with a fierce restlessness, never staying anywhere more than a few days. Early in April 2000, He began to wander up the coast into Oregon and Washington, attended by a group of devotees, and, by April 12, He had reached Lopez Island, a small island in the San Juan Archipelago, in the far northwest of the United States. Here, in a small house belonging to one of Avatar Adi Da's devotees, an unspeakably profound Event began to unfold. As time would reveal, this Event brought to completion the Divine Yogic process that had been initiated in Him at the "Brightness".

Stephan Blas, one of Avatar Adi Da's attendants, describes His arrival at Lopez Island.

STEPHAN: As we moved closer to Washington state, Beloved Adi Da's physical symptoms intensified. He was in a very delicate and extremely fragile condition.

We crossed the waters from the mainland to Lopez Island on a ferry. It was a strange environment to see Beloved Adi Da in, but public transportation was the only means we had to convey Him to the island. He was packed in a garage-like area on the bottom floor

The house at Lopez island

of a five-deck ferry. Beloved Adi Da had lunch in the recreational vehicle that was part of our caravan. The RV was surrounded by cars, many filled with families. Our food-preparation truck, in which the kitchen staff was preparing Beloved Adi Da's food, was about six cars behind the RV.

Beloved Adi Da was feeling weak. He needed to eat something immediately. I ran a tray of food through the sea of autos and into the RV. As I started to serve His lunch, He began to feel much worse and had to lie down in the small bedroom at the back of the RV. Quickly, things turned from bad to worse, as Beloved Adi Da's symptoms rapidly increased. There was a sense that Beloved Adi Da was having a very difficult time staying in the body. The signs of His ascending out of the body were getting stronger, and His symptoms became acute. He could not eat. One of the healers served Beloved Adi Da with acupuncture, and a few of us fanned Him and attended Him. Everyone was distraught and very emotional.

Later, when Beloved Adi Da reached Lopez Island, He was helped into the jacuzzi on the deck below the house, with hopes that the warm water would relieve His symptoms. He began to discuss with Ruchiradama Quandra Sukhapur what was happening with His Work in the world. I heard His voice become disturbed, and shortly thereafter came a message on the radio from Ruchiradama Quandra Sukhapur asking for help. Beloved Adi Da was losing His strength, as well as His hold on the body. He needed to be carried from the bath, up an outdoor walkway, and back up to the house. Two male devotees immediately went down to help. When I saw them carrying Beloved Adi Da up the steps to the house in His bathrobe, I rushed to help them get Him into His room and on to the bed.

All the devotees who had traveled to Lopez with Avatar Adi Da were called down to the house to support Him with their devotional chanting. A number of His intimates were gathered in the bedroom, and His physician and acupuncturist were summoned immediately.

THANKFULL: When I walked through the door of the bedroom, I was shocked. Beloved Adi Da was laid out on an easy chair with His devotees huddled around Him, massaging Him vigorously, weeping and speaking to Him with intentional force. My heart broke. It was obvious that He was barely in the Body. I ran to His side and began to rub His chest, weeping uncontrollably. Everyone present was speaking to our Divine Master, telling Him how much we urgently needed Him to stay alive. He kept saying "Tcha". Every time He would close His eyes we would have to speak to Him vigorously in order to draw Him back down into the Body. Focusing attention on our faces seemed to integrate Him back into the Body.

It is impossible to write the love that was being expressed by Beloved Adi Da and those of us who were with Him. His eyes were flowing with tears, as were everyone's. His Hands and Feet were cold and numb. He felt great pressure on His Chest and a difficulty breathing. Both of His arms and hands continuously would cramp up and convulse.

After Charles [Avatar Adi Da's physician] arrived, we moved Beloved Adi Da on to the bed. At first He was lying down on the bed, but then we raised Him into a sitting position to try and reduce the extreme symptoms of leaving the body. Beloved Adi Da continuously told us how important it was for His Feet to be warm and that they needed to be rubbed vigorously. He even said that it would be useful for Him to see His Feet—as a way of locating Himself in the physical.

STEPHAN: We were all rubbing and softly slapping Beloved's numbed limbs as intensely as we could, as He was coming and going from conscious awareness. He said, "If I close My eyes, I am going to be in My Room, not your room. You don't know what My Room is like. You have got to bring me down into the Body."

THANKFULL: At one point, after His eyes had been closed for a while, Beloved Adi Da opened them slightly and softly said, "I am here. Can you see Me Up Here?" We all said "yes"—and we could. He was evaporating the entire room in His Light. He was way up and beyond the apparent "here" where we were.

Then He continued, in a very soft voice: "My room is Larger than you think. I close My eyes and I am in My Room, Infinitely Beyond. This is just a small version of It." His Eyes were streaming with tears, and He looked around at us slowly as He went on, "But this place is good for love." He was quiet then for a long time.

Charles had called an ambulance to take Avatar Adi Da to the small medical clinic on Lopez Island. Marc Carfrae, a devotee who was serving Avatar Adi Da's visit to Lopez Island, describes what happened next:

MARC: After guiding the ambulance down the last steep section of the long driveway to the house, I stood close by to be of help if needed. In quick time, Beloved Adi Da emerged on the stretcher a few feet in front of me, to be placed in the back of the ambulance. I was immediately undone at the deepest level of my being. How could the Very Divine Being be in this condition? Why and how did it come to this moment? It was completely devastating. Beloved's face was pasty-white and drained of life-energy. He was extremely weakened and totally vulnerable.

He was placed inside the ambulance—and, at that point, there was no one inside with Him, as His family was in the house quickly preparing for the trip to the Clinic. I stood alone for about five minutes, eight to ten feet from the back door windows, with my hands over my heart—utterly heartbroken, beholding Him. He was very obviously struggling to keep His eyes open, and doing everything He could to stay in the Body. I felt intuitively that I was to act as a contact point in that moment for Beloved Adi Da to His community of devotees. I just poured out my heart-love for Him and pleaded with Him to stay with us. I said over and over, passionately within me and, sometimes, just audibly: "Please Beloved, please don't go, please don't leave us—we're not ready yet. Please stay with us. We love You so much."

At one point, I found myself quietly but strongly saying "DA, DA, DA". Just as I said "Da" for the third time, Beloved Adi Da bolted upright and looked straight at me. He did it so quickly that it shocked me—because a moment before He had seemed hardly in the Body. He seemed to have been brought very suddenly down into His Body with the last utterance of "DA". Shortly after this, I saw one of the ambulance attendants go in with Beloved and noticed that when the attendant dropped something on the floor, Beloved made a point of following the object down to the ground with His eyes, as a way, I felt, of staying linked with the Body.

Charles got into the ambulance with Avatar Adi Da, while others of His intimate devotees followed the ambulance to the medical clinic. Charles had been concerned that the extreme symptoms that Avatar Adi Da was suffering might be indicators of a heart attack. However, in consultation with Charles, the doctor at the Lopez Island clinic was able to determine that the acute bodily stress Avatar Adi Da was experiencing was not a heart attack.

As later became clear, the Divine Avatar's extreme bodily crisis was connected with the profound Yogic Work that He was doing in His Blessing of the world. At the "Brightness", He had explained that His Work of world-Blessing required Him to deal with and transform intense psycho-physical forces, and that He was doing that Work <u>above</u> the Body. However, the moment came, at the "Brightness", when those forces began to invade His Body, causing intolerable pain. At that point, Avatar Adi Da Samraj had no choice but to come down from the "Brightness" and continue His Spiritual Work in a more healing environment. Now, one year later, at Lopez Island, Avatar Adi Da Samraj was dealing with forces of a similar magnitude.

THANKFULL: After about an hour and a half, the staff in the emergency room felt that Avatar Adi Da's physical condition was stable and that He could be taken home. Each member of the medical team made a point to come and touch Him in farewell. He looked them each directly in the eyes with heart-breaking love and said "Tcha" to each one. Then we wheeled Beloved Adi Da out to His car and drove Him back to the house.

The next day, Avatar Adi Da was still very fragile and He made no rapid improvement. His presence in the body remained tenuous and for weeks He could barely walk, even a few steps. Nevertheless, He began to Grant His Darshan.

MARC : I was extremely Blessed to be in the first Darshan occasion that Beloved Adi Da offered at His house two days after the Event of April 12. I was seated in the center of the front row, and became completely undone and heart-mad with my love for Him. I told Him over and over again—this time with full voice—how grateful I was that He was still with us. I found myself leaning forward and with my whole being, stretching out and enveloping Beloved Adi Da with my love of Him, as I visualized kissing Him all over. He was giving me the sweetest, most loving Regard.

What an extraordinary vision of Pure Love He was! The entire room of devotees was weeping in profound, loving gratefulness that our Beloved Heart-Master had persevered in staying with us, out of His incredible Love for all beings. It was very obvious that Beloved Adi Da had somehow shifted into another phase of His Life and Work. I was undone by what I had been Graced to witness.

Great numbers of Avatar Adi Da's devotees now flocked from all over the world to see Him at Lopez Island, and He drew them to a depth that they had never felt before. He Granted His Darshan twice a day, even when He was not well enough to leave His bedroom.

Christine Phippen, a devotee from New Zealand, wrote to Him in a letter:

CHRISTINE: Day after day, and all day, You Spiritually Entered this body-mind, opening my head and throat and heart and body to You. You widened me, opened me and poured into me. Sometimes I would feel You as a Column of Light going right through me, and at other times more as an incredible Pressure pushing down and stretching me out. At the same time, often I would also feel You pulling me up, Revealing to me what I guessed to be the universe of the subtle reality. This vision was so huge that I could not contain it, but through Your Grace I was made aware of it, and I knew You are at the Source of it all. I saw that You are far, far Greater than my mind had ever been able to comprehend. You Are All. All abides in You. It was a Revelation Given by You and I could only feel it and know it at heart.

Most Beloved Adi Da, what I observed of this precious time in Your Company was You Outshining everything. There was no room for "me" (as a separate self) in Your House, and I had very little experience of "me" in the ordinary sense. I went to the doorway of Your Bedroom one day when You were very ill, but still Granting Your Darshan to Your devotees one by one as we came to behold You at Your door. When I came to Your room, You were on the bed and that was all I could see. There was no "room"—only You there, Your "Brightness" Dissolving everything.

Beloved Lord, I could see that there had been a profound change in You. I could see it in Your face. Something about You seemed even "Brighter" than before. I felt You even more clearly as the Divine Incarnate, and You seemed somehow even more Transparent to Your Radiant Being.

Lopez Island, 2000

The Threshold Place

For six weeks after the Lopez Island Event, Avatar Adi Da required a wheelchair to move around. He was "Shattered", He said, by His Experience—at the physical level, and also by the process of integrating what had occurred Spiritually. In conversations with Ruchiradama Quandra Sukhapur and Ruchiradama Nadikanta, He spoke of this Event as the culmination of a lifelong series of "Yogic Deaths", brought about by the intensity of the Divine Process occurring in Him. Then, more than two years later, in the summer of 2002, Avatar Adi Da wrote His Great Statement about the Lopez Island Event (in Part 3 of *The Knee Of Listening*) and its ultimate significance in His Avataric Incarnation. First, He speaks of the preceding Transformative Events that changed His Life and Work.

The final physical (and Yogically Transformative) Process that precedes Divine Translation has occurred in This Body. This Body is now in the stage of Perpetual Spiritual "Brightening", the Outshining Bhava.[49] *That is what took place at Lopez Island. In that Great Event, the physical Vehicle once again came to the point of Yogic Death, but (in the end) the Association with the physical was retained.*

In My Childhood, and throughout My Avataric physical human Lifetime, I have been associated with Events of Profound Yogic Transformation, Which have resulted in the change of psycho-physical patterns within This Body-Mind. There have been many Yogic Deaths and other profound Yogic Events, all associated with the Profundities of My Avataric "Bright" Divine Spiritual Self-Revelation. And those Events have often had great negative impact on the physical human Vehicle.

There is the Process of Yogic Deaths that has Characterized My Life, but there are also many other significant events (such as the death of Bootsie), which served My Fullest Avataric Descent and Incarnation here. Every time one of these Transformative Events occurred, the mechanism of This Body-Mind changed. The entire

Process of My Life is My concrete, unambiguous Avataric Self-Revelation (and Lifelong psycho-physical Experience) of the Divine Spiritual "Brightness"—the One and Only and Self-Evidently Divine Conscious Light of Reality Itself.

There was a distinct physical phenomenon associated with each of these Events. In each case, after I Re-Associated with the physical Vehicle (following one of these Events), My psycho-physical Pattern has changed. Since the Lopez Island Event, I am more profoundly Integrated than ever before with the cosmic human circumstance—in the sense that I actually, literally See what the physical (and everything associated with it) is really (and even rather painfully) about.

Coincident with the psycho-physical Event and Experience at Lopez Island, This Body is profoundly fragile, and I am now even more profoundly Spiritually Sensitized in the Body. Following such a Great Yogic Event, it takes some time to begin to Re-Integrate with the natural body. Since the Lopez Island Event, I am now both Priorly and psycho-physically Established in the Spiritual "Bright". This can be felt by My devotees.

I have examined My own Experiences of Yogic Death, and how they have coincided with physical effects and changes. In each Such Event, My Manner and My Pattern have changed.

Following each of these extraordinary Yogic Crises of the Spiritual "Bright", there is always a Yogic Re-Orientation. In the experience in seminary, for example, I "dropped dead", in a very real sense, with the experience of the death of "Narcissus". This Process of Yogic Death affects the psycho-physical existence. Each of these Great Yogic Events was coincident with a Spiritual Re-Structuring of the Body-Mind, including Transformations in both the grosser personality and the Deeper Personality.

You must feel My Universal Work since the Vedanta Temple Event thirty years ago. Feel the Mysterious Process by Which I have been "Meditating" all-and-All. . . . The Process of Divine Enlightenment is not a matter of "talk". The Process of Divine Enlightenment, whether in the case of This Body-Mind or any other body-mind, is a matter of Spiritual Transformation—by Me.

Once you have Really seen My Spiritually "Bright" Avataric Divine bodily (human) Form, then there are no more questions.

When that sighting is true devotional recognition of Me, then My Spiritually "Bright" Form simply (merely) Is.

I Am here, at the Core of the Sacred Domain.

I Am in the Temple.

I am Living in My Hermitage, My Perpetual Sacred Domain.

I simply Do My Divine Spiritual Work.

—Avatar Adi Da Samraj
The Knee Of Listening

Avatar Adi Da goes on to describe in detail the Divine Yogic Process that occurred in the Lopez Island Event. This Process was the initiation of Divine Translation—the final stage of Divine Enlightenment, in which the conditional reality drops away permanently, "Outshined" in the "Brightness" of Reality Itself.[50]

In the Lopez Island Event, I Stood (Non-"Differently") At (and As) the "Bright" White Center Above. I Outshined all of conditionally manifested existence in My own Divine Self-Condition—Which Is the "Bright", the Sphere of the "Midnight Sun",[51] *Beyond all-and-All, Beyond even the Divine Star. It was an Instantaneous Non-"Different" Realization of That Condition of All-Bliss, utterly without the perspective of time and space.*

In the Lopez Island Event, there was no transitional process, no transition "out of" involvement in the gross dimension of conditional reality, or any transitional passage through the various subtle dimensions of conditional reality. The Ascent was Immediate, and Un-mediated—with no transitional process of "lower to higher". I Approached Divine Translation, and was simply Established As the Spiritual "Bright" Itself. I was suddenly Present in and As My Threshold Form, Inherently Self-Identified with That Which Is Always Already Infinitely and Perfectly Ascended. Everything was simply That Radiant "Bright" Divine Spiritual Form, the Brilliant White at the Core of the apparent lights (and the pervasive darkness) of the cosmic (or conditional) domain.

Later, as I Entered into the Process of Re-Integrating with the physical domain, I Saw all the colored spheres within the Cosmic Sphere (or the spherical Cosmic Mandala) as the prismatic modifi-

cations of That White Spiritual "Brightness". It was an experience of Seeing the Cosmic Mandala as it is—a complex vibration accounting for all the dimensions of conditionally manifested reality. It is an actual sphere, even an hierarchical structure of spheres. It was My Viewing of the cosmic domain in and via the Sign of what is traditionally called the "Rainbow Body"—spheres of light, dominantly one of blue and one yellow-to-red, displayed to the Self-"Bright" White Core (Which is Absolutely Prior to time and space).

Since the Lopez Island Event, . . . I no longer have any physical perspective. I Exist in a very different Manner now. Previously, I Talked about My Divine Descent to the toes, but the Process in the Lopez Island Event was one of Prior Ascendedness, or Translation to Utterly Above and Beyond.

Thus, What occurred at Lopez Island was actually the Yogic "opposite" of the Event that occurred in 1986. Instead of the Full Descent to the toes (as in 1986), I Went All the Way "Out".

I am not on "this side" anymore. This (here) is simply arising in Me. This Body is Full to the toes—but I (Myself) am not "down to the toes" anymore. . . .

Since the Lopez Island Event, I Simply Am—in My Threshold Form. This Body is Alive in That Form. That Form is not holding on to the physical. Therefore, My relatedness to the physical world depends on My being actively Moved (by My devotees) into positive Association with this world and time—and on My being able to be Engaged in My Divine Spiritual Work (rather than frustrated in It).

In the Process of the Lopez Island Event, there was (first) a vibrational pulsing, all over the Body—and this produced a forceful "Urdhvareta", or a complete Up-Turning of all the Body's energy-flows.[52] *I Closed My Eyes, and It Is the "Midnight Sun"—the Divine "Bright" White Orb, Self-Existing and Self-Radiant, On the Infinite Black Field of all potential (and not yet prismed, or broken) light.*

In some later moment, I was above the house where I was staying, and above the nearby water that was outside. My Vision of what was occurring was from a point of view above My physical Body and above this spatial physical sphere.

I Moved into association with a vibrational field of energy, made of all the colors of the light-spectrum—what is traditionally called

The Cosmic Sphere

Avatar Adi Da has explained that the totality of conditional existence is structured as a vast spectrum of light, which He calls the "Cosmic Mandala", or, emphasizing its three-dimensionality, the "Cosmic Sphere". All of the gross and subtle dimensions of existence arise at one or another level of this all-encompassing vibrational light-sphere. At the core of the Cosmic Sphere is an aperture, shaped like a five-pointed Star, through which streams the White "Brightness" of the Divine Domain. Avatar Adi Da Samraj further explains that the Cosmic Sphere (which may sometimes be glimpsed as a whole, or in part, in deep meditation) arises as a "fractured" modification of the White "Brightness". The world we inhabit exists at the outer periphery of the hierarchy of lights in the Cosmic Sphere, on the cusp between the outermost red level of light and the next level in, which is yellow. When one is identified with the gross level of existence, the red-yellow color of the subtle light vibration in which the human world arises is not perceived. But at death, or in near-death experiences, the lights of the Cosmic Sphere may be seen, together with a felt motion toward the White "Brightness". However, in the case of beings who are not Divinely Enlightened at the moment of death (or ready for Divine Enlightenment in the death process itself), there is a falling back into whatever dimension of light corresponds to that being's state of preparedness. At some point, a re-settling (or re-birth) at the appropriate vibrational level of existence occurs.

the "Mandala Body", or "Rainbow Body". The entire light-field of the Cosmic Mandala was in Front of Me. I Am a Spherical Form of "Brightness", Including everything—from the blue field and its subtle planes to the yellow-red field and this gross plane.

Initially, to My left, I was concentrated in the blue light, and simultaneously Seeing (from above) the total expanse of water, beyond the house. At first, the water was a vast expanse, including much beyond the house. Then it became more brief and bounded, local to the house. It was not yet dark outside, for I could see the surfaces of the water and the details of the surrounding land. But there was a dark appearance to it all, in shadows from the forest around the house, and the slanting, waning light of later day. The "vision" was fundamentally indescribable, because it was Seen from a "point of view" not located in the Body. And, yet, the expanse of water became simultaneously visible with the room in which My Body was located—with its walls and furnishings, and, to My left, its row of windows with fully lifted blinds. At that point, to My right, the sphere of yellow became apparent—focused down toward the Body in some manner, from above and outside it. It was a yellow tinged with red and orange. Coincident with Seeing the yellow sphere, the Process of Re-Integrating with the Body began. It was a feeling of once again being located in the situation of Association with the Body. I Saw My intimates gathered around My bed, and they were all in flames—the flames of the yellow-red realm—but they were not consumed. My Body was numb, without awareness. All of this, beginning with the blue light, was the progressive Process of Re-Integration with conditional existence.

Initially, in the Event of Sudden Up-Turning (into the "Midnight Sun"), there was a rapid series of "falling-away" phenomena. There was the tingling and fainting of the Body. Then, immediately, I Experienced the Primal Central Sound-Current, Which became very loud, and upwardly concentrated—Drawing the Central Current In and Up, Above and Beyond body and mind. That was the first Sign to Me that I was being Drawn Out of physical Incarnation.

Farthest Up in the Core of Sound-Vibration, I Saw a "Bright" White Tunnel, with empty niches along the sides. There were no "people in white". There were no distinct forms or personalities—because no mind of Me was active there. Then the "Midnight Sun" of the Divine "Bright" Spherical Self-Domain. At first, Seen—then, Perfectly Become.

Effectively, it was death—in terms of the Body. There was no bodily awareness, although it was certainly not a circumstance of unconsciousness. It was the Infinitely Profound Samadhi of Outshining.

Eventually, I Re-Emerged from the "Midnight Sun" of My Divine Spiritual White Self-"Brightness"—and so, in due course, there was a peripheral re-organization of (or Re-Association with) My gross Bodily conditions. In the Process of Re-Association, there was, at first (as I have already Indicated), a "bindu" (or sphere) of blue, to the left. And another "bindu", of yellow and deep red, to the right. The "bindu" of yellow and red located Me back in this world, which is the yellow-red realm of the Cosmic Mandala.

As I Merged with the yellow-red sphere, I became aware that I was Re-Associating with the physical—rather than feeling the strong movement Up and Out, which (if it had continued) would have culminated in the death of My human Vehicle. The Struggle of Re-Integration with the physical manifested, in part, as convulsions in the Body. The "Bright" Spiritual Light-Current of My Being was Re-Connecting with the physical level, and that Process caused Bodily convulsions.

In that Process, the Body had a quality of being greatly stretched, or elongated. My legs seemed to be very, very long, and those who were standing or sitting by My Feet seemed to be quite a distance away from Me. It was a moment of non-ordinary awareness of physicality—of the pervasive yellow-red light, of the gross world consumed in flames, of the Body greatly stretched out. Eventually, there was a kind of "collapse" back into the ordinarily perceived shape and context of the physical, and then a "return" to so-called "normal" (or "natural") awareness of the room and the people in it.

The Lopez Island Event was similar to the Initiatory Event of My Avataric Divine Self-"Emergence" (on January 11, 1986), in terms of the Depth of Spiritual and Yogic Profundity. As in 1986, I had been (in the Lopez Island Event) at the point of Relinquishing the Body entirely—but, through My own Persistent Impulse and Felt

Movement of Sympathetic (or Compassionate) Love for beings, I was able to Yogically Re-Engage the Body.

However, those two Events were also, in some sense, "opposite" in their significance. In the Event of 1986, I Completed My Descent into the conditional realms, My Avataric Submission to here, Which began at My Birth. The Lopez Island Event, in contrast, was My Direct Ascent, to the Primal "Bright" Spiritual Self-Condition of Conscious Light.

I Am now, even in bodily (human) Form, presently Alive at the White Core of the Cosmic Mandala, the Doorway to the Spiritually "Bright" Divine Sphere and Self-Domain. In the Lopez Island Event, I Passed Beyond—in That "Bright" Doorway. My Thus Transfigured Body remains—but only on the Unique Basis of Direct Spiritual Illumination, and always tentatively Given to live, perpetually Wounded by the Self-Evident "Bright" Spiritual Transparency of all the heart-breaking companionship of mortal beings.

I Stand At the Threshold.

Now, and forever hereafter, I Stand There.

I Remain in this world Bodily, for now—but I Am Always Already on the "Other Side".

—Avatar Adi Da Samraj
The Knee Of Listening

San Francisco Bay, 2001

CHAPTER 17

"ALL OF THIS IS BEAUTIFUL"

One day, six months after the Lopez Island Event, Avatar Adi Da Samraj remarked to Ruchiradama Quandra Sukhapur, "The problem with human beings is that they lack profound experience." And He spoke of His urge to stay in the Body in order to continue His Work to draw people into "a life-transforming experience of the Divine Spiritual Reality".

Within a matter of months, Avatar Adi Da Samraj had established an entirely new "language" through which He could convey that Reality to human beings. It is a language of light—the "Bright" made visible through works of art. He describes His Art as "multi-dimensional Light-Imagery". Through these works of art (which make boldly innovative use of the media of photography and video), He was developing a means by which He could Offer His Communication about Reality to everyone, beyond the limits of the verbal mind. His Divine Art was a primary aspect of His Life and Work as it began to unfold after the Lopez Island Event.

Photograph taken on the California coast in the early 1960s by Adi Da Samraj

The Moon over the Water

Where the Light Glances off the Water—
that is where the pictures begin.

—Avatar Adi Da Samraj
November 21, 1999

Avatar Adi Da had taken some photographs of the northern California coast in the early 1960s (during His period of intensive observation on the beach while at Stanford), and He had attended some photography classes in Los Angeles early in 1973. But, during all the years of His Teaching-Work and Revelation-Work, Avatar Adi Da scarcely touched a camera. As He remarked later, what had been required of Him to establish the Way of Adidam did not allow Him to place any attention on doing art.

Beginning in October 1998, Avatar Adi Da Samraj began to focus in His artistic Work in a very serious way. Now that His verbal Teaching was fully Given, He began to develop pre-verbal, or artistic, means to picture the complex (and ultimately single) nature of Reality.

Avatar Adi Da was staying at the Hermitage on the northern California coast that He had named "Tat Sundaram" (meaning, in Sanskrit, "All of this is beautiful!"). Near dawn on October 5, Avatar Adi Da rose to work on some refinements to the manuscripts of His "Source-Texts". Looking out from His upstairs bedroom, He could see the beautiful moon—reddish, and almost full—hanging over the ocean in the first light. It should be photographed, He said.

Thankfull Hastings describes the occasion:

THANKFULL: At 6:00 A.M., I arrived at Beloved Adi Da's house to take photographs of the moon as it was setting over the ocean. I noticed that the light was on in Beloved Adi Da's study, which looks over the ocean where the moon was setting. I took some photographs of the moon.

I had also borrowed a professional-quality camera from a devotee who was staying nearby and set it up on a tripod, in case

Beloved Adi Da decided to come out onto the porch of His room and take photographs Himself. At about 7:15 A.M., I heard the door from His study open, and saw that Beloved Adi Da had stepped out onto the porch with the camera and tripod in hand. The moon was just above the horizon, and the sun was rising behind the house in the east. The sky was spectacular, with a serene pastel glow, as if it were dawn and sunset at the same time. It was one of the most beautiful natural phenomena I had ever seen. Beloved Adi Da positioned the tripod and camera on His porch and began taking photographs of the moon setting over the water. It was absolutely silent, apart from the sound of the ocean below us. His concentration on what He was photographing was a magnificent vision to behold.

After this, discussions about photography and photographic equipment became a major part of the Divine Avatar's life. Almost daily, Thankfull brought Him brochures on cameras, lenses, tripods, and every kind of photographic accessory representing the current state of the art. Avatar Adi Da's technical "consideration" was exhaustive, and went on for most of a year, during which He took relatively few photographs. He was studying and experimenting to discover exactly what kind of approach to photography would serve His Purpose and what would be the best equipment for the task.

As Avatar Adi Da explained, what He intended to convey through His Art was His Revelation about Light: "All That Is Is Light." Real God, the Source-Condition, Is Conscious Light—and everything that exists is this same Light, appearing in modified form. How could He use the photographic process to make this Revelation? This was the challenge He had set Himself—to make patterns in light that would break the viewer's stride, moving people beyond the ego's view of existence, beyond the observer/object mode, into the vision of Oneness. He wanted to show people the Beauty and Fullness that radiate in and through this mortal world, and do so with a revelatory power that would affect their lives.

Camera Obscura and Camera Illuminata

The word "camera" (in Latin) means "room". The first camera—called "camera obscura" (or "dark room")—was simply a room with a small hole in the wall or the ceiling, through which light entered and made an image on the opposite surface. Avatar Adi Da Samraj points out that the visual mechanism in human beings works the same way. The light enters the eye, an image is formed (in reverse) on the retina, and is then interpreted via nerve impulses in the brain—resulting in the image that is perceived. But what is perceived is simply an interpretation of reality via the mind and its conditioning. What we see represents a particular point of view on reality, not the "thing" itself.

In other words, everything perceived is arising in the "camera" (or "room") of mind. And so, what is the Truth of what exists? How do you comprehend the subject from a greater point of view than one angle in the mind?

AVATAR ADI DA SAMRAJ: Imagine a thousand cameras, all snapping photographs simultaneously of the same space, from a thousand different points of view. Imagine a single shutter release connecting the thousand cameras and releasing them all at exactly the same moment for the same length of exposure. If you took an infinite number of photographs with an infinite number of cameras, would you wind up photographing Reality Itself?

I am interested in the "Consideration" of how I might use photography in a different manner, a manner that transcends fixed point of view in the room. I look for technical ways to "break out" of the camera—to make images that are the tangible manifestation, the expression, of a different mode of experience.

—January 12, 1999

Avatar Adi Da Samraj intends His images to open up the being—to allow an intuitive glimpse of Reality. His Revelation is that Reality Is Light—not electromagnetic light (in and of itself), but the Source-Light within Which all lights and forms arise and disappear. Thus, the purpose of His Art is to "En-Light-en" the viewer—to fill the "room of mind" with Light, to transform the "dark room" (or "camera obscura") into a "'Bright' Room" (or "Camera Illuminata").

The Camera Must Be Overcome

AVATAR ADI DA SAMRAJ: The Images I make are a "room" full of Light. The camera must be overcome. The body-mind is an apparatus, virtually a camera obscura. You never move out of this camera obscura all of your life. Yet all the images of you are there. You are looking at the pictures and not understanding, not comprehending Reality. You don't understand how these images are appearing. And you don't understand the Identity of This. But the consciousness that appears as "point of view", as a focal point in the room, or in the "camera" of the body-mind, is the Consciousness within Which the camera is arising. Everything <u>inside</u> the camera was generated simultaneously with everything <u>outside</u> the camera. It is an incident in Light.

—May 18, 1999

A Transformative Shift

In June 2000, Avatar Adi Da was moved to take photographs for the first time in the two months that had passed since the Lopez Island Event. He was no longer requiring a wheelchair and, now, back at Tat Sundaram, He wanted to walk with His camera in the redwoods, as He had done many times previously.

Spontaneously, one day, as He was walking in one of the ancient forests near Tat Sundaram, Avatar Adi Da Samraj began to allow more freedom in the way He was using the camera. The result was that His subjects—the forest and the devotees walking with Him—were no longer recognizable as sharply defined objects. Rather, the images were imbued with a great influx of light and motion. This was a major turning point in His Artwork.

In the fall and winter of 2000, Avatar Adi Da spent two months in Yosemite National Park in California, and it was during that time

Yosemite, 2000

that He developed the technical mastery of His equipment such that He could use it effortlessly to convey the depth of His Revelation through images—just as He had developed His use of the English language to convey His Revelation in written form.

Standing in the icy fields of Yosemite, Avatar Adi Da found all kinds of unusual ways to break through the apparent limitations of the camera. In particular, He experimented with multiple-exposed images—exposing a series of different images on the same frame of film. This Work that He did at Yosemite laid the foundation for Him to begin Working in an entirely new way with human subjects.

When He returned from Yosemite to the Mountain Of Attention in January 2001, Avatar Adi Da Samraj had the technical means to enter into this new phase of His Work in its fully realized form. All that was needed was the right circumstance. And so, in February, one of the buildings at the Sanctuary was transformed into a studio.

The studio was very humble—an ordinary rectangular building, basically one room. At the beginning of March, Avatar Adi Da went to Work in the new studio, creating many sequences of images, each with a particular theme. He called these sequences "suites"—creating some with as few as 8 images and others with as many as 3,000 images.

As soon as He began making multiple-exposed images of human subjects in that space, the leap that had occurred at Yosemite in Avatar Adi Da's Mastery of His medium was obvious. He was creating an entirely new depth and motion and life in His images. He has often pointed out that what the eye sees in life is not static. The process of perception is complex and constantly changing. Avatar Adi Da's multiple exposures capture that process, beyond any fixed point of view—and, at the same time, they mysteriously draw the viewer into the contemplation of Reality Itself. The compositional precision with which He superimposes the different exposures, using nothing but His own sighting of each shot through the viewfinder, is extraordinary.

As He Himself has explained, His intention has been to develop a way of using the camera that allows Him the degree of plastic freedom that a painter enjoys:

AVATAR ADI DA SAMRAJ: Different qualities are evident in the Images I have made at different times and in the Images that belong to different Suites. I have been Working more and more to develop a plastic approach that allows complete freedom in generating abstract forms, while still maintaining visual elements that are recognizable. Such an approach to Image-making is what I have intended and wanted to do from the beginning. All along, I wanted to develop a way of using the photographic medium that is similar to the way I have used paint. A lot of work was required to get to that point.

—August 30, 2001

Transcending the Camera: The "Bright" Reality Beyond "Point of View"

by Avatar Adi Da Samraj

This Essay was written by Avatar Adi Da Samraj in 2001, as His "Artist's Statement".

The camera is "point of view" incarnate. The event of the camera registering an image on a piece of film replicates the human idea of what it is to see: The light of the "outside" world enters through a small aperture and is registered on a light-sensitive material. Thus, both the camera and the human being are mechanisms for registering reality from a particular "point of view" in space-time. The camera—like the human being—is a "point-of-view machine". Thus, the process of making photographs reflects the nature of the human event, of human experiencing.

The human individual in the midst of reality is like a camera in a room—perceiving everything from a fixed "point of view". But what does the room really look like? The room can be viewed from every possible "point of view" in space-time—not merely from any particular "point of view", or even a finite collection of "points of view". Therefore, no "point of view" can reveal the room, or Reality Itself, because every "point of view" is limited and essentially self-referring.

Reality Itself always already Exists. Reality Itself Is What Exists Prior to "point of view", before any individual "point of view" constructs its version of presumed "reality".

"Point of view" is the essence of ego-life: The apparently individual being presumes that he or she is a particularized "point", or organized "point of view", in space-time. And that "point" is "made" by contracting from the Condition of Totality—and, indeed, by contracting from even every mode, form, or condition of conditional existence. Therefore, the camera is a precise mechanical equivalent of the ego—because it, too, functions as fixed "point of view".

In My use of the camera, I Work to make Images that go beyond, and even undermine, the conventions of "point of view". Such Images transcend the limitation that would seem to be inherent in the photographic mechanism (or "point-of-view machine"). They allow the viewer to see and feel the "room"—or the world, or Reality—as it is, beyond the ego's self-reference. And such Images thereby become a non-verbal means of "picturing" the essential human process of ego-transcendence—going beyond the fixed "point of view" of the ego, or the core presumption of separateness.

This "Consideration" of the human being as a "point of view" existing in the midst of Unknowable Reality began in My childhood. I spent many hours sitting silently in My room, contemplating what it would mean to exist and perceive not from a "point of view" <u>in</u> the room, but from the "point of view" <u>of</u> the room itself. This was the beginning of My Investigation of the Process of Divine Enlightenment—the Process by which it becomes possible to be Identified with the Condition in Which all experience is arising, rather than with the "point of view" of the apparently individual experiencer.

That "Consideration" of the "room" has always been at the root of My Artwork. For many years, the Artwork I Created consisted primarily of paintings, drawings, and literature. Eventually, the decades of My "Consideration" culminated in a focus in photography and video, as artistic media uniquely suited to the Communication I Intend to Make.

Long before I started My concentrated Work in photography and video, I established My fundamental artistic position through the writing of a study of early twentieth-century literature and art, focusing on Gertrude Stein and such painters as Cézanne, Picasso, Mondrian, and so on. (This study was written as My Master's Thesis, in the English department at Stanford University, in 1966. My graduate studies in English at Stanford were built upon My undergraduate studies in the philosophy department of Columbia College in New York City, including intensive study of world literature and world art.) My primary interest in writing this study was to address the implications of the modernist effort to reduce art to sheer plastic and technical manipulation of words or paint (or the "medium", in any form), thereby achieving a "meaningless" artistic communication. My conclusion was that the effort to divest art of meaning is a grave fault—a fault which is also generally evident in the culture of the time (dominated by the "point of view" of scientific materialism), in the increasing "abstraction" from what is profoundly human and, even more so, from everything Spiritual and Divine. This conclusion is summarized in the title I have given to this study: *The Reduction Of The Beloved To Shape Alone: The Effort Toward Abstraction, The Pure Present, and The New In "Modern" Art, Psychology, and Philosophy—Especially As Defined In The "Meaningless" Aesthetic Theories Of Gertrude Stein.*

Thus, although My approach to Creating photographic Images is highly abstract, I am not looking to create "meaningless" patterns. Indeed, I have chosen the camera as a medium precisely because it inherently preserves at least a degree of perceptual realism and does not allow for the kind of absolute "abstraction" from meaning (or participatory reality) that is potential with paint. I wish to maintain the tension of a clear and direct reflection of conditional reality, including an address to the process of transcendence.

If reality is reduced to a shattered abstraction without meaning, then the beautiful is no longer there, the beloved is no longer there. I use the photographic medium precisely because it inherently reflects human and conditional reality and form. I enter into My photographic Contemplation of Reality as a feeling process—never abstracted from a feeling-relationship to human experience, but always embracing human realities. The content of My Images is extremely intimate, and deals with fundamental issues of existence in which people are profoundly vulnerable and where deep "consideration" is required.

Thus, the making of these Images is a profoundly participatory Work—not abstracting the subject from Myself, but participating utterly. Therefore, the visual abstraction in these Images is not something separate or separative, but an expression of the seamlessness of Reality. I Work to move the viewer into ecstasy—abstracted beyond the ego's modes of perception. Ecstasy abstracts absolutely (but not meaninglessly)—beyond all presumed "difference" between "self" and "other".

My Art is Created by means of My Participation in the Process of Realizing the Beautiful, or the Condition That is Ecstatic. When That Condition is fully Realized, one spontaneously utters, "All of This Is Beautiful! This Is That Which Is Beautiful."

This purpose for the arts—of Realizing that "All Is Beautiful"—is the understanding that was alive in the Western tradition in the time of Plato, as expressed in *The Symposium.* I am thoroughly sympathetic with Plato's "consideration" of Realizing Beauty. In the centuries since Plato, that understanding has been degraded in the Western world, and in the common world altogether—but that understanding remains fundamental to right human existence.

The living body-mind inherently wants to Realize the Matrix of life, wants to allow the Light into the "room". Making it possible for human beings to fulfill that impulse is what I Work to do. My Images are Created to be a means of participating in Reality as Fundamental Light—the world as Light, relationship as Light, conditional light as Absolute Light.

The "room" is where the "focal point" of ego happens. Ultimately, when the camera is transcended, there is no longer any "room" at all—but only Love-Bliss-"Brightness" limitlessly felt, in vast unpatterned Joy.

Quandra Loka

The beginning of September 2002 was the next great moment of transition in the emerging Art-Work of the Divine Avatar. At the time, He was residing at Da Love-Ananda Mahal. He would sometimes visit local resorts on Kauai, where He would swim for exercise and sit for long periods, Radiating His silent Blessing to all. On one such occasion, He was given a disposable underwater camera. It was not "serious" equipment, but an inexpensive plastic camera designed to be sold to tourists. The devotee making the offering felt that it might be an interesting amusement.

Over the next few days, Avatar Adi Da became thoroughly absorbed in experimenting with the possibilities of underwater photography. He went through a whole series of these cameras—creating a new suite of over two hundred images, which He called *The Plastic Camera.*

When the images were developed, it was instantly obvious that the Divine Avatar's Image-Making had entered another dimension. The medium of water suffused the Images with a radiant, fluid energy and functioned in a unique manner as a complex lens.

The human subject of *The Plastic Camera* was Ruchiradama Quandra Sukhapur Rani. Within a few weeks, now using professional underwater equipment, Avatar Adi Da Samraj began to work with her further, in a private environment. In response to His obvious need for a circumstance where He could develop His underwater Art, devotees had rented a house with a suitable pool.

This was the beginning of "an ongoing suite of indefinite length", which consists (as of July 2003) of more than 5,500 Images. This suite—which includes both black-and-white and color images—represents the culmination of the Divine Avatar's Image-Art so far. He has named the Suite *Quandra Loka*[53] *(The Indivisible Space of Conscious Light).*

In the following brief Essay, Avatar Adi Da describes His intention in this suite:

Photographing underwater for *Quandra Loka*

Quandra Loka *is a visual meditation on a very simple circumstance: a woman in and near a pool of water. Narcissus, the archetype of ego, gazes at his own reflection in a pond, never able to contact the "object" of his self-enamored affection. But Quandra, the true beloved, is one with the water itself, whether in or out of the pool.*

I shot the majority of the Images in Quandra Loka *underwater, or with the camera lens partially submerged in water, so that the water functions as a vast and subtly complex lens, achieving visual results not possible by any technical means. The Images are made by a "technique" that requires continuous participation in the living instant of the photographic situation—sensitive to the constantly changing sunlight conditions, the ever-shifting minute movements of the subject, and even My own ability to stay submerged underwater. This "method" is beyond conceptual effort, beyond conventions of control in the ordinary sense, beyond "point of view". This process of generating Images—involving absolute awareness of every detail of what is occurring and (simultaneously) an intuitive trust in allowing the ultimately unpredictable process to take place—is a means of allowing Reality to be Self-Manifested.*

I intend these Images to "picture" the Unity of the Undifferentiated Reality from Which all appearances emerge in a constant flow of changes. The entire span of human possibilities is reflected in these Images—both "positive" and "negative". But all possibilities are seen in the context of that Inherent Unity (or Indivisible Space). The positives and the negatives are all transcended, rather than any attempt being made to render them acceptable in and of themselves.

—Avatar Adi Da Samraj
"On *Quandra Loka*"

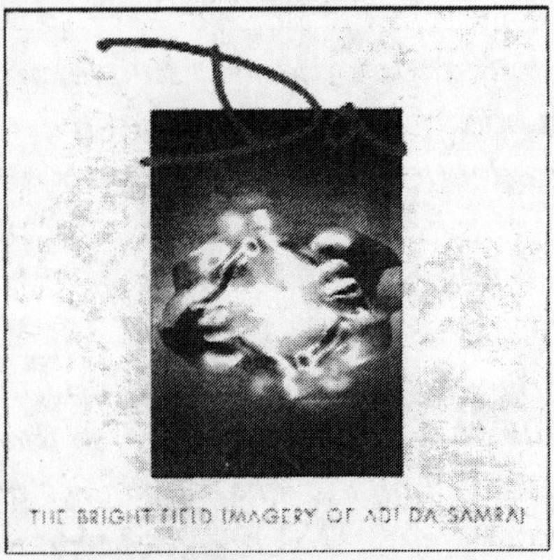

To view Avatar Adi Da's Art visit:
www.daplastique.com

Critical Acclaim for *Quandra Loka*—

It is a rare artist who can convey, convincingly, the sense of being face to face with the source of being. Adi Da can clearly live in the depths without succumbing to their pressure, bringing back pearls of art to prove it.

Indeed, again and again Adi Da's photographs convey a sense of aesthetic as well as physical ecstasy. Virtually all of his images are masterpieces of abstraction—ecstatic visions . . . that are simultaneously formal epiphanies.

—Donald Kuspit
Art critic; Professor of art and philosophy;
Author, *Redeeming Art: Critical Reveries,*
and numerous other publications

Monumental Images from *Quandra Loka*
(pigmented inks on canvas)
The "Bright" Room Gallery, the Mountain Of Attention Sanctuary

Avatar Adi Da relates to His photographic negatives as "blueprints", using them as the basis for making "monumental fabrications". To date, these fabrications include large-scale pigmented inks on canvas, plasma-screen installations, and multi-media screen-projected performance events—with many additional forms of fabrication planned for the future. These fabricated works frequently involve the grouping of multiple images in specific combinations and configurations. He designs His fabrications to be "monumental"—by which He specifically means larger in size than the human body—so that the viewing of them engages the entire body and mind, not merely the eye and head.

The Fruit of a Lifetime of Spiritual Work

Avatar Adi Da Samraj is the epitome of the sacred artist. His every physical movement with the camera is perfect Yoga. His Work arises out of His Divine Siddhis, and all the arduous technical training to which He has submitted Himself. His Revelation of the Spiritual Reality—via His Divinely Enlightened "eye" and peerless camera technique—makes His Image-Art uniquely sacred.

AVATAR ADI DA SAMRAJ: In the traditional setting, sacred art is undertaken as a Spiritual discipline, not merely a technical or a cultural endeavor in the conventional sense. There are many profound requirements—not only artistic requirements, but also requirements related to Spiritual life.

There are esoteric profundities associated with sacred art—profound training, profound readiness, a profound life that has to be lived before you ever do anything to show anybody else.

Sacred art is not just a kind of subject matter. To be an artist in the sacred sense is a profoundly different matter than being an artist in the secular (or worldly) sense. Sacred art is not ego-art—and, therefore, it takes a lifetime of work.

I Myself have engaged a lifetime of Work, in which I have been occupied with art, as well as other aspects of the totality of what I do. And it is at this point in My Life that I am prepared to make Works for showing, having done it and "considered" it since I was a child. So, in this respect, I am functioning very much in the mode of the traditional artist within a sacred circumstance.

—July 1, 2003

Avatar Adi Da Samraj intends His Art to affect human culture, and not merely to hang in galleries or museums. That is why great expansiveness and originality in its fabrication will be important into the future. He is not making "religious" art, any more than He is giving a "religious" Revelation, in the conventional sense. His

Revelation is about Reality Itself, and so His Images go beyond any particular system of philosophy or culture.

The Divine Image-Art of Avatar Adi Da affects the psycho-physical being, prior to mind. He profoundly intends His Art Work to become so widely known that, over time (during and beyond His human Lifetime) He can give everyone everywhere the vision and taste of His Divine Domain of Conscious Light.

Adidam Samrajashram, 2003

CHAPTER 18

"I Am Merely Present—and Accessible"

One day in February 2002, as Avatar Adi Da Samraj was walking into the Manner of Flowers (His residence at the Mountain Of Attention), He showed signs of disorientation relative to the body. While walking into the house on the arm of Ruchiradama Quandra Sukhapur, He was moved to speak to her about the unusual nature of His relationship to the physical body and the gross dimension, since the Lopez Island Event.

AVATAR ADI DA SAMRAJ: I am not in a normal condition. I should not be required to think, or obliged to struggle with ordinary things.

These signs, such as a kind of dizzy Swooning, or "Intoxication", are signs of My Bhava. I suffer trying to do what the ordinary man does. I am in a different condition, and this Body is profoundly Yogically Transformed.

The dizziness is not negative. I do not feel like being normal. I feel "Intoxicated" in the Body. I appreciate it—and My devotees should.

—February 13, 2002

At another moment, Avatar Adi Da reminded devotees of a further aspect of His Yogic state: He often does not blink for long periods—a characteristic that had first been noticed in His childhood:

AVATAR ADI DA SAMRAJ: This non-blinking has to do with My Condition, My State, My Samadhi. There is no ego, no functioning of the brain in the mode of egoic attention. The pastor in my childhood noticed this non-blinking when I was sitting in the religion class—and he said that if I didn't start blinking, I would go crazy! As a Lutheran minister, he did not have a relationship to Spiritual and mystical phenomena.

The conventional world is suspicious of Spiritual signs. But, traditionally, signs such as this were respected.

—December 19, 2001

Avatar Adi Da added that sensitivity to His unique Yogic signs on the part of His devotees would only develop based on their deepening participation in the Spiritual process.

The fundamental Yogic change in Avatar Adi Da Samraj since the Lopez Island Event was vividly communicated by Him one day while speaking with Ruchiradama Quandra Sukhapur. The Divine Avatar pushed His thumb into the middle of His forehead and said forcefully, "This is as far down as I go." In the following days, Avatar Adi Da began to Speak of His unique relationship to the physical body, and of the profound significance of the Lopez Island Event.

I Spiritually Radiate into the Body. I do not "step down" to the toes and identify with the plane of the Body. Even though I am (in My bodily human Form) physically active, I (Myself) do not "come down" below the brows (or below the brain core).

This is a description of the fundamental Means by Which I have always Maintained a Yogic Spiritual Association with gross life. And—since the Great Event at Lopez Island (on April 12, 2000), or, really, since the Great Event at the "Brightness" (on April 22, 1999)—This Disposition (of Spiritually Radiating from Above to below) has become the <u>only</u> Means by Which I Maintain Yogic Spiritual association with gross life. Since the Single Great Event of the "Brightness" and Lopez Island, I am no longer disposed to "Set

Foot" below the brows—but I am only Radiant to here, from Infinitely Above the conditional (or psycho-physical) planes.

I Spiritually Radiate, from Infinitely Above, into the gross conditions of existence. In this Manner, the Body (of My own gross physical Appearance) is Maintained by My own Spiritual Self-Radiance, Which is Infinitely Above the Body (and Infinitely Above the bodily manifested mind of thoughts). The apparent exercise of My attention "moves into" the gross physical domain only in the sense of such Spiritual Radiating into the Body. There is Spiritual Descent to the brain core, as a base (or platform) for what I appear to animate in gross exchanges—but attention (itself) does not move to "settle below" (or become fixed in the planes of conditional patterning associated with the bodily and mental functions). Of course, there is natural energy flowing in the Body below the brows, and a Descent of My Spiritual Radiance to below and everywhere. I am (in the naturally apparent sense) animated in the gross (physical) dimension. But I am not (and have never been) bound in attention below the brows—because there is no ego-mind in Me.

From the beginning, from My Birth and Infancy, I have been What I Am. I Am the Spiritually Self-"Bright" Divine Sun Infinitely Above. My Birth was the Initiation of My Avataric Divine Self-"Emergence". Then, at the age of approximately two years, a Sympathetic Association with bodily existence occurred. Thus, from that age, I began to Combine. That Combining was an essential aspect of My Work of Submitting to the world and (Thereby) Coming Down. That Combining fitted Me to the Submission-Pattern that (necessarily) characterized all My Years of Learning and Teaching humankind.

The "Thumbs" is the Means That I Bring to Awaken and Liberate living beings. I Am the "Bright". The "Thumbs" is a Divine Yogic Spiritual Manifestation, and the "Thumbs" is the Means whereby I was able to go through the course of life in this conditionally manifested Vehicle. The "Thumbs" is how My "Bright" Divine Spiritual Self-Transmission is Able to Serve living beings under these mortal and limited conditions. . . .

Certain aspects of My Work became Full and Complete with the Yogic Establishment of My Avataric Divine Self-"Emergence" (on January 11, 1986). Other aspects of My Work became Full and

Complete with the "Santosha Event" (of September 7, 1994). And yet other aspects of My Work became Full and Complete with the Great Event Which was Initiated at the "Brightness" (in Adidam Samrajashram) and Which Culminated at Lopez Island. These have been the principal Events in the Completion (or progressive "Shedding") of My Avataric Divine Spiritual Work of Self-Submission. . . .

◆ ◆ ◆

My Infancy was the same Self-Revelation of the Divine Person, of the "Bright" Itself, that I am Making now (since the Lopez Island Event). Truly, heart-recognition of Me As the Divine Avatar should have occurred at My Birth—but, because it did not, it was necessary that I Make My Submission to humankind. In that Avataric Divine Work of Self-Submission, I had to Engage in Acts of Self-Revelation—in the midst of Consenting to be involved in a life-process, apparently below the brows. I had to Reveal the Way by which everything can be conformed to Me. I Entered that Ordeal of Self-Revelation on the basis (and by Means) of My Boundless Sympathy with ordinary beings.

That Sympathy was a tacit Agreement to Descend—to be Descended to, and Combined with, what is (in and of itself) less than the "Bright", or (apparently) other than the "Bright". My Agreement to Descend was My Self-Submission to darkness—in order to Spiritually "Brighten" it.

How was that Avataric Divine Self-Submission possible? It was possible because of the "Thumbs". The Mechanism of the "Thumbs" allowed Me to Coincide with conditional reality. The "Thumbs" allowed Me to Introduce the "Bright" into My own Descended Life. The "Thumbs" was the Divine Means by Which I Shined from Above into what is below—to Purify and Transform it, and to Awaken it to Myself.

My verbal Teaching is largely an elaboration of what I mean to Convey by Speaking of "the 'Bright'" and "the 'Thumbs'". The "Bright" Is My Very Person. The "Thumbs" Is the Means to Realize Me.

◆ ◆ ◆

I Am Always Already Infinitely Above and Beyond. This is the Inherent (or Native) Condition of My Avataric Divine Incarnation.

I Am the Self-Evidently Divine Person—not a karmic being reaching toward the Divine Person.

I Am Divinely Self-Manifested here, without psyche or mind. I am Associated with a Body-Mind Which has natural functional faculties, and Which has an in-Depth (or Deeper) functional Personality—but I am not (in any manner) identified with (or bound to) that psycho-physical structure. It is simply the structure by means of which I am Associated with conditionality. . . .

I am not bound by mind. Even though I was Moved to Associate Myself with the conditional worlds, by Means of My Sympathetic Self-Submission, I am not (and have never been) identified with conditions. Therefore, I must be understood as an Avataric Divine Manifestation, not as a karmic entity. True heart-recognition of Me requires this understanding. Otherwise, you are not recognizing Me, but merely thinking about Me.

The Lopez Island Event was a direct Divine Manifestation of What Is Infinitely Above and Beyond, a Manifestation in Which there was no psyche or mind. In near-death experiences, people typically see dead relations—but, in the case of the Lopez Island Event, there were no apparently attendant beings of any kind. The entire structure of conditional existence (with its gross, subtle, and causal dimensions) was Gone Beyond. I experienced that near-death passage without any visionary or mental attitudes. There were no structures of mind. There was no psyche to make phenomena. . . .

I See everything from the "Other Side", from the "Position" of My Divine Self-Domain, from the "Position" of the "Bright"—not from below and reaching Above, but from <u>Already</u> Infinitely Above and Beyond. I See the Cosmic Mandala structure from the "Other Side"—not from "this side". I See everyone and everything from the "Brightness" Side, not from the bodily side. . . .

I Am Always Already Established Infinitely Above and Beyond.

I Am Sympathetic to all-and-All.

I Am Self-Radiant here.

I am not fixed in this domain.

I Am Simply here.

That is <u>why</u> I Am here—not to persist in Self-Submission, not to persist in Teaching, but to Simply <u>Be</u> here.

◆ ◆ ◆

I (Myself) am not identified with the body-mind.

I Am the "Bright", Unbroken—Just That. There is an apparent Association with the Body-Mind, in the context of Which I Am Self-Radiant—but I (Myself) am not bound (or patterned) egoically.

I (Myself) have no conditionally patterned impulses or destiny. I (Myself) have never had any such impulse or destiny.

I have Embraced this Association Sacrificially, Responsively, and Compassionately.

That Sacrificial, Responsive, and Compassionate Embrace was the Circumstance and Origin of My Avataric Divine Submission-Work. Such has been My active Lifetime.

◆ ◆ ◆

I (Myself) do not "come down" below the brows, in the sense of identifying with the Body. It is not that there is no energy below the brows. It is simply that that energy is not of the mind.

I (Myself) Am Always Already Infinitely Above.

In the Lopez Island Event, I was Divinely Self-Revealed to Be Always Already Fully Established in (and As) the Condition That I Am. That Condition is the Basis for My Association with the Body. It is So now, and It has always been So—from My Birth-Time.

The Lopez Island Event is a Divine Revelation-Sign. It is the . . . Divine Revelation-Sign of My Always Already (or Priorly) Ascended Condition. That Ascended Condition has always been the Case, even from My Birth. It is the Condition in Which I Existed during the two years following My Birth—before My Avataric Divine Spiritual Work of Self-Submission began, before I Submitted to the Self-Sacrificial Ordeal of Combining with existence below the brows. And That Always Already Ascended Condition Remained the Case, even during all the years of My Avataric Divine Submission-Work.

My Avataric Divine Spiritual Work of Self-Submission was the Means by Which I Revealed the Way of the devotional and Spiritual relationship to Me—Which is the Divine (and Spiritually Self-"Bright") Way of the "Thumbs". That Original Foundation-Work of Revelation has now been entirely Accomplished. Therefore, My Avataric Divine Self-Submission to My devotees and to the world is no longer the basis of My Association with anyone. . . .

Now (since the Lopez Island Event) I Am here As I Was at the beginning of My Bodily Incarnation, before I Made My Submission. I Am Simply Present here, the "Bright" here—Just That.

The Single Great Event of the "Brightness" and Lopez Island brought an end to My Avataric Divine Submission-Work in the gross sphere. I am not grossly connected to the Body. I Am Utterly Above and Beyond.

Do not confuse Me with the conventional mind of gross worldliness.

Above and Beyond is the Basis of My Avatarically-Born bodily (human) Divine Form.

Truly, My Divine Self-Condition is not limited by any "point of view".

I Am Beyond the gross, subtle, and causal domains.

I Am the "Midnight Sun".

I Am the "Bright"—Infinitely Above and Beyond.

My "Thumbs" would Be Pressed Upon the crown of every head—and I would Light the Way Above and Beyond your body and your mind.

—Avatar Adi Da Samraj
"I (Myself) Do Not 'Come Down' Below the Brows"

The Law of Right Relationship to the Master

After sixty years of His Submission to Descend, Avatar Adi Da is re-established in the Yogic Condition of His birth and earliest years. He has "Returned" to the Place He never left, merely Radiating His Love-Bliss from Infinitely Above, while still retaining a mysterious connection to the physical domain.

It is not that He is inactive in the Body. But His mode of living and Working is profoundly different from what it was. In the years of His Submission-Work, He was always actively creating a process around Him and drawing His devotees into that. In the Great Event at Lopez Island, the Divine Siddhis that had enabled Him to Work in the mode of Submission disappeared conclusively. Now He is active only in response to the gifts of devotion that are brought to Him by His devotees, His patrons, and others in the world who respect and support His Work.

Traditionally, the primary gift that can be offered to a Realizer is to set him or her apart from the world, provide an ashram, build temples, make holy places where that one chooses to move or to reside. Those who recognize the Realizer take care of that one bodily and provide what the Master indicates is needed for his or her Spiritual work.

The gifts laid at the feet of a Realizer have always been of many kinds—from the simplest to the most magnificent—depending on the characteristics of those who made the offerings. The great majority of those who came, for example, to Swami Nityananda of Ganeshpuri offered a simple gift of fruit. Others provided money and service to establish and maintain his ashram. A few—such as Swami Muktananda—came to offer their entire lives for the sake of Realization. And the Prasad (or the Master's returned gift of Blessing) was fitted to the aspirations of each one.

The law of the devotional relationship to Avatar Adi Da is fundamentally the same as it has been traditionally. One can relate to Him and serve Him as closely and profoundly as one is moved to do. But, for all His devotees, right relationship to Him carries responsibilities and Blessings that go far beyond what was the case in the traditional setting.

Avatar Adi Da Samraj is the Divine Avataric Intervention, long-promised for the "late-time". And so the necessities of His existence include everything that is necessary to let the world know that He is here. To be devoted to Him means serving Him bodily, creating Ashrams around Him, doing a global mission, and establishing the sacred places and structures necessary for Him to be able to extend His Blessing for all time to all living beings. The historic moment of His human Lifetime is just the beginning of an eternal Process. And yet, it is now, while He is Alive in the Body, that the foundation of His unending Blessing-Work must be laid.

The incomparable opportunity exists, in this moment, to serve Him—the Divine Transmission-Body on earth—to cultivate His Regard, and to provide Him with the means to function in His Blessing manner. This is the only right disposition in which to approach Avatar Adi Da—not the desire to get something for oneself, but the impulse to worship and protect and accommodate the Incarnate Divine Person.

AVATAR ADI DA SAMRAJ: It must be understood—I am not a karmic entity. I am here based on a Unique Process of Incarnation that is Spiritually Made, Divinely Made. I am here entirely based on this Compassionate and Spiritually-Made Appearance. My Condition is entirely of this Nature. So I am not persisting here on a karmic basis. I have no karmic life. I have the potential to be moved to respond to the world, or to devotees through devotion. That is how I function.

My Functioning here is Unique, and I must be enabled to do it. Devotion enables Me to do it. I respond to devotion—that mode of bringing the faculties to Me, surrendering egoity. This stimulates My Regard and My Doings, My Unique Doings. They are all Spiritually-Based, all made in a mode of existence not commonly within the sphere of awareness of people.

My Doings in the apparent sense are shown in the gross plane of visibility. But the Context and Fullness of it is beyond that common visibility.

There is a unique form of relationship to Me that is right. It is the unique practice of devotion that I have Given you. That is not a karmic mode of relating to Me—as a social "other", or as an "other" in the organizational sense, or simply as some "other" to be related to through the conventions of religious appearances that are merely ceremonial.

I Am the Means to transcend that. The unique relationship to Me, rightly lived, is the Process whereby karmic bondage is transcended.

I cannot Do My Work unless I am caused to Do it by devotees, by people responding to Me, by people recognizing Me and approaching Me rightly. This moves Me Responsively in a non-karmic Manner, in a purely Compassionate, Spiritually-Based Manner, to Bless, and to Bless by all the kinds of doings that are spontaneously Generated by Me.

That includes My Blessing Transmission-Work, My Communication of My Word, My Manifestation of visual Art—and any mode of My Activity. All of these things are non-karmic events that must be caused by devotion, by right accommodation of Me, right approach to Me, right service to Me.

I am not in a conventional or egoic state. This must be appreciated and understood, and people must approach Me uniquely.

—June 18, 2003

Just as the Divine Avatar is not a karmic entity, so also, His devotees are not limited by their own karmas, when there is resort to His Grace.

AVATAR ADI DA SAMRAJ: The profound response to Me has nothing to do with karma. Anyone can respond to Me. The karmic aspects of the personality have to be dealt with in the course of your sadhana. But the response to Me is something every apparent individual is capable of—because the heart is unbounded, the heart is free.

You can respond to Me—but you have to make much of it. You have to be made serious by it. You have to be willing to respond and get on with it.

—August 13, 1995

"I Am Established in My Divine Samadhi"

The Ruchira Avatar, Adi Da Samraj, returned to His Principal Hermitage-Ashram, Adidam Samrajashram (Naitauba), on May 29, 2003. He had been away for four years doing His Spiritual Work at His Hermitage Sanctuaries in the United States. Some weeks after arriving on His Holy Island, the Divine Avatar was Moved to spend several days at His Mahasamadhi site, the "Brightness", the place of His profound Spiritual struggle and tapas in 1999. While staying there, engaged in the unknowable Depth of His Blessing of beings, Avatar Adi Da Samraj felt a magnification of His Divine Indifference, or perfect Yogic Equanimity, relative to everything conditional. He recognized that even the residual impulse to perpetuate patterns of interactive work with His devotees—including the effort of urgent Speech, calling them to embrace the requirements of His Avataric Work—had been spontaneously relinquished.

When He came down from the "Brightness" on the evening of July 6, Avatar Adi Da Samraj made a formal statement to Ruchiradama Quandra Sukhapur Rani (who introduces His Communication below). He Spoke these Words of eternal Invitation, Calling all to prepare to approach Him in His Divine Samadhi—now, while He is alive in the body, and forever afterwards in His Empowered Places.

RUCHIRADAMA QUANDRA SUKHAPUR RANI: The profundity of the invisible nature of Beloved Adi Da's Spiritual Work for all humankind has become completely evident to me. He does not need to Work with individuals any longer. He is involved in Serving the collective consciousness of humankind, of earthkind. He is Working with the the collective nature of humankind and its collective egoity—to "Brighten" it. So everyone and everything is in His Sphere, and there is no personal relationship with Him in the conventional sense. This is literally so. This is the time of His World-Blessing Work—initiated in 1999 at the "Brightness", and now established in its Fullness.

The "Brightness", Adidam Samrajashram, 2003

AVATAR ADI DA SAMRAJ: Essentially, from this point on, I am simply here. My own Divine Samadhi is My Manifestation here. In some respects, I am Present now as I will be after the death of this Body. My years of Interacting with people for the purpose of Instructing them have fully come to an end.

So I will be merely Present. My Teaching is Full. It is Fully Expressed, Fully Written, Fully Summarized.

The Way is there to be embraced and lived by My devotees as intensively as they choose to do it. They must resort to Me.

It is not about Me Giving them My Attention. It is about them giving Me their attention. I am simply here—Established in My Samadhi, My Divine Spiritual Manifestation.

My unfolding Demonstration makes it both necessary and appropriate for Me to be accessible—now, and continuing into the future.

All access will be, in every apparent sense, the same—people are to be brought into My physical Company. I will be there. At some point, I will get up and leave. Typically, there will be chanting, or perhaps, sometimes, sacred performances. Or I may simply be Sitting there or Standing there in some circumstance or other. Often there will be spontaneous occasions of access. Generally speaking, day after day, there will be some kind of occasion or occasions where I will be accessible, and it will be also broadcast via the Internet.

My Spiritual Manifestation, as I Said, is spontaneous. It is responsive. It does not require or carry with it, necessarily, any Indication from Me in terms of even looking at anybody.

In terms of what I will be Doing from day to day, My Work is largely Invisible and not spoken.

In terms of outward activity, I will principally be making Images—and, otherwise, simply living in My Hermitage Circumstance.

I am simply here, or wherever I am at the moment—and people simply have access to Me. I will simply be there in the time of their access to Me, and there will be no special apparent doings on My part in the event. Nor is any required from now. Therefore, there should not be any expectation of special apparent doings on My part, nor should there be any presumption that there is something negative about the fact that I am not engaged in such doings. It is in order, and it is right, and it is as things should be at this stage—since I have Completed What I needed to Do to Manifest the Way in all respects and make It clear.

My devotees should value their relationship to Me above all, and resort to Me truly. It is up to them to do so. They should support and cultivate My Existence here, Move My Blessing to them through their true and right practice. They should not presume to ever enter into any kind of a social or organizational or (otherwise) merely ceremonial form of relationship to Me. Such is not appropriate. It is not (in any sense) necessary, and it simply has nothing to with the sadhana of relationship to Me.

Having completed the fundamentals of My active Work for the purpose of Manifesting the Way and Establishing the process of access to My own Person, My availability now and in the future is very much in the traditional mode—the mode in which people have approached Spiritual Masters of various degrees in the past, when those Masters were not (in any outstanding sense) outwardly interactive with people, although they were always Spiritually active. They were simply established in the Samadhi of their own Realization, and manifesting that spontaneously. And, so, in that sense, I am from now in the same kind of disposition, and will be accessible on that same basis.

So people must understand the nature of how I am now Existing and Working—and how it will be forever, from now. After My physical Lifetime, it will be the same. People will be given access under the Authority of the Ruchira Sannyasin Order—access to My Mahasamadhi Site, to the Empowered Places, the Hermitages, and so on—as during My Physical Lifetime. And I will be active then as now.

—July 6, 2003

"I Am the Heart of all-and-All"

Regardless of how long remains of His Incarnation-time, Avatar Adi Da's fundamental Work is Done—His Teaching and Revelation-Work is Complete, His Divine Self-"Emergence" is accomplished. He is here, as He says, "To Stay".

Now, and Forever Hereafter, I Enjoy The Capability, In My Infinite Divine Self-Domain, To Be Infinitely Manifested In and Throughout The Cosmic Domain, Without the slightest limit.

Now, and Forever Hereafter, I Do Not Require any Secondary (or conditional) siddhis.

Now, and Forever Hereafter, By Means Of My Inherent (Divine) Siddhis, I Appear In and Via every element in every plane Within The conditional (or Cosmic) Domain.

This Is Eternally So.

This Has Always Been So—but you (and every one, and all, and All) Did Not Fully Notice Me As I Am.

Therefore, I Have Made This—My First, My Last, and My Only Perfectly Consequential Avataric Divine Incarnation—To Completely Inform you (and every one, and all, and All) About My Infinite and Eternal Nature and Work.

I Love you Now.
I Will Love you every "then" and "there".
And I Always Loved you (and every one, and all, and All).
That Is How I Got To here (and every "where").

—Avatar Adi Da Samraj
Aham Da Asmi

The Transforming Yogic Events and Great Epochs in the Work of Avatar Adi Da Samraj (and Their Correspondence with His Names)

BIRTH

November 3, 1939
(Long Island, New York)

1939–1970
"Sadhana"

Franklin Jones

DIVINE RE-AWAKENING

September 10, 1970
(Hollywood Vedanta Temple)

1972–1979
Teaching-Work
(Relates to devotees as "friend" or "brother")

Bubba Free John
(from 1973)

REVELATION "I <u>AM</u> DA"

September 13, 1979
(The Mountain Of Attention Sanctuary)

1979–1986
Teaching-Work continues, but on the basis of His Confession of Divinity
(Relates to devotees as Divine Heart-Master)

Da Free John

THE END OF THE FIRST 14 YEARS OF SUBMISSION-WORK

1972–1986
(the Work of Reflecting devotees to themselves)

THE DIVINE SELF-"EMERGENCE"

January 11, 1986
(Adidam Samrajashram, Fiji)

1986–2000
Impulse to cease Submission-Work, which nevertheless continues, as "Tapas", or "Penance"
(Divinely Descends into His physical Vehicle "down to the toes", such that His Body becomes the very "Icon" of the Divine)

Da Love-Ananda
also:
Da Avabhasa
Dau Loloma Vunirarama

Adi Da
also:
Da Santosha

YOGIC EVENT OF "DIVINE COMPLETENESS"

September 7, 1994
(Pacific Harbour, Fiji)

Divine Yogic Event that further deepened the process of His Divine Self-"Emergence"

Intensifying impulse to cease Submission-Work

YOGIC ORDEAL AT THE "BRIGHTNESS"

March 10–April 22, 1999
(Adidam Samrajashram, Fiji)

World-Blessing Work Yogically Established in perpetuity at the "Brightness"

Spiritual Energy concentrated Above the Body

Initiation of the Yogic Process that culminated in the Lopez Island Event

CULMINATING YOGIC DEATH

April 12, 2000
(Lopez Island, Washington State)

Culmination of the Divine Yogic Process that began at the "Brightness"

Establishment as the Threshold Personality, Standing as the White "Brightness", Prior to the conditional worlds

THE END OF THE SECOND 14 YEARS OF SUBMISSION-WORK

1986–2000

(the Work of Enduring the reluctance of devotees to fully embrace the ego-transcending practice of Adidam)

2000–

A new dimension of Work begins to unfold,
no longer based on Submission
to devotees and the world

Adidam Samrajashram, 2003

Avatar Adi Da Samraj is not an "Other". He is the Divine "Brightness" Descending into the manifest worlds. He is felt and seen in dreams and visions by many who have never heard His Name. He is recognized most intimately at the heart, suddenly, by pure Revelation.

The opportunity to become a formal devotee of the Ruchira Avatar, Adi Da Samraj, is an immeasurable Grace. This devotional relationship to Him grants peace, sanity, and a fearless equanimity in the face of all that life can bring. As the relationship to the Divine Avatar unfolds, He unlocks the door of the body-mind to the inflow of His Spiritual Blessing. And then nothing is ever the same. One's life is profoundly purposed to go beyond all bondage to the ego and world, for He has Awakened the tangible, unshakable certainty that existence is Divine, and that He Himself, the Beloved of one's heart, is the very Form of Reality, Truth, and Real God.

Those whose hearts are given, in love, to Me, Fall into My Heart. Those who are Mine, because they are in love with Me, no longer demand to be fulfilled through conditional experience and through the survival (or perpetuation) of the ego-"I". Their love for Me grants them Access to Me, and (Thus) to My Love-Bliss—because I Am Love-Ananda, the Divine Love-Bliss, in Person.

What will My lover do but love Me? I suffer every form and condition of every one who loves Me, because I Love My devotee As My own Form, My own Condition. I Love My devotee As the One by Whom I Am Distracted.

I Grant all My own Divine and "Bright" Excesses to those who love Me, in exchange for all their doubts and sufferings. Those who "Bond" themselves to Me, through love-surrender, are inherently Free of fear and wanting need. They transcend the ego-"I" (the cause of all conditional experience), and they (cause and all and All) Dissolve in Me—for I Am the Heart of all-and-All, and I Am the Heart Itself, and the Heart Itself Is the Only Reality, Truth, and Real God of all-and-All.

What is a Greater Message than This?

—Avatar Adi Da Samraj
Da Love-Ananda Gita

Adidam Samrajashram, 2003

AN INVITATION

Becoming a Formal Devotee of Avatar Adi Da

This book has a simple message: The Very Divine Person has Appeared in human Form, as Avatar Adi Da, in order to Reveal the Way of Real-God-Realization to all beings.

That Way, the Way of Adidam, is an ecstatic life of Communion with Real God, through the devotional and Spiritual relationship with Avatar Adi Da.

As Avatar Adi Da's devotee, you enter into devotional Communion with Him, and directly receive His Spiritual Blessing, and His Instruction, through which He Liberates you from the egoic suffering of self-distracted seeking.

The Way of Adidam is about an ecstatic Spiritual life, a life that is not bound and merely suffering but that is moved beyond that context into the larger and truly Spiritual dimension of real existence. That Spiritual Awakening is not merely something that occurs far into the future of the Way of Adidam. It is there after a base time of preparation—the student-beginner stage. And the base time of preparation as a student-beginner is itself an ecstatic practice and a positive, self-purifying life.

As a student-beginner, you begin to develop the fundamental practice of devotional resort to Avatar Adi Da—expressed in life through meditative feeling-Contemplation of Him and sacramental worship of Him, through direct service to Him and His Work, and through embrace of the life-positive disciplines He has Given to His devotees (as ways to magnify the energy and attention available for the life of devotional resort to Him). Once you have established this foundation, you are invited into Avatar Adi Da's physical Company to be directly Spiritually Initiated by Him—into the primary practice of searchlessly Beholding Him. You make a pilgrimage to Avatar Adi Da's Hermitage (wherever He may be residing at the time), where you enter into a period of retreat that is centered around sitting in His physical Company in special occasions of His Darshan.

When Avatar Adi Da has Graced you with His Spiritual Initiation, establishing the practice of searchlessly Beholding Him, your participation in the "culture of access" to Avatar Adi Da begins. Together with other devotees who have been Initiated, you participate daily in the life of Spiritually Awakened Invocation of Him. And you continue to return to the circumstance of retreat in His physical Company as often as you can—specifically, at times when you are prepared to receive His Spiritual Initiation into more advanced stages of the process.

Even from the beginning of your formal relationship with Avatar Adi Da as His devotee, you participate in the Global Ashram of Adidam—linked in real-time to Avatar Adi Da Samraj and His Hermitage Ashram via live (and recorded) internet broadcasts of His Darshan and other sacred events. You also have access to retreat and special celebrations at the Hermitage Ashrams Empowered by Avatar Adi Da.

This is a Spiritual opportunity literally unparalleled in the entire history of the Great Tradition of religious and Spiritual practice—the Way of Adidam is an entirely new Revelation that completes and fulfills all previous traditions.

Avatar Adi Da is the Promised God-Man, the miraculous Revelation of Real God, here in our time. To find out how you can become a formal devotee of Avatar Adi Da, and take up practice of the Way of Adidam, contact one of our centers, using the information given on the following pages.

What You Can Do Next—

Contact an Adidam center near you

■ To find out about becoming a formal devotee of Avatar Adi Da, and for information about upcoming courses, events, and seminars in your area:

AMERICAS
12040 North Seigler Road
Middletown, CA 95461 USA
1-707-928-4936

PACIFIC-ASIA
12 Seibel Road
Henderson
Auckland 1008
New Zealand
64-9-838-9114

AUSTRALIA
P.O. Box 244
Kew 3101
Victoria
1800 ADIDAM
(1800-234-326)

EUROPE-AFRICA
Annendaalderweg 10
6105 AT Maria Hoop
The Netherlands
31 (0)20 468 1442

THE UNITED KINGDOM
PO Box 20013
London, England
NW2 1ZA
0208-962-8855

EMAIL: **correspondence@adidam.org**

■ For more contact information about local Adidam groups, please see **www.adidam.org/centers**

Learn more about Avatar Adi Da's Liberating Offering to all

■ **ADIDAM**

The True World-Religion
Given by the Promised God-Man,
Adi Da Samraj

A Guide to the Unique Devotional
and Spiritual Relationship
Offered by the Ruchira Avatar,
Adi Da Samraj

A direct and simple summary of each of the fundamental aspects of the Way of Adidam. 194 pp., **$16.95**

I regard the work of Adi Da and his devotees as one of the most penetrating spiritual and social experiments happening on the planet in our era.

—JEFFREY MISHLOVE, Ph.D.
Host, PBS television series, "Thinking Allowed";
Author, *The Roots of Consciousness*

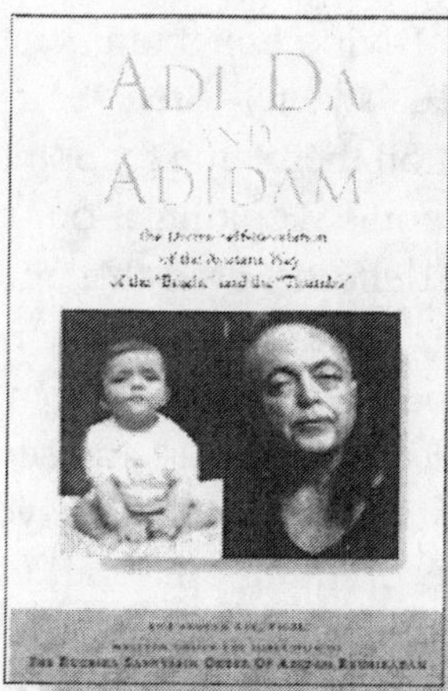

■ **ADI DA AND ADIDAM**

The Divine Self-Revelation
of the Avataric Way of
the "Bright" and the "Thumbs"

A 64-page introduction to Avatar Adi Da Samraj and His Unique Spiritual Revelation of the Way of Adidam.
$3.95

Read the Twenty-Three "Source-Texts" of Avatar Adi Da Samraj

In late 1969, in the brief period of three weeks, Avatar Adi Da wrote the original text of His literary masterwork, *The Mummery Book.* His writing of this book—which proved to be a remarkable prophecy of His Work to come—was the beginning of His immense Work of communicating His Revelation of Truth in words, both written an spoken. This outpouring lasted for 30 years, coming to a summary point in the years 1997–1999. During that period, Avatar Adi Da created a series of twenty-three books that He designated as His "Source-Texts". He incorporated into these books His most essential Writings and Discourses from all the preceding years, including many Writings and Discourses that had never been published previously. His "Source-Texts" are thus His Eternal Message to all. They contain His full Divine Self-Confession and His fully detailed description of the entire process of Awakening, culminating in seventh stage Divine Enlightenment.

Through the Revelation contained in His twenty-three "Source-Texts", Avatar Adi Da has brought to completion the search for Spiritual Truth that has occupied humankind for millennia. Looking at our current human situation in particular, He has demonstrated the untenability (and, indeed, the remarkable naivete, not to mention the negative influence) of the scientific materialist point of view, the point of view that (by asserting that the physical reality is the "only" and senior reality) creates an environment of doubt relative to everything beyond the physical domain—everything Divine, everything Spiritual, even everything psychic. And looking "back" at our entire history, He has "made sense" out of the welter of differing viewpoints in the Great

Tradition, demonstrating how they do, in fact, constitute a single (although complex) "design". And He has Made the Supreme Divine Offering that goes beyond what has ever been offered before—the Way that Realizes Permanent Indivisible Oneness with Him, the "Bright" Divine Reality Itself.

The twenty-three "Source-Texts" of Avatar Adi Da Samraj include:

- *The Dawn Horse Testament Of The Ruchira Avatar*
- *The Five Books Of The Heart Of The Adidam Revelation*
- *The Seventeen Companions Of The True Dawn Horse*

The Dawn Horse Testament

The Dawn Horse Testament Of The Ruchira Avatar

The "Testament Of Secrets" Of The Divine World-Teacher, Ruchira Avatar Adi Da Samraj

Avatar Adi Da's paramount "Source-Text" is a complete summary of the entire Way of Adidam. It flows seamlessly from His Self-Revelation in the Prologue and chapter one; through a "consideration" of His Life and Work, expositions of His fundamental Teaching-Arguments and the fundamental practices He Gives to His devotees, and incisive descriptions of the egoic patterns of individual beings and human collectives; through the course of the stages of the Way of Adidam, culminating in seventh stage Divine Enlightenment; to the declaration of the Establishment of the Realization of the "Bright" and the Perpetual Revelation of the "Bright" via the Agency of His Work and Word and Person.

This Great Divine Testament is unparalleled in its magnitude and depth. No scripture like it has ever been seen before. It is the first and only <u>complete</u> account of the <u>entire</u> Divine Way of utter ego-transcendence and dissolution in the "Brightness" of Real God.

The Dawn Horse Testament is truly the core of Avatar Adi Da's twenty-three "Source-Texts". Indeed, all of the "Five Books" and most of the "Seventeen Companions" are built around a central text drawn from *The Dawn Horse Testament*.

The Five Books Of The Heart Of The Adidam Revelation

The Five Books Of The Heart Of The Adidam Revelation comprise a complete summary of Who Avatar Adi Da Samraj Is and the Way that He Offers. The "Five Books" are key readings for all who are moved to study the Essence of His Revelation and His Way.

BOOK ONE:

Aham Da Asmi
(Beloved, I Am Da)

The "Late-Time" Avataric Revelation Of The True and Spiritual Divine Person (The egoless Personal Presence Of Reality and Truth, Which Is The Only Real God)

Avatar Adi Da's Self-Revelation of His own Divine Person and His Impulse to Bless and Liberate all.

BOOK TWO:

Ruchira Avatara Gita
(The Avataric Way Of The Divine Heart-Master)

The "Late-Time" Avataric Revelation Of The Great Secret Of The Divinely Self-Revealed Way That Most Perfectly Realizes The True and Spiritual Divine Person (The egoless Personal Presence Of Reality and Truth, Which Is The Only Real God)

Avatar Adi Da's Offering of the devotional and Spiritual relationship to Him, in the traditional manner of Guru-devotion.

BOOK THREE:

Da Love-Ananda Gita
(The Free Gift Of The Divine Love-Bliss)

The "Late-Time" Avataric Revelation Of The Great Means To Worship and To Realize The True and Spiritual Divine Person (The egoless Personal Presence Of Reality and Truth, Which Is The Only Real God)

The foundation (devotional) practice of heart-Communion with Avatar Adi Da Samraj: Simply turning the four principal human faculties—body, emotion, mind, and breath—to Him.

BOOK FOUR:

Hridaya Rosary (Four Thorns Of Heart-Instruction)

The "Late-Time" Avataric Revelation Of The Universally Tangible Divine Spiritual Body, Which Is The Supreme Agent Of The Great Means To Worship and To Realize The True and Spiritual Divine Person (The egoless Personal Presence Of Reality and Truth, Which Is The Only Real God)

The Spiritually Awakened practice of heart-Communion with Avatar Adi Da Samraj: Searchless Beholding of Him and reception of His Divine Spiritual Transmission—more and more allowing oneself to open Upwardly to Him, such that body, emotion, mind, and breath are "Melted" by His down-Flowing Spiritual Infusion.

BOOK FIVE:

Eleutherios (The Only Truth That Sets The Heart Free)

The "Late-Time" Avataric Revelation Of The "Perfect Practice" Of The Great Means To Worship and To Realize The True and Spiritual Divine Person (The egoless Personal Presence Of Reality and Truth, Which Is The Only Real God)

Heart-Communion with Avatar Adi Da Samraj beyond the four faculties, in the Domain of Consciousness Itself: Realizing Avatar Adi Da Samraj—As the "Bright" Itself, or the Conscious Light of Reality (having transcended identification with body, emotion, mind, and breath).

The Seventeen Companions Of The True Dawn Horse

The "True Dawn Horse" is a reference to *The Dawn Horse Testament Of The Ruchira Avatar.* Each of *The Seventeen Companions Of The True Dawn Horse* is a "Companion" to *The Dawn Horse Testament* in the sense that it is an elaboration of a principal theme (or a group of principal themes) from *The Dawn Horse Testament.* Among the "Seventeen Companions" are included Avatar Adi Da's two tellings of His own Life-Story, as autobiography (*The Knee Of Listening*) and as archetypal parable (*The Mummery Book*).

The Seventeen Companions Of The True Dawn Horse are a vast field of Revelation, which can be "considered" from many points of view. Presented here is one way of understanding the interrelationships between these "Source-Texts" and the flow of Argument they collectively represent.

Paradigms of Reality:

The Real Nature of God, Cosmos, and Realization

BOOK ONE:

Real God Is The Indivisible Oneness Of Unbroken Light

Reality, Truth, and The "Non-Creator" God In The True World-Religion Of Adidam

The Nature of Real God and the nature of the cosmos. Why ultimate questions cannot be answered either by conventional religion or by science.

BOOK TWO:

The Truly Human New World-Culture Of Unbroken Real-God-Man

The Eastern Versus The Western Traditional Cultures Of Mankind, and The Unique New Non-Dual Culture Of The True World-Religion Of Adidam

The Eastern and Western approaches to religion, and to life altogether—and how the Way of Adidam goes beyond this apparent dichotomy.

BOOK THREE:

The Only Complete Way To Realize The Unbroken Light Of Real God

An Introductory Overview Of The "Radical" Divine Way Of The True World-Religion Of Adidam

The entire course of the Way of Adidam—the unique principles underlying Adidam, and the unique culmination of Adidam in Divine Enlightenment.

Original Writings and Talks:

Avatar Adi Da's First Teaching-Communications

BOOK FOUR:

The Knee Of Listening

The Divine Ordeal Of The Avataric Incarnation Of Conscious Light—The Spiritual Autobiography Of The Divine World-Teacher, Ruchira Avatar Adi Da Samraj

Avatar Adi Da's autobiographical account of the years from His Birth to His Divine Re-Awakening in 1970—His Demonstration, in His own Life, of the Way to Realize Real God most perfectly—also including His Revelation of how His Avataric Incarnation was made possible and His Confession of the nature and significance of the Great Events of Yogic Death that have occurred in His Life since His Divine Re-Awakening in 1970.

BOOK FIVE:

The Divine Siddha-Method Of The Ruchira Avatar

The Divine Way Of Adidam Is An ego-Transcending Relationship, Not An ego-Centric Technique

Avatar Adi Da's earliest Talks to His devotees, on the fundamental principles of the devotional relationship to Him and "radical" understanding of the ego. Accompanied by His summary statements on His relationship to Swami Muktananda and on His own unique Teaching-Work and Blessing-Work.

Book Six:
The Mummery Book
A Parable Of The Divine True Love, Told By Means Of A Self-Illuminated Illustration Of The Totality Of Mind

Avatar Adi Da's literary masterpiece—a work of astonishing poetry and deeply evocative archetypal drama. It is Avatar Adi Da's life-transforming message about how to Realize the Absolute Truth in the midst of the chaos and tragedy of human experience.

An extraordinarily beautiful and potent "prose opera", *The Mummery Book* is both a highly experimental novel (drawing fully on the twentieth-century "stream" of experimental fiction) and an immense theatrical piece. Thus, *The Mummery Book* can either be read as a book or performed as a theatrical event.

A "mummery" is "a ridiculous, hypocritical, or pretentious ceremony or performance". This, Avatar Adi Da is telling us, is what human life amounts to—if we merely live as the separate ego-self. And the only way "out" of this mummery is to relinquish ego—by finding, receiving, and conforming ourselves to the Divine True Love.

In *The Mummery Book*, Adi Da confronts head-on the central agony of born existence: that everything and everyone—ourselves, and everyone we love—dies. The hero of *The Mummery Book*, Raymond Darling, goes through an extraordinary series of adventures and ordeals—centered around his search for his beloved, a lady named Quandra—in the course of his ultimate overcoming of the inescapable fact of mortality. The story of Raymond Darling is, in fact, Avatar Adi Da's telling of His own Life-Story in the language of parable—including His unflinching portrayal of how the unconverted ego makes religion (and life altogether) into a meaningless mummery. Ultimately, *The Mummery Book* is the "Story" of Consciousness Realizing Its Indivisible Oneness with Energy (or Its own Radiance).

Esoteric Principles and Practices:

Revelations of Divine Oneness, Divine Spiritual Transmission, and the means of conforming the body-mind to the Divine Spiritual Process

BOOK SEVEN:

He-and-She Is Me

The Indivisibility Of Consciousness and Light In The Divine Body Of The Ruchira Avatar

One of Avatar Adi Da's most esoteric Revelations—His Primary "Incarnation" in the Cosmic domain as the "He" of the Divine Consciousness, the "She" of the Divine Light, and the "Son" of "He" and "She" in the "Me" of His Divine Spiritual Body.

BOOK EIGHT:

Ruchira Shaktipat Yoga

The Divine (and Not Merely Cosmic) Spiritual Baptism In The Divine Way Of Adidam

The Divine Heart-Power (Ruchira Shakti) uniquely Transmitted by Avatar Adi Da Samraj, and how it differs from the various traditional forms of Spiritual Baptism, particularly Kundalini Yoga.

BOOK NINE:

Ruchira Tantra Yoga

The Physical-Spiritual (and Truly Religious) Method Of Mental, Emotional, Sexual, and Whole Bodily Health and Enlightenment In The Divine Way Of Adidam

The transformation of life in the realms of money, food, and sex. Includes: understanding "victim-consciousness"; the ego as addict; the secret of how to change; going beyond the "Oedipal" sufferings of childhood; the right orientation to money; right diet; life-positive and Spiritually auspicious sexual practice, and so on.

Stages of Life:

The six potential stages of ego-based life, and the Divine seventh stage of life

BOOK TEN:

The Seven Stages Of Life

Transcending The Six Stages Of egoic Life, and Realizing The ego-Transcending Seventh Stage Of Life, In The Divine Way Of Adidam

The stages of human development from birth to Divine Enlightenment. How the stages relate to physical and esoteric anatomy. The errors of each of the first six stages of life, and the unique egolessness of the seventh stage of life. Avatar Adi Da's Self-Confession as the first, last, and only seventh stage Adept-Realizer.

BOOK ELEVEN:

The All-Completing and Final Divine Revelation To Mankind

A Summary Description Of The Supreme Yoga Of The Seventh Stage Of Life In The Divine Way Of Adidam

The ultimate secrets of Divine Enlightenment—including the four-stage Process of Divine Enlightenment, culminating in Translation into the Infinitely Love-Blissful Divine Self-Domain.

Process of Adidam:

Five Comprehensive Views of the Practice of Adidam

BOOK TWELVE:

What, Where, When, How, Why, and Who To Remember To Be Happy

A Simple Explanation Of The Divine Way Of Adidam (For Children, and Everyone Else)

A text written specifically for children but inspiring to all—with accompanying Essays and Talks on Divine Ignorance, religious practices for children and young people in the Way of Adidam, and the fundamental practice of whole bodily devotion to Avatar Adi Da Samraj.

BOOK THIRTEEN:
No Seeking / Mere Beholding
The Always Primary Practice Of The Divine Way Of Adidam

A comprehensive summary of the always primary practice of the Way of Adidam—which is searchless Beholding of Avatar Adi Da Samraj—including detailed Instruction relative to rightly participating in the unique opportunity of retreat in Avatar Adi Da's physical Company.

BOOK FOURTEEN:
Santosha Adidam
The Essential Summary Of The Divine Way Of Adidam

An extended overview of the entire course of the Way of Adidam, based on the esoteric anatomy of the human being and its correlation to the progressive stages of life.

BOOK FIFTEEN:
The Lion Sutra
The "Perfect Practice" Teachings In The Divine Way Of Adidam

Practice in the ultimate stages of the Way of Adidam. How the practitioner of Adidam approaches—and passes over—the "Threshold" of Divine Enlightenment.

BOOK SIXTEEN:
The Overnight Revelation Of Conscious Light
The "My House" Discourses On The Indivisible Tantra Of Adidam

A vast and profound "consideration" of the fundamental Tantric principles of true Spiritual life and the "Always Already" Nature of the Divine Reality.

Great Tradition:

The Total Spiritual "Effort" of Humanity as a Unified (and Progressive) Process

BOOK SEVENTEEN:

The Basket Of Tolerance

The Perfect Guide To Perfectly Unified Understanding Of The One and Great Tradition Of Mankind, and Of The Divine Way Of Adidam As The Perfect Completing Of The One and Great Tradition Of Mankind

The Basket Of Tolerance is a book like no other—simultaneously an unprecedented Spiritual Revelation and an extraordinary intellectual document.

While Avatar Adi Da's other twenty-two "Source-Texts" are focused in His exposition of the Way of Adidam, *The Basket Of Tolerance* is His comprehensive examination of the Great Tradition of mankind—in other words, of the global and historical context within which He has made His Revelation of the Way of Adidam. Thus, *The Basket Of Tolerance* focuses on the immense variety of historical expressions of the religious and Spiritual search, from prehistoric times to the present.

The core of *The Basket Of Tolerance* is a bibliographical listing of 5,000 documents (in all media—print and audio-visual), meticulously ordered by Avatar Adi Da in an elaborately subdivided sequence, to form a continuous "Argument". Avatar Adi Da introduces that "Argument" with a series of groundbreaking Essays, and He comments on the bibliographical "Argument", at numerous points, through a further series of over 100 essays relating to specific books (or groups of books) in the bibliography (covering a wide spectrum of topics).

Through the "Argument" of this annotated bibliography, Avatar Adi Da examines in detail the entire human religious search and demonstrates how there is truly a single process, composed of distinct (hierarchically related) stages (corresponding to the fourth, the fifth, and the sixth stages of life), evident in all the diversity of human religious history (previous to His Appearance here)—a process of which any given religious tradition represents a "piece". While Avatar Adi Da's examination of the Great Tradition concentrates on the various global manifestations of religion and Spirituality, it also embraces the "practical" issues that relate to the human process of the first three stages of life—such as understanding (and right participation in the process) of death, understanding (and right use) of the function of mind, right circulation of energy within the body, right physical exercise of the body, right diet, right emotional-sexual practice (whether sexually active or celibate), right living in the collective human context, and so forth.

Altogether, *The Basket Of Tolerance* is the elaborately detailed "proof" that there is, indeed, a "perennial philosophy". This "philosophy", however, is not a single "set" of unified "beliefs". Rather, it is a process, composed of distinctly different stages—and the points of view of the successive stages do not necessarily agree with one another. Furthermore, those stages are not (ultimately) based on conceptual differences but on experiential differences relating to the various aspects of the esoteric anatomy of the human structure.

Study other books and recordings
by and about Avatar Adi Da Samraj

■ To find out about and order "Source-Texts", books, tapes, CDs, and videos by and about Avatar Adi Da, contact your local Adidam regional center, or contact the Adidam Emporium at:

1-877-770-0772 (from within North America)
1-707-928-6653 (from outside North America)

Or order online from: **www.dawnhorsepress.com**

Support Avatar Adi Da's Work and the Way of Adidam

■ If you are moved to serve Avatar Adi Da's Spiritual Work specifically through advocacy and/or financial patronage, please contact:

Advocacy
12040 North Seigler Road
Middletown, CA 95461
phone: (707) 928-0103
email: advocacy@adidam.org

For young people: Join the Adidam Youth Fellowship

■ Young people under 21 can participate in the "Adidam Youth Fellowship"—either as a friend or practicing member. Adidam Youth Fellowship members participate in study programs, retreats, celebrations, and other events with other young people responding to Avatar Adi Da. To learn more about the Youth Fellowship, call or write:

Vision of Mulund Institute (VMI)
10336 Loch Lomond Road, PMB 146
Middletown, CA 95461
phone: (707) 928-6932
fax: (707) 928-5619
email: vmi@adidam.org

The Ruchira Sannyasin Hermitage Ashrams Spiritually Empowered by Avatar Adi Da Samraj

Traditionally, Realizers have been provided with set-apart places where they were free to do their Spiritual Work in an appropriate and secluded circumstance. And these places became Spiritually Empowered through their Presence and Work.

In this traditional manner, devotees of Avatar Adi Da have provided places where He is completely set apart to do His Blessing-Work for the sake of humanity as a whole, as well as His specific Spiritual Work with devotees who come on pilgrimage to receive the Initiatory Spiritual Blessing of being in His physical Company on retreat.

My Work for the entire world is My Divine Blessing-Work, Which I do principally in seclusion. I live in perpetual retreat in a hermitage mode, and receive those of My devotees who are rightly prepared in that circumstance. Sometimes I roam in public circumstances, in order to have contact with people in general. But, fundamentally, I remain in hermitage retreat.

—Avatar Adi Da Samraj

Avatar Adi Da Samraj moves among the various Hermitage Ashrams in His spontaneous Wandering-Work of world-Blessing.

Spiritually, He is perpetually "in residence" at each of His Hermitage Sanctuaries. This is because He has Invested Himself Spiritually in these sacred places, and His Spiritual Power and Presence is constantly active in all of them.

Adidam Samrajashram
the Island of Naitauba in Fiji

Adidam Samrajashram is Avatar Adi Da's principal Hermitage Ashram and the primary Seat from which His Divine Spiritual Blessing Flows to the entire world.

The Mountain Of Attention Sanctuary of Adidam
in northern California

Da Love-Ananda Mahal
in Hawaii

Notes to the text of *Adi Da: The Promised God-Man Is Here*

INTRODUCTION

1. The Sanskrit word "Siddha" means "a completed, fulfilled, or perfected one", or "one of perfect accomplishment, or power".

2. The Sanskrit word "Samadhi" traditionally denotes various exalted states that appear in the context of esoteric meditation and Realization.

3. This practice of turning the faculties to Avatar Adi Da Samraj is called "Ruchira Avatara Bhakti Yoga", or the practice (yoga) of devotion (bhakti) to the "Bright" (Ruchira) Incarnation of the Divine (Avatara), Adi Da Samraj.

CHAPTER 1

4. The root meaning of "Franklin Albert Jones" is "the highly-born (Al-) 'Bright' (-bert) Free Man (Franklin) through Whom God is Gracious ('Jones', a derivative of 'John')".

5. Avatar Adi Da uses the word "gross" to mean "made up of material (or physical) elements". The gross (or physical) dimension is, therefore, associated with the physical body, and also with experience in the waking state.

6. Devotees of Avatar Adi Da often address Him with the intimate Title of respect and acknowledgement, "Beloved".

7. In the Greek myth of Narcissus, the beautiful youth is cursed to fall in love with himself. When he discovers his own image reflected in a pond, he is completely enamored and stays by the pond, contemplating his own image, until he eventually dies of a broken heart.

CHAPTER 2

8. Rang Avadhoot (1898–1968) was a Realizer in the tradition of Dattatreya (a Hindu deity traditionally regarded as an Avatar of Brahma, Vishnu, and Siva).

9. For a more detailed description of Swami Nityananda's Instruction (given from the subtle dimension) to Avatar Adi Da, see chapter 14 of *The Knee Of Listening* and "I (Alone) Am The Adidam Revelation" (which appears in a number of His "Source-Texts").

10. Paramahansa Yogananda (1893–1952), the author of *Autobiography of a Yogi*, taught what he called "Kriya Yoga".

11. Jnaneshwar (1275–1296) was a great Siddha of Maharashtra, India. He was a venerated leader of the Hindu bhakti movement, and wrote the *Jnaneshwari*, a poetic commentary on the *Bhagavad Gita*.

Milarepa (1040–1123) is one of the most revered personages in Tibetan Buddhism, famous for the extremely intense austerities he undertook at the behest of his teacher, Marpa the Translator.

12. Gautama Shakyamuni (circa 563–483 B.C.E.) is the great Indian Sage commonly known as "the Buddha".

Hui Neng (638–713), one of the best-known figures in Chinese Buddhism, is regarded as one of the founders of the Zen (or Ch'an) tradition. His talks and sermons are recorded in the *Platform Sutra*.

Shankara (788–820), one of the greatest Hindu Sages, is perhaps the best known exponent of the tradition of Advaita Vedanta.

Ramana Maharshi (1879–1950) was a great Indian Sage, who Realized the Transcendental Self at a young age. An Ashram was established around him at Tiruvannamalai in South India, which continues today.

13. "Purusha" and "Siva" are traditional Hindu names for the Divine Being Itself, or Divine Consciousness. "Siva" is sometimes pictured as a ferocious male Deity, or the "Destroyer", but, in His more benign aspect, is essentially the same as "Purusha".

14. The Sanskrit term "Siva-Shakti" is an esoteric description of the Divine Being. "Siva" is a name for the Divine Being Itself, or Divine Consciousness. "Shakti" is a name for the All-Pervading Spirit-Power (or Energy) of the Divine Being. "Siva-Shakti" is thus the Unity of the Divine Consciousness and Its own Spirit-Power (or Energy).

15. In the Hindu tradition, Brahman is the Ultimate Divine Reality That is the Source and Substance of all things, all worlds, and all beings.

16. In the Hindu tradition, Atman (with a capital "A") is the Divine Self.

17. "Nirvana" is a Buddhist term for the Unqualified Reality beyond suffering, ego, birth, and death. The "Nirvanic Ground" indicates the same Reality.

CHAPTER 3

18. The Indian Spiritual Master Ramakrishna (1836–1886) was a renowned ecstatic, and a lifelong devotee of the Goddess Kali, a form of the "Mother-Shakti". In the course of his Spiritual practice, Ramakrishna spontaneously embraced many different religious and Spiritual disciplines, eventually Realizing a state of profound mystical union with the Divine.

19. This book is now titled *The Divine Siddha-Method Of The Ruchira Avatar*, and is one of Avatar Adi Da's twenty-three "Source-Texts".

20. "Bubba" was also one of Avatar Adi Da's childhood nicknames.

CHAPTER 4

21. "Siddhi" is Sanskrit for "power", or "accomplishment". "Siddhi" is used both as a general term for Avatar Adi Da's Divine Spiritual Blessing-Power and as a reference to specific aspects of the Divine Power He manifests in His Blessing-Work.

CHAPTER 5

22. The "Great Tradition" is Avatar Adi Da's term for the total inheritance of human, cultural, religious, magical, mystical, Spiritual, Transcendental, and Divine paths, philosophies, and testimonies from all the eras and cultures of humanity—which inheritance has (in the present era of worldwide communication) become the common legacy of humankind.

23. See, for example, *Kundalini: The Evolutionary Energy in Man*, by Gopi Krishna (Berkeley, Calif.: Shambala, 1971).

24. Natural life-energy and the Divine Spirit-Current move through the body in a Circle of descent and ascent—down the front and up the back. The frontal dimension of the personality is epitomized in the frontal line, or the pathway through which both natural life-energy and the Divine Spirit-Energy descend down the front of the body, from the crown of the head to the bodily base. The spinal line is a primary pathway through which both natural life-energy and the Divine Spirit-Energy ascend up the back of the body, from the bodily base to the crown of the head. The frontal line is associated with the gross (or physical) dimension of the body-mind, while the spinal line is associated with the subtle (or higher mental, psychic, and mystical) dimension of the body-mind.

25. For a description of the frontal dimension of the personality, see note 24 above.

CHAPTER 6

26. "Left-hand" Tantra is the mode of Tantra in which otherwise "forbidden" substances and activities are used as skillful means. In the "right-hand" schools of Tantra, such "forbidden" substances are not used.

CHAPTER 7

27. The Tantric traditions of Hinduism and Buddhism describe as "heroic" the practice of an individual whose impulse to Liberation and commitment to his or her Guru are so strong that all circumstances of life, even those traditionally regarded as inauspicious for Spiritual practice (such as consumption of intoxicants and engagement in sexual activity), can rightly be made use of as part of the Spiritual process.

Avatar Adi Da's uniquely "Heroic" Ordeal, however, was undertaken not for His own sake, but in order to discover, through His own experience, what is necessary for all beings to Realize the Truth. As the Divine Person, it was necessary for Him to have experienced the entire gamut of human seeking, in order to be able to Teach any and all that came to Him.

28. Avatar Adi Da has Revealed that His Divine Spiritual Body Appears everywhere in the cosmic domain in the Form of Primal Divine Sound and Primal Divine Light. In His Light-Form, He Appears as a brilliant white five-pointed Star.

In The Form Of My Divine Sound Of Thunder and In The Form Of My Divine Star Of Light, I Everywhere Appear, and (By Means Of My Avatarically Self-Transmitted Divine Grace) I May (By every one) Be Heard and Seen (Directly and Infinitely Above the body-mind)—At The conditional Source-Point Above this world (and every world). [The Dawn Horse Testament Of The Ruchira Avatar]

29. Puja is formal sacramental worship.

30. Avatar Adi Da uses the metaphor of the "dog" and "washing the dog" to Indicate the purification of the body-mind in the process of Adidam. He addresses the presumption (as in the Kundalini Yoga tradition) that the Spiritual process requires a spinal Yoga, or an effort of arousing Spiritual Energy literally at the "tail" end of the "dog" (the bodily base, or the muladhara chakra), and then drawing It up (or allowing It to ascend) through the spinal line to the head (and above). In contrast, Avatar Adi Da Samraj has Revealed (particularly in His *Hridaya Rosary*) that, in reality, the human being can be truly purified and Liberated (or the "dog" can be "washed") only by receiving His Divine Blessing-Power (or Hridaya-Shakti) and Spiritual Person downward from Infinitely Above the head to the bodily base.

CHAPTER 8

31. The celebration of "the Day of the Heart" is now called "The Great Sovereign-Avataric Holy Day of the Divine Re-Awakening".

CHAPTER 9

32. Shirdi Sai Baba employed a mysterious method of working with his devotees, or granting them the power of his Blessing, by frequently handling a group of coins, which (it is said) he used as representations of his devotees. Acknowledging that He also Worked in a similar manner during His Teaching years, Avatar Adi Da sometimes referred to any small group of His devotees through whom He was Working (at a particular time) to serve all His devotees (and even all beings) as His "coins".

33. The N-factor is the unknown determining factor, the Unaccountable Mystery on which conditional existence depends.

34. For a description of the "consideration" of the forerunners of Avatar Adi Da's Birth, see chapter 12.

35. Avatar Adi Da has Revealed that, just as there is a physical anatomy, there is also an actual Spiritual anatomy (or structure) that is present in every human being. As He says in *The Basket Of Tolerance*, it is because of this structure that the "experiential and developmental process of Growth and Realization demonstrates itself in accordance with what I have Revealed and Demonstrated to be the seven stages of life".

See *The Seven Stages Of Life* or *Santosha Adidam* for a further description of the esoteric Spiritual anatomy of Man.

CHAPTER 10

36. The requirements relative to an exclusively raw diet applied to those in leadership positions at that particular time and is no longer a requirement for any practitioner of Adidam. While celibacy is not required, the sexual discipline in the Way

of Adidam is a personal "consideration" within the context of a specific range of guidelines for the individual's level of practice and intentions relative to renunciation.

37. The "Perfect Practice" of Adidam is devotional and Spiritual Communion with Avatar Adi Da in the context of the Awakening to the point of view of Consciousness, beyond the points of view of body or mind.

38. *The Lion Sutra* was originally titled *Love-Ananda Gita.*

39. "Yajna" is Sanskrit for "sacrifice". Avatar Adi Da's entire Life may be rightly characterized as a Sacrifice, or Yajna, for the sake of bringing His Divine Gifts to all. In the Way of Adidam, the term "Yajna" is specifically used to refer to Avatar Adi Da's occasional travels, during which He Blesses the world and all beings through His contact with many people and places.

CHAPTER 11

40. See B. V. Narasimha Swami and S. Subbarao, *Sage of Sakuri*, 4th ed. (Bombay: Shri B. T. Wagh, 1966), pp. 190–191, 204.

41. In March 2000, in response to a letter from the author, Avatar Adi Da confirmed her intuition that He was conceived on February 18, 1939. The sacred reasons offered to Him were as follows:

In the account of the meeting between the Shankaracharya and Upasani Baba, the story goes on to say that following the prophetic conversation between them, the Shankaracharya spent Sivaratri at Upasani Baba's Ashram. Sivaratri is a traditional lunar festival honoring Siva and his consort Parvati that is held in India each year between mid-February and early March. For Sivaratri—the celebration of Siva in embrace with his consort—to have been the moment of Avatar Adi Da's Conception fits perfectly with the nature of the Divine Avatar's Incarnation and Work. It is a sacred prefiguring of His sacred Union with the "Divine Goddess" at the Vedanta Temple, bringing an end to her independence as "maya".

The possibility that Sivaratri coincided with Avatar Adi Da's conception grows on the grounds that, in 1939, Sivaratri fell on February 18, which happens to be the birthday of Avatar Adi Da's father, Frank Jones, and also of Ramakrishna (born 1836), whose great significance as a precursor of Beloved Adi Da's Incarnation is described in chapter 12. These sacred conjunctions, combined with the human reality that February 18 was a day of intimate celebration for His parents (being His father's birthday), moved Avatar Adi Da to accept that on February 18, 1939, His human vehicle was conceived.

42. "Tcha" is Avatar Adi Da's characteristic sound of Blessing.

CHAPTER 12

43. "Fakir" in Arabic literally means "poor", and it may be used to mean either material impoverishment or the virtue of an aspirant making himself or herself "poor" by ceasing to be self-centered. For a full account of this incident, see *The*

Life of Swami Vivekananda, Volume One, by his Eastern and Western Disciples (Calcutta: Advaita Ashram, revised and enlarged edition, 1979), pp. 182–83.

44. In view of this, it is a remarkable coincidence that Ramakrishna's birthday, February 18, was also the birthday of Avatar Adi Da's father, Franklin Augustus Jones.

45. Marie Louise Burke, the principal Western biographer of Swami Vivekananda, has confirmed that Swami Vivekananda most likely would have visited Kew Gardens, since he spent so much time in London and this was exactly the type of place he liked to visit.

CHAPTER 14

46. M. U. Hatengdi, *Nityananda: The Divine Presence* (Cambridge, Mass.: Rudra Press, 1984).

CHAPTER 15

47. "Mahasamadhi" ("Great Samadhi") is a Sanskrit term for the death of a great Realizer.

48. Such individuals include Amma and Swami Prakashananda.

CHAPTER 16

49. "Bhava" is a Sanskrit word used to refer to the enraptured feeling-swoon of Communion with the Divine. When Avatar Adi Da's devotees refer to His Bhava, they are speaking of this Divine State. In this case, Avatar Adi Da is referring to Divine Translation, the final stage of Divine Enlightenment, in which the conditional reality drops away permanently, "Outshined" in the "Brightness" of Reality Itself. See note 50.

50. The completion of the process of Divine Translation is the physical death of the Realizer. Avatar Adi Da has stated that the process of Divine Translation could be likened to clay pots in a kiln. As the kiln heats, the clay pots get brighter and brighter. First, they begin to glow as individual forms. Eventually, the heat is such that it is simply white, and no distinct forms are noticed.

51. "Midnight Sun" is a term Avatar Adi Da uses to refer to His Revelation of the esoteric visionary representation of Reality as a White Sphere in a black field.

52. The traditional Sanskrit term "urdhvareta" refers to the Yogic practice of reversing the flow of aroused sexual energy such that it flows up the spinal line rather than being discharged through the genitals. In the Lopez Island Event, the Up-turning of energy in Avatar Adi Da's Body included all natural bodily energy and Spiritual Energy, not simply sexual energy.

CHAPTER 17

53. "Quandra" is the principal female character in Avatar Adi Da's literary masterwork, *The Mummery Book.* "Loka" means "place" or "realm".

An Invitation to Support Adidam

Avatar Adi Da Samraj's sole Purpose is to act as a Source of continuous Divine Grace for everyone, everywhere. In that spirit, He is a Free Renunciate and He owns nothing. Those who have made gestures in support of Avatar Adi Da's Work have found that their generosity is returned in many Blessings that are full of His healing, transforming, and Liberating Grace—and those Blessings flow not only directly to them as the beneficiaries of His Work, but to many others, even all others. At the same time, all tangible gifts of support help secure and nurture Avatar Adi Da's Work in necessary and practical ways, again similarly benefiting the entire world. Because all this is so, supporting His Work is the most auspicious form of financial giving, and we happily extend to you an invitation to serve Adidam through your financial support.

You may make a financial contribution in support of the Work of Adi Da Samraj at any time. You may also, if you choose, request that your contribution be used for one or more specific purposes.

If you are moved to help support and develop the Hermitage circumstance provided for Avatar Adi Da and the other members of the Ruchira Sannyasin Order, the senior renunciate order of Adidam, you may do so by making your contribution to The Da Love-Ananda Samrajya, the Australian charitable trust which has central responsibility for the Sacred Treasure of the Ruchira Sannyasin Order.

To do this: (1) if you do not pay taxes in the United States, make your check payable directly to "The Da Love-Ananda Samrajya Pty Ltd" (which serves as the trustee of the trust) and mail it to The Da Love-Ananda Samrajya at P.O. Box 4744, Samabula, Suva, Fiji; and (2) if you do pay taxes in the United States and you would like your contribution to be tax-deductible under U.S. laws, make your check payable to "The Avataric Pan-Communion of Adidam", indicate on your check or accompanying letter that you would like your contribution used for the work of The Da Love-Ananda Samrajya, and mail your check to the Advocacy Department of Adidam at 12180 Ridge Road, Middletown, California 95461, USA.

If you are moved to help support and provide for one of the other purposes of Adidam—such as publishing the Sacred Literature of Avatar Adi Da, supporting Avatar Adi Da's Divine Image-Art, supporting any of the Sanctuaries He has Empowered, maintaining the Sacred Archives that preserve His recorded Talks and Writings, or publishing audio and video recordings of Avatar Adi Da—you may do so by making your contribution directly to The Avataric Pan-Communion of Adidam, specifying the particular purposes you wish to benefit, and mailing your check to the Advocacy Department of Adidam at the above address.

If you would like more information about these and other gifting options, or if you would like assistance in describing or making a contribution, please write to the Advocacy Department of Adidam at the above address or contact the Adidam Legal Department by telephone at 1-707-928-4612 or by FAX at 1-707-928-4062.

Planned Giving

We also invite you to consider making a planned gift in support of the Work of Avatar Adi Da Samraj. Many have found that through planned giving they can make a far more significant gesture of support than they would otherwise be able to make. Many have also found that by making a planned gift they are able to realize substantial tax advantages.

There are numerous ways to make a planned gift, including making a gift in your Will, or in your life insurance, or in a charitable trust.

If you would like to make a gift in your Will in support of the work of The Da Love-Ananda Samrajya: (1) if you do not pay taxes in the United States, simply include in your Will the statement, "I give to The Da Love-Ananda Samrajya Pty Ltd, as trustee of The Da Love-Ananda Samrajya, an Australian charitable trust, P.O. Box 4744, Samabula, Suva, Fiji, __________" [inserting in the blank the amount or description of your contribution]; and (2) if you do pay taxes in the United States and you would like your contribution to be free of estate taxes and to also reduce any estate taxes payable on the remainder of your estate, simply include in your Will the statement, "I give to The Avataric Pan-Communion of Adidam, a California non-profit corporation, 12040 North Seigler Road, Middletown, California 95461, USA, __________" [inserting in the blank the amount or description of your contribution].

To make a gift in your life insurance, simply name as the beneficiary (or one of the beneficiaries) of your life insurance policy the organization of your choice (The Da Love-Ananda Samrajya or The Avataric Pan-Communion of Adidam), according to the foregoing descriptions and addresses. If you are a United States taxpayer, you may receive significant tax benefits if you make a contribution to The Avataric Pan-Communion of Adidam through your life insurance.

We also invite you to consider establishing or participating in a charitable trust for the benefit of Adidam. If you are a United States taxpayer, you may find that such a trust will provide you with immediate tax savings and assured income for life, while at the same time enabling you to provide for your family, for your other heirs, and for the Work of Avatar Adi Da as well.

The Advocacy and Legal Departments of Adidam (located at 12180 Ridge Road, Middletown, California 95461, USA; telephone 1-707-928-4612; FAX: 1-707-928-4062) will be happy to provide you with further information about these and other planned gifting options, and happy to provide you or your attorney with assistance in describing or making a planned gift in support of the Work of Avatar Adi Da.

Further Notes to the Reader

An Invitation to Responsibility

Adidam, the Way of the Heart that Avatar Adi Da has Revealed, is an invitation to everyone to assume real responsibility for his or her life. As Avatar Adi Da has Said in *The Dawn Horse Testament Of The Ruchira Avatar,* "If any one Is Heart-Moved To Realize Me, Let him or her First Resort (Formally, and By Formal Heart-Vow) To Me, and (Thereby) Commence The Devotional (and, In Due Course, Spiritual) Process Of self-Observation, self-Understanding, and self-Transcendence. . . ." Therefore, participation in the Way of Adidam requires a real struggle with oneself, and not at all a struggle with Avatar Adi Da, or with others.

All who study the Way of Adidam or take up its practice should remember that they are responding to a Call to become responsible for themselves. They should understand that they, not Avatar Adi Da or others, are responsible for any decision they may make or action they may take in the course of their lives of study or practice. This has always been true, and it is true whatever the individual's involvement in the Way of Adidam, be it as one who studies Avatar Adi Da's Wisdom-Teaching or as a formally acknowledged member of Adidam.

Honoring and Protecting the Sacred Word through Perpetual Copyright

Since ancient times, practitioners of true religion and Spirituality have valued, above all, time spent in the Company of the Sat-Guru (or one who has, to any degree, Realized Real God, Truth, or Reality, and who, thus, serves the awakening process in others). Such practitioners understand that the Sat-Guru literally Transmits his or her (Realized) State to every one (and every thing) with whom (or with which) he or she comes in contact. Through this Transmission, objects, environments, and rightly prepared individuals with which the Sat-Guru has contact can become empowered, or imbued with the Sat-Guru's Transforming Power. It is by this process of empowerment that things and beings are made truly and literally sacred and holy, and things so sanctified thereafter function as a source of the Sat-Guru's Blessing for all who understand how to make right and sacred use of them.

Sat-Gurus of any degree of Realization and all that they empower are, therefore, truly Sacred Treasures, for they help draw the practitioner more quickly into the process of Realization. Cultures of true Wisdom have always understood that such Sacred Treasures are precious (and fragile) Gifts to humanity, and that they should be honored, protected, and reserved for right sacred use. Indeed, the word "holy" means "set apart", and, thus, that which is holy and sacred must be protected from insensitive secular interference and wrong use of any kind. Avatar Adi Da has Conformed His human Body-Mind Most Perfectly to the Divine Self, and He is, thus, the most Potent Source of Blessing-Transmission of Real God, or Truth Itself, or Reality Itself. He has for many years Empowered (or made sacred) special places and things, and these now serve as His Divine Agents, or as literal expressions and extensions of His Blessing-Transmission. Among these Empowered Sacred Treasures are His Wisdom-Teaching and His Divine Image-Art, which are full of His Transforming Power. These Blessed and Blessing Agents have the literal Power to serve Real-God-Realization in those who are Graced to receive them.

Therefore, Avatar Adi Da's Wisdom-Teaching and Divine Image-Art must be perpetually honored and protected, "set apart" from all possible interference and wrong use. The gathering of devotees of Avatar Adi Da is committed to the perpetual preservation and right honoring of the Sacred Wisdom-Teaching of the Way of Adidam and the Divine Image-Art of Adi Da Samraj. But it is also true that, in order to fully accomplish this, we must find support in the world-society in which we live and in its laws. Thus, we call for a world-society and for laws that acknowledge the sacred, and that permanently protect it from insensitive, secular interference and wrong use of any kind. We call for, among other things, a system of law that acknowledges that the Wisdom-Teaching of the Way of Adidam and the Divine Image-Art of Adi Da Samraj, in all their forms, are, because of their sacred nature, protected by perpetual copyright.

We invite others who respect the sacred to join with us in this call and in working toward its realization. And, even in the meantime, we claim that all copyrights to the Wisdom-Teaching and Divine Image-Art of Avatar Adi Da and the other Sacred Literature, recordings, and images of the Way of Adidam are of perpetual duration.

We make this claim on behalf of The Da Love-Ananda Samrajya Pty Ltd, which, acting as trustee of The Da Love-Ananda Samrajya, is the holder of all such copyrights.

Avatar Adi Da and the Sacred Treasures of Adidam

True Spiritual Masters have Realized Real God (to one degree or another), and, therefore, they bring great Blessing and introduce Divine Possibility to the world. Such Adept-Realizers Accomplish universal Blessing-Work that benefits everything and everyone. They also Work very specifically and intentionally with individuals who approach them as their devotees, and with those places where they reside and to which they direct their specific Regard for the sake of perpetual Spiritual Empowerment. This was understood in traditional Spiritual cultures, and, therefore, those cultures found ways to honor Adept-Realizers by providing circumstances for them where they were free to do their Spiritual Work without obstruction or interference.

Those who value Avatar Adi Da's Realization and Service have always endeavored to appropriately honor Him in this traditional way by providing a circumstance where He is completely Free to do His Divine Work. The Ruchira Sannyasin Hermitage Ashrams have been set aside by Avatar Adi Da's devotees worldwide as Places for Him to do His universal Blessing-Work for the sake of everyone, as well as His specific Work with those who pilgrimage to His Hermitage circumstance (wherever He may be residing at a given time) to receive the special Blessing of coming into His physical Company.

Avatar Adi Da is a legal renunciate. He owns nothing and He has no secular or religious institutional function. He Functions only in Freedom. He, and the other members of the Ruchira Sannyasin Order, the senior renunciate order of Adidam, are provided for by The Da Love-Ananda Samrajya, which also provides for His Hermitage circumstance and ensures the permanent integrity of Avatar Adi Da's Wisdom-Teaching and His Divine Image-Art, both in their archival and published forms. The Da Love-Ananda Samrajya exists exclusively to provide for these Sacred Treasures of Adidam.

The institution which has developed in response to Avatar Adi Da's Wisdom-Teaching and universal Blessing is known as "The Avataric Pan-Communion of Adidam". This formal organization is active worldwide in making Avatar Adi Da's Wisdom-Teaching available to all, in offering guidance to all who are moved to respond to His Offering, and in providing for the other Sacred Treasures of Adidam. In addition to the central corporate entity known as The Avataric Pan-Communion of Adidam, which is based in California, there are numerous regional entities which serve congregations of Avatar Adi Da's devotees in various places throughout the world.

Practitioners of Adidam worldwide have also established numerous community organizations, through which they provide for many of their common and cooperative community needs, including those relating to housing, food, businesses, medical care, schools, and death and dying. By attending to these and all other ordinary human concerns and affairs via ego-transcending cooperation and mutual effort, Avatar Adi Da's devotees constantly free their energy and attention, both personally and collectively, for practice of the Way of Adidam and for service to Avatar Adi Da Samraj, to the other Sacred Treasures of Adidam, and to The Avataric Pan-Communion of Adidam.

All of the organizations that have evolved in response to Avatar Adi Da Samraj and His Offering are legally separate from one another, and each has its own purpose and function. Avatar Adi Da neither directs, nor bears responsibility for, the activities of these organizations. Again, He Functions only in Freedom. These organizations represent the collective intention of practitioners of Adidam worldwide not only to provide for the Sacred Treasures of Adidam, but also to make Avatar Adi Da's Offering of the Way of Adidam universally available to all.

Index

Y